BOUNDARIES OF TOUCH

BOUNDARIES OF TOUCH

Parenting and Adult–Child Intimacy

JEAN O'MALLEY HALLEY

UNIVERSITY OF ILLINOIS PRESS
URBANA AND CHICAGO

Library of Congress Cataloging-in-Publication Data
Halley, Jean O'Malley, 1967–
Boundaries of touch: parenting and adult-child intimacy /
Jean O'Malley Halley.
p.   cm.
Includes bibliographical references and index.
ISBN-13: 978-0-252-03212-7 (cloth: alk. paper)
ISBN-10: 0-252-03212-8 (cloth: alk. paper)
1. Touch—Psychological aspects.
2. Boundaries—Psychological aspects.
3. Parent and child.
I. Title.
BF275.H27   2007
155.6'46—dc22   2006100922

For Jacob, and for Isaiah and Lena, with so much love

Contents

Preface

Several years ago, I told a colleague of my concern about a very sweet young student who persisted in hugging me whenever she saw me. I had attempted to avoid her hugs like the plague, ducking into doorways, bathrooms, and offices when I saw her coming. Usually she spotted me anyhow, and came rushing over, smiling sweetly, friendly and as pleased as ever to see me. Her arms were inevitably outstretched for a hug. She had no shame; she hugged me in front of other students, in front of faculty and staff, in front of the college day-care children out on a field trip across campus. I liked this student immensely. She was very bright, enthusiastic, friendly, and kindhearted. Her hugging involved no weird overtones, nothing sexual—nothing but a friendly, happy-to-see-you greeting. Nonetheless, her hugging made me extremely uncomfortable. This was not because I have anything against hugging, whether it be friendly or sexual, greeting or supportive, or any of the other myriad forms in which hugging may come. Actually, I quite like hugging.

No, this student's hugs bothered me because of the school's vigilance over potentially "wrong" or "inappropriate" touch. In a recent mandatory sexual harassment seminar with other faculty and staff, we had been briefed about how to avoid being sued. Surprisingly, the training had very little to do with gender, power, or violation. In a nutshell, we were told *not to touch* our students. We should not touch them publicly. We should not touch them privately. Indeed, we were never, ever, to touch them, if it could be helped, anywhere, in any way at all.

A 1996 episode of the popular television series *Buffy the Vampire Slayer* reflected my experience. Buffy, a high school girl, speaks with her school principal in the hallway about a traumatic event. She had seen her teacher's beheaded body hanging in the cafeteria refrigerator. In response to this unquestionably upsetting experience, the principal told Buffy that if she *ever* needed a hug she could come to him. Yet, he continued, "Not a real hug, of course, because there is no touching in this school. We are sensitive to wrong touching."[1]

If Buffy's principal could not make an exception and *really* hug her in that moment, then I certainly had better not be hugging my students during the very run-of-the-mill events making up our days. As my colleague and I discussed my concern, it became clear that this vigilance seemed to be every-where. Wherever I worked or was myself a student, it was impossible not to notice how guarded people were about touching, particularly the touching of those more vulnerable, and, more particularly, the touching of children by adults. The more I looked into it, the more I realized it was everywhere. Touching had become dangerous. And it seemed dangerous in a way that had very little to do with the ways in which touching actually *can be* a violation. So, at the suggestion of my colleague, I made touching—specifically, ways of thinking about touching—the topic of this study.

Erving Goffman describes my problem when he writes that a "'definition of the situation' is almost always to be found, but those who are in the situation ordinarily do not create this definition, even though their society often can be said to do so; ordinarily, all they do is to assess correctly what the situation ought to be for them and then act accordingly."[2] My book illuminates how we act according to definitions that we do not create in terms of touch. It explores the social history of our touching "situation" and contemplates its implications. Most of us in the United States today are extremely wary about physical contact. We are especially wary about touching anyone who might be perceived as in some way less powerful. This touching prohibition appears to come from everywhere and to define most situations. Albeit perhaps intensi-fied in places of learning—places of the mind where being in a body seems oddly inappropriate—it is not only in academic, scholarly, and school situa-tions but also in many others, such as day cares, restaurants, offices, subways, and city parks, that touching is deeply regulated. Most of us don't spend a lot of time thinking how strange this is, how strange to feel uncomfortable putting a hand on a student's shoulder or giving them a hug, or letting a small child at the summer camp where one works sit on your lap, or even simply how strange it is to make sure to leave one's office door wide open while speaking with a subordinate so that no one even *thinks* touching happened.

As much as I enjoy hugging, I did not and do not hug my students. I as-sessed the situation, as Goffman writes, and now forego hugging, arm touch-ing, hand squeezing, and any other form of friendly physical contact. The fear seems to be that touch is always sexual, and that sexual equals abuse and violation. Second-wave radical feminism was a movement that exposed widespread violent touch in the United States. From personal experience, but also as the child of a second-wave radical feminist and a feminist myself,

I knew well the ways touch could be used as a medium for abusive power. Yet, whereas power is always an issue in any human interaction, touching contains multiple meanings, meanings that move above and beyond and between questions of power. Maybe it was my grounding in feminism, maybe it was my own personal experience of abusive touch—something led me to wonder why so many of my daily life situations demanded that I not touch at all, and, moreover, that I experience feelings of anxiety about the possibility of touch, any touch, be it gentle, loving, accidental, helpful, thoughtful, friendly—*any* touch at all. The focus of feminism had been abusive touch, not *all* touch. So where did this paranoia come from? What was it really about?

Over time, the topic of my book became even more focused. Because of events in my own life, I became increasingly interested in touching children—or, rather, in ways of thinking about touching children.

Acknowledgments

I am very grateful to so many people. My students have been an endless source of inspiration and insight. I only hope they have learned as much from me as I have learned from them. The members of my four writing groups including my Scholarship Circle at Wagner College, Pam Donovan, Robin Isserles, Mathew Jecker Byrne, Melissa Ditmore, Dina Pinsky, Betsy Wissinger, Anne Schotter, Sarah Donovan, Mark Elliott, Maria Gelabert, Mary Lo Re, Kim Worthy, Rafael de la Dehesa, Grace Mitchell, and Salvador Vidal-Ortiz were all incredibly helpful. My department chair at Wagner College, John Esser, has been very supportive of my work on this project and in general. Lynn Chancer read my work and gave me extremely helpful feedback. I could not have had more inspiring, more supportive, kinder guidance from my mentors, Stuart Ewen, Patricia Ticineto Clough, Hester Eisenstein, and the late Bob Alford; they have all been teachers and friends whom I could never thank enough. Without them, in so many ways, this book quite literally would not have happened.

The women I interviewed added immensely to this book and my understanding of ways of thinking about touching children. My editor at the University of Illinois Press, Laurie Matheson, was both kind and efficient, making this anxious person's life a little less anxious. The press's outside readers offered me very smart guidance as to how to sharpen and improve the book. I am also grateful for financial support in working on this project from the Woodrow Wilson National Fellowship Foundation, the Leopold Schepp Foundation, the Helena Rubinstein Foundation, the Jewish Foundation for Education of Women, and the Wagner College Maureen Robinson Fellowship.

Pat Horn and Sarah L. Hartman have both been extremely helpful. My dearest friends, Rich Holland, Wendy Gannett, Amy Gateff, Janet LeMoal, Monica Lichtmer, Carol Quirke, Quinn Cushing, Amy Eshleman, and Ramya Vijaya, and my beloved family, Kathleen O'Malley, Janet Spector, Andrew Maxfield, Sharon Saydah, Sean Maxfield, Kate Maxfield, Judson Byrd Finley, Kevin Maxfield, the late Franzi Groszmann, Lore Segal, Beatrice Segal, David Segal, Benjy Segal, Rakesh Rajani, Maggie Bangser, Amar Rajani-Bangser, and Chhaya Rajani-Bangser, all gave me so much love, so much support. Finally,

I am so grateful to my partner, my closest friend and critical reader, my love, Jacob Segal. Jacob patiently read draft after draft (after draft) of this book; whatever of this is compelling or well written is largely because of him. And, of course, I owe many thanks to my research assistant, my sweet child, Isaiah Halley-Segal. Also, many thanks to Kathleen Halley-Segal, just for showing up in all of her plump and delicious touch-ability.

BOUNDARIES OF TOUCH

ONE

To Touch or Not to Touch

While working on this book, I stayed overnight at a hospital for the first time. I came home exhausted, pale after massive blood loss, and very afraid. On top of all of that, someone came home with me. He was noisy, demanding, easily dissatisfied, constantly hungry, and apparently never tired, at least not at night. Where he came from and what I was to do with him seemed a complete mystery. I thought my life was over. And it was. At least my life as I knew it.

In all the conflicting advice I got, whether and how to touch my son seemed to be one of the biggest issues.

"Put him down and let him cry it out. That's his exercise."

"Never leave a baby to cry alone. Pick him up, hold him, and comfort him."

"Feed him whenever he wants."

"Make him learn to wait. Don't feed him every time he cries; you'll spoil him."

"Keeping him in the bed with you is very dangerous. You could roll over on him and crush him. And besides, if you let him stay in your bed now, you will never get him out."

"Of course he doesn't sleep well. He's in a crib. He needs to be with you in your bed at night. No one likes to sleep alone."

This study explores such conflicting child-rearing advice and the ideologies that underlie prescriptions about when, where, and how to touch children.

Using self-help books on child rearing, popular scientific thought, media representations, and political discourse, I examine the ambiguities of ideologies of adult–child touch and the ways in which these ideologies are bound up with larger cultural issues. By "ideologies of touch," I mean ways of thinking about adult–child physical contact and when this is interpreted as good or bad, helpful or harmful to children. Here, the term "ideology" refers to taken-for-granted practices and normalizing belief systems.

I shed light on why touch is sometimes understood to be fundamentally necessary to human well-being and, at other times, potentially deeply harmful. I argue that ideologies of adult–child touch are part of larger patterns of social "power" that reveal and reproduce mainstream conceptions of gender, sexuality, race, and class. In other words, these ways of thinking are normative; they expose social power "in action." And social power *happens* through them.

In thinking about power this way, I clearly reveal my debt to Michel Foucault. Foucault shows us how power operates to form choice in various networks that normalize. Normalization is the process through which people come to demand of themselves, as the larger society demands of them, that they reproduce "normal" standards of action—that is, standards upheld by their larger social and historical context as normal—and shun that which is considered "abnormal." Foucault writes, "The judges of normality are present everywhere. We are in a society of the teacher-judge, the doctor-judge, the educator judge, the 'social worker'-judge; it is on them that the universal reign of the normative is based; and each individual, wherever he may find himself, subjects it to his body, his gestures, his behaviour, his aptitudes, his achievements."[1]

Foucault argues that networks of power operate to support this normalization. By networks of power, Foucault means how power flows through society, and how human beings are both acted upon by power and reproduce it. Through this normalization, we become subjects—subjects who, for example, touch or don't touch. Foucault claims, "Power must be analysed as something which circulates. . . . It is never localized here or there, never in anybody's hands, never appropriated as a commodity or piece of wealth. Power is employed and exercised through a net-like organisation. And not only do individuals circulate between its threads; they are always in the position of simultaneously undergoing and exercising this power."[2]

Foucault shows us the relationship between normalization and networks of power and knowledge. Knowledge and "truth" are not facts that we gather separate from culture. Truth is always born from a cultural context, and with that context, it changes. What we understand to be "true" about touching changes as culture changes. Ultimately, that which we know, that which we believe to be true, is the expression of social power within our own cultural situation. Indeed, our ways of thinking about the world, our ideas about truth, and our knowledge in any given historical time both articulate and are embedded in social power. As Foucault makes clear, we must "abandon a whole tradition that allows us to imagine that knowledge can exist only where power relations are suspended and that knowledge can develop only outside its injunctions, its demands and its interests. . . . We should admit rather that power produces knowledge . . . that power and knowledge directly imply one another."[3] Knowledge, or what Foucault also calls "discourses of truth," are created through power. "In a society such as ours . . . there are manifold relations of power which permeate, characterize and constitute the social body, and these relations of power cannot themselves be established, consolidated nor implemented without the production, accumulation, circulation and functioning of a discourse. We are subjected to the production of truth through power and we cannot exercise power except through the production of truth."[4] In this book, I explore how elite discourses of truth about adult–child physical contact function as such forms of power in shaping parents' attitudes about "normal" touch. Indeed, these "touching truths" shape more than attitudes. They shape *us* as parent-subjects and child-subjects, people who live and think in particular, culturally bound ways. More broadly, these normalizing discourses of truth about touch both spring from and help reproduce our social order.

One important way in which ideologies of touch reproduce social power is that they replicate a dualistic framework in Western thought and culture. They tend to enforce an either/or rather than a more inclusive both/and orientation. Dualisms demand that individuals conform to limited models of what it means to be human and prescriptions for living. Because of this dualistic rigidity, a binary framework makes parenting—already a difficult job—even harder, as within it parents can never act "correctly." From the perspective of one side of the binary frame, parents are always parenting badly. Another effect of binary thinking is that dualistic ideologies of touch tend to shift attention away from the real problems that far too many parents and children face: they inadequately take into account families' struggles with poverty, the time constraints of a mother's second shift,[5] and violence in the lives of many women and children. The slippery boundaries surrounding touch are especially important to explore if we see the dualisms as constructed, not natural. By examining the binary nature of ideologies of adult–child touch, my study challenges the power of dualisms to govern our lives.

This does not mean that mainstream ideologies of touch are merely "bad," or that the ideologies as expressed, for example, in popular child-rearing literature have nothing to offer. Rather, we must be vigilant as to the multiple and problematic meanings that the ideologies contain, and wary as to the normalizing ways they shape us as human-subjects in our social world. Foucault writes, "My point is not that everything is bad, but that everything is dangerous, which is not exactly the same as bad. If everything is dangerous, then we always have something to do. So my position leads not to apathy but to . . . activism."[6]

Foucault makes clear the relevance of my book. Issues of social power lie beneath many current debates about adult–child touch in child rearing, such as breastfeeding versus bottle-feeding and sleeping with the baby versus insisting on the crib. In the spectrum of touching ideologies, "good" touching might range from unlimited touching to none. "Bad" touching might be all forms of physical contact or just forms defined as "violent," as in the case of child sexual abuse; finally, no form of touch might be seen as problematic. Here Foucault challenges us to loosen the binds of these ideologies by examining the social and historical context of their development. Maybe then we could see the ideologies, at least in part, as just that—ideologies—rather than absolute truths demanding from us "good" parenting and naming us "bad" parents. Foucault suggests a critical stance whereby we can reject the ideologies that work to shape us as parent-subjects. In this way, for example, women who mother are released from the reified categories of "good" mother, "bad" mother, "instinctual" mother, or "scientific" mother.

In this book I explore *ideologies* rather than behaviors, and I focus on mainstream cultural ideologies because they are the ideas of any given time period that legitimize the interests of the more powerful groups in society. Ideologies do not evolve by themselves; they are rooted in social conditions and connected to the ways people actually live. Ways of thinking about touch spring from and reinforce the real touching that happens between human beings. In the contemporary mainstream United States, this seems to signify comparatively little touching.[7] "Cross-cultural studies have revealed that the United States has one of the lowest rates of casual touch in the world—about two times an hour (although this does not hold for Puerto Ricans, who claim one of the highest rates of casual touch—about 180 times an hour). French parents touch their children three times more often than American parents."[8]

Mainstream ideologies of adult–child touch act as a window into the dominant culture. They expose ways of thinking about our bodies and the meaning of being human while highlighting social power structures. For example, without at least a middle-class income, many of the prevailing prescriptions are impossible to fulfill. Some experts against touching insist, for example, that each child have a room of his or her own. Others who champion extensive touching require women to stay home full time with their children, conveniently ignoring that many women can't afford to.

White middle-class ways of thinking about touch in the twentieth- and twenty-first-century United States replicate dualistic Western thinking within which mind–body is the most basic dualism. The mind–body dualism informs all the binary patterns apparent in mainstream ideologies of touch. The Western medical model is one important place where such dualistic thinking is both articulated and reproduced. Peter Freund and his colleagues write, "The medical model assumes a clear dichotomy between the mind and body"; for example, "physical diseases are presumed to be located solely within the body."[9] In the twentieth century, as we began to assume the human body was an object to be understood, cared for, and cured by science and the medical model, "increasing numbers of areas of life were brought under medicine's purview and control."[10] In other words, increasing areas of life were, in Foucault's terms, brought under the normalizing domain of medicine and "medicalized." Child rearing is such an area of life; it was medicalized in the early twentieth century. Medicalization of child rearing meant that people generally understood child rearing as an issue "needing doctors' attention, regardless of whether the medical approach was more effective than the nonmedical."[11]

Throughout the twentieth century, such medical or expert child-rearing advice split along pro- and anti-touch lines. Because women are associated with the body and men with the mind, during pro-touch periods, when touch was understood to be "necessary" to children's health and well-being, it was women's physical presence that was considered most important. During anti-touch periods, when touch was taboo and seen as dangerous, dirty, and threatening to children's healthy development, it was women's touch that was most dangerous and in need of surveillance. Experts then focused on the dangers of mothers touching children.

On Dualisms and Gender in Contemporary Touch Debates

Science versus Nature Dualisms

The tension between pro- and anti-touch experts must be understood in light of another dualism, science versus nature. In this book, I show how experts use science, but also sometimes just the rhetoric, whether of science or the preeminence of the "natural," to argue their positions. With enough good scientific research, we often do come closer to a kind of truth. For example, much scientific research has concluded that "breast is best" when it comes to infant feeding. Many studies have found that breastfed infants stay healthier and as adults have lower rates of cancer and other illnesses. Some studies have even suggested that breastfed infants score better on intelligence tests, such as a Danish study that concluded that the "longer infants are breastfed the higher they are likely to score on intelligence tests as adults."[12]

But science, like any other truth-telling endeavor, springs from a socio-cultural and historical moment, too. As Foucault shows us, science is never value-free, purely objective, or separate from questions of power. Every scientific conclusion comes from a power-laden position. For instance, as will be discussed in a later chapter, child-rearing expert and scientist Richard Ferber claims that people sleep better when they sleep alone. This "knowledge" is not simple truth (as many people throughout the world might testify). Rather, it is a normative position located in a particular place and time. The "scientific" truth that claims we sleep better alone merges with the middle-class belief in individualism and independence. This idea holds that it is morally superior to sleep alone because it makes one more independent.

Knowledge and ideas about truth are also bound up directly with the political economy. "Knowledge" can be used to blatantly further economic interests. For example, other studies, particularly those sponsored by the powerful formula industry, have shown that formula, like breastfeeding, is also good for infants and, in certain circumstances, even better than the breast. Given this scientific research, the widespread use of formula, in no small part, has been a result of its endorsement by an important component of the scientific community—the American Academy of Pediatrics. The formula industry has even conducted breastfeeding research. Ross Laboratories, a major formula company, collects and publishes national breastfeeding statistics. Indeed, they are the "only group that tracks national breastfeeding statistics—via a survey generated by their Marketing Department and subsequently presented as unbiased research."[13]

Rhetoric of the "natural" and natural truths is likewise grounded in a particular context. In some ways, such rhetoric is more dangerous because it has no official community, like the scientific community, from which it must gain approval. The "natural" is appealing to the white middle-class United States in this particular cultural moment. Our "instincts," common sense, and feelings are all frequently used to legitimize ideas of the "truth." Where this knowledge comes from is debatable. I claim that it is sociocultural knowledge—"in the air," so to speak—of one's social context. We know these commonsense things because we simply live and breathe in our society's "truths." These social "truths," this "instinctual" knowledge, can be useful and informative. It can also be wrongheaded and dangerous.

One example of an important—and questionable—"truth" is that for the past couple of centuries, we in Western cultures have considered women "natural" parents. In one sense, this was a self-fulfilling prophecy. Women were understood to be naturally nurturing, and were raised to be so. In another sense, of course, this thinking is incorrect and deeply limiting to both men and women. As we begin to think of men as nurturing too, the culture has begun to raise and socialize men to *be* nurturing. Indeed, much like that which we believe to be "truth," we *ourselves* are, as Judith Lorber writes, "transformed by social practices to fit into the salient categories of a society."[14]

Another "truth" imagined to be natural is the assumption of heterosexuality. This assumption that heterosexuality is "natural" (much like the idea that women mothering is "natural") lies at the core of mainstream United States culture. The result of this assumption is compulsory heterosexuality, a social system grounded in heteronormative ideology that reinforces (indeed, *forces,* as the penalties are severe for many who challenge heteronormativity) heterosexuality in all aspects of social life. Adrienne Rich argues in her seminal essay "Compulsory Heterosexuality and Lesbian Existence" that the issue is not one of "simple 'gender inequality,' nor the domination of culture by males, nor the mere 'taboos against homosexuality,' but the enforcement of heterosexuality for women as a means of assuring male right of physical, economical, and emotional access."[15]

Experts use different rhetorics to make their truth-telling and heteronormative arguments. In this book, I explore how these arguments are grounded in larger ideologies and the ways in which power is acted out through them. I am less interested in "truths" (or in debating what might be "true") than in illuminating how ideas come to be seen as truths and how they are linked to power.

My own experiences play a role in my thinking about my study.[16] One of the problems with the ideological form of our conversations about touch is that because of the binary framework the conversations exist within, individuals refrain from speaking about their own experiences if speaking risks subverting ideologies of touch. For example, people who practice extended breastfeeding often will not talk about their practice in public, even though, as I have found, many, many people practice extended breastfeeding. Breastfeeding a child until she or he is three or four years old is still seen as very strange—as if it was quite unusual—in the mainstream United States. Thus, because of the larger cultural prohibition against long-term breastfeeding, people stay in the closet, so to speak, about their own practice.[17] On the other hand, women who follow a pro-touch practice within a pro-touch community also have trouble expressing their ambiguous feelings about so much touch (maybe they don't want the child in the bed with them) either to their community or to themselves. The same happens for women who decide not to breastfeed at all, or for the current commonly recommended twelve months. One women in a mothering group I was a member of discussed her decision to wean her infant at six months because she did not like how her breasts looked or felt. The mother sitting next to me pursed her lips and whispered, "That is so selfish." There is little room for dissent when it comes to touching practices.

My experiences reveal to me the constraints our society places on talk about touch. Thus, these personal experiences play an important role in the background of this book. First, I have a violent childhood history, one in which I was sexually abused. Albeit a far too common experience (of touch) in the contemporary United States, child-rearing literature almost never *explicitly* addresses the issue of sexual abuse—even though anxiety about sexual abuse underlies many of the proposed touching practices in child-rearing literature. And, despite studies that show that from one out of three to one out of six women have a history of child sexual abuse,[18] this issue never came up in any of the three mother–infant groups I took part in. Nor did I feel comfortable or that it was "appropriate" for me to raise my own child sexual abuse history as a topic of conversation in the context of the groups, even though this history deeply affected my experience of my own body, of touching, and, when I had a child, of parenting.

Second, while working on this book, reading a plethora of child-rearing and other expert literature, talking to new mothers, and sitting in on parenting groups, I had a baby. I breastfed. I flip-flopped between eschewing the crib, to using it, to giving it up again. I worried about my own to some extent unavoidably erotic connection with my child. Partly because of my experience of sexual abuse, I struggle with being extremely uncomfortable in my own body. And parenting, perhaps more than any other human experience, is fundamentally embodied. In some sense, I live with the dualisms I examine, the mind–body split, in an extreme way.

My history, body, and social context helped drive my choices about how to parent. Yet my own preferred style of parenting is really not the topic of this book. I do not believe that my parenting choices are the right ones for everyone. Indeed, it is central to my argument that, contra the demands of the child-rearing literature, there is no one right choice for everyone. I intend to be honest about my own choices—and my insecurities, doubts, and anxieties—while focusing on the options that exist in mainstream ways of thinking about touching children and analyzing how those options are tied to larger social structures.

Gender–Body Dualisms and Heteronormativity

Other central dualisms engendered by ideologies of touch are those that construct gender and sexuality. These constructions are fundamentally linked to how Western culture has split its conception of the human being into two parts: the body and the soul or mind. The body is identified with the earth, other animals, and the primitive, and the mind is identified with the spirit, God and the heavens, civilization, rationality, and control. Feminist scholar Susan Bordo writes that "disdain for the body, the conception of it as an alien force and impediment to the soul, is very old in our Greco-Christian traditions."[19] The body is understood to be whatever the soul is not. It is alien and confining to the soul; it is like an enemy cage from which the essential self struggles to escape. The mind is, or aspires to be, rational, but the body is wildly passionate. In its animalistic nature, the body perpetually verges on losing control.

Americans are obsessed with their bodies, Bordo notes. She cites a study in which 190 out of 500 people, when asked what they feared most in the world, replied: "Getting fat."[20] Why do we experience this obsession, and why is American culture in particular so preoccupied with making the body slim, thin, tight, and young? "In an age when our children regularly have nightmares of nuclear holocaust, that as adults we should give this answer—that we most fear 'getting fat'—is [truly] bizarre," Bordo writes. She argues that "the nightmares of nuclear holocaust and our desperate fixation on our bodies as arenas of control—perhaps one of the few available arenas of control we have left in the twentieth century—are not unconnected of course."[21] Whereas many people experience the modern world as deeply out of control, one's body offers the possibility of gaining concrete control over something—oneself.

We fixate on our bodies as a literal territory to be dominated in an out-of-control world. Gender and sexuality cement this connection, playing an essential role in the mind–body split, because women (who are always assumed to be heterosexual) are associated with the body, and men ("real men," who are never gay) with the mind.

This body association is costly for women. "For if, whatever the specific historical content of the duality, *the body* is the negative term, and if woman *is* the body, then women *are* that negativity, whatever it may be: distraction from knowledge, seduction away from God, capitulation to sexual desire, violence or aggression, failure of will, even death."[22] And for women of color there is a double burden of bodily associations. Besides being female, they are by virtue of their race understood in the dominant culture to be animalistic and of the body.

Along with race, sex, and gender, dualistic thinking also helps construct normative sexuality. Lorber argues,

> In Western societies, we see two discrete sexes and two distinguished gen-
> ders because our society is built on two classes of people, "women" and
> "men." Once the gender category is given, the attributes of the person
> are also gendered: Whatever a "woman" is has to be "female"; whatever a
> "man" is has to be "male." Analyzing the social processes that construct
> the categories we call "female and male," "women and men," and "homo-
> sexual and heterosexual" uncovers the ideology and power differentials
> congealed in these categories.[23]

As Lorber indicates, along with gender dualities, the binary structure also plays out in categories of sex—male versus female—and (hetero)sexuality. Indeed, our society is built on heterosexual culture as much as on, as Lorber argues, binary gender and sex categories. Michael Warner writes that heterosexual culture "thinks of itself as the elemental form of human association, as the very model of intergender relations, as the indivisible basis of all community, and as the means of reproduction without which society wouldn't exist."[24] Drawing on Foucault, Warner argues that "the logic of the [hetero]sexual order is so deeply embedded by now in an indescribably wide range of social institutions, and is embedded in the most standard accounts of the world, queer struggles aim not just at toleration or equal status but at challenging those institutions and accounts."[25] The family is such an institution. And for families, along with the culture at large, one important function of child-rearing advice has been the reproduction of normative sex (female versus male), gender (femininity, body, mother–wife, nurturing caretaker versus masculinity, mind, father–husband, rational breadwinner), and (hetero)sexuality—in other words, the reproduction of heteronormative culture.[26]

In heteronormative Western thought, particularly within the Judeo-Christian tradition, one version of the body-as-female duality portrays women as sexual/evil temptresses. The temptress reproduces heteronormativity. She (the bad body-woman) endangers men (the good rational-man) through seducing them to evildoings. Biblical figures such as Eve and Jezebel play out this tempt-ress theme. And the female seductress lives on in innumerable contemporary secular stories. The *Fatal Attraction* femme fatale is common in television and films. Even girls are suspect, as various versions of the novel *Lolita* demonstrate. Bordo argues, "These depictions of women as continually and actively luring men to arousal (and, often evil) work to disclaim male ownership of the body and its desires. The arousal of those desires is the result of female manipula-tion and therefore is the woman's fault. This construction is so powerful that rapists and child abusers have been believed when they claimed that five-year-old female children 'led them on.'"[27] Girls and women often internalize this thinking, considering themselves responsible for unwanted advances and even sexual assault. This guilt plays into a deep discomfort with femaleness, self-hate of female bodies, and shame.

Women live with the daily threat of rape, battering, and other harassment. But in the midst of so much that is out of control, the body is not only a site for violation, it is also a sphere, albeit contested, of female control. Women cannot ignore a world that demands their bodies take a specific form. Yet they may focus themselves on that form, and choose—in a sense—to make their life largely about it. In doing so, they gain a kind of control.

One way for women to focus on their bodies is through eating problems such as anorexia nervosa or bulimia.[28] Other ways include believing in and attempting to live out gendered female roles associated with the body and the "natural." One of these contemporary roles is the "natural mother."

Ideologies of touch replicate the dualistic natural mother theme. Ways of thinking about adult–child touch swing toward the pro-touch end of the continuum during times when the body and the "natural" are seen as "good" and "wholesome." Being good and wholesome, much like being rational and controlled in anti-touch times, has meant being heterosexual (even as this has also often meant being *asexually* heterosexual for mothers).

Because women are associated with the body, their touch matters most dur-ing pro-touch periods. During such times, mothers are encouraged to touch their children—and child-rearing thought, like the "naturalist" school called attachment parenting, urges mothers to touch their children as much as pos-sible. Attachment "parents"—really, mothers—believe that bodies touching bodies, mothers touching babies, is central to good mothering. In this think-ing, babies need touch at least as much as any other need in order to grow up to be physically and psychologically healthy. And it's very important that it is the mother who does the touching.

At the anti-touch end of the continuum, the body and the "natural" are understood to be dangerous, unclean, uncivilized, and potentially out of control. Because of their association with the body, women are especially dangerous. During these ideological moments, we must be vigilant of women's bodies and women's touch. There is to be less touching between parents (mothers) and children. John B. Watson, founder of the behaviorist school in the 1920s, took this thinking to an extreme. Watson believed mothers should virtually never touch their children. The ideal way to raise children, he insisted, was in a scientific laboratory. For the dominant culture at the time, and for Watson, science represented the opposite of the out-of-control female/body. Science, like the male mind, was understood to be rational, ordered, and in control. Children raised by science/men would grow up in the image of science and men. They would be controlled and controlling, strong, rational, and firm. Watson believed that children, raised—as almost all children were—by women/bodies, were weak, emotional, and out of control. It's easy to dismiss Watson as a misogynist and an extremist, and in fact he was both. But he also founded one of the most influential strains of thinking about how mothers should (or shouldn't) touch their children, giving rise to social practices recommended and followed to this day.

Dualisms and the Debate over Touch and Raising Children

These two extremes at either end of the touch continuum run through the twentieth century. They correspond to the two child-rearing schools of thought that Barbara Ehrenreich and Deirdre English call the "behaviorist" and the "permissive" schools.[29] Behaviorists are, more or less, anti-touch. Permissivists, or what I call the "naturalists," are fundamentally pro-touch. This study examines these two dominant schools of thought on child rearing in the twentieth-century United States.

The behaviorist and naturalist schools mirror the mind–body split. The behaviorists believe in the mind and the power of the rational scientific world; the naturalist school has faith in the body and the power of nature to teach us how to live. I contrast these two schools with the radical feminist analysis of touch and its focus on violence. The behaviorist school begins with Watson in the 1920s and threads through the century to contemporary child-rearing expert Richard Ferber. The naturalist school begins with Benjamin Spock in the 1940s and La Leche League International in the 1950s, and can be followed to contemporary child-rearing expert William Sears. Each school has fundamentally different ways of thinking about child rearing and the touching of children.

   Underlying the differences between behaviorist and naturalist child-rearing experts are two distinct ways of thinking about what it means to be human and the ideal goal of human development. Watson, the founder and, in many senses, the father of behaviorism, argued that human beings begin life as un-molded clay to be shaped by behaviorist training. He thought a child could be trained to do or be anything. He did not believe in the influence of genetic disposition toward a particular characteristic or skill, and argued against the possibility of "natural" or "instinctual" knowledge.

   The behaviorists turned to science rather than nature or human instinct for guidance about how to live. Nature was dangerous and not to be trusted because nature and the natural body could run amok. That which was associated with nature—the corporeal world of women, animals, sexuality, and bodies—was to be contained and managed by science. In terms of child rearing, Watson and other behaviorists argued that only through science could society learn how to parent. "Parenthood," wrote Watson, "instead of being an instinctive art, is a science, the details of which must be worked out by patient laboratory methods."[30] Watson argued, *"No one today knows enough to raise a child.* The world would be considerably better off if we were to stop having children for twenty years (except those reared for experimental purposes) and were then to start again with enough facts to do the job with some degree of skill and accuracy."[31]

   Both the behaviorists and the naturalists reproduced the connection of the feminine with the natural body. Watson thought that science taught us how to manage the body and the children and women who were associated with it. Early behaviorists openly argued that women were dangerous. "Mother love," Watson wrote, "is a dangerous instrument."[32] Women were understood to be particularly dangerous if they did not listen to science—that is, to men—and from it learn how to live their lives and raise their children.

   The behaviorist goal in child rearing was to train children (who in Watson's work always seemed to be boys) to be "masculine" adults: independent, rational, individualist, under control, unemotional, and, importantly, heterosexual. Here we learn as much from the positive desire of behaviorists *for* masculinity as from the *fear of* effeminacy. Watson wrote that an unfit mother will "inevitably bring up a weakling." Not only is a weakling the opposite of masculine, but he is a "petted, spoiled, sullen, shy youngster who [will] grow up a liar and a thief."[33] In these goals for human development, and in their way of understanding what it means to be human, twentieth-century behaviorists joined a larger mainstream United States and European masculine ideal.[34] And insofar as behaviorist thinking springs from, and reproduces, a larger

American ideology that idealizes both masculinity and heteronormativity, behaviorists have been inextricably connected to mainstream white middle-class American ways of thinking.

Behaviorists focus squarely on masculinity and boys. Early twentieth-century behaviorist writing in particular seems to be solely about boys and their development to manhood. Reading Watson, one wonders what happened to all the girl babies. Watson considers females only as grown women, and then only in the role he considers appropriate for them: as mothers. Like most people in his world, Watson believed that men and women were fundamentally different creatures. He focused his discussion on male characteristics and development. True to his culture, Watson valued the masculine traits ascribed to men and not the feminine ones ascribed to women.

In contrast to the behaviorists, who believe that children must be trained to become useful, modern, masculine adults, naturalists view human beings as already perfect in their most "natural" state. Whereas behaviorists overtly champion science over the "natural," naturalists explicitly understand themselves as trusting in nature *instead* of science. Naturalists believe in, and idealize, "nature." They assume that human beings are born "knowing" how to live. With respect to child rearing, naturalists trust the baby, whom they believe naturally knows what she or he needs. Naturalists celebrate and idealize the body and that which they associate with the body: women and children. But despite their faith in nature, naturalists also use science to bolster their arguments. This points to the incredible power of science in our culture today and over the past one hundred years. In truth telling, science is the bottom line, the god of our contemporary quest for wisdom. Even those who claim to be the fundamental critics of science and its experts—the naturalists—ultimately use science to confirm their own beliefs. Indeed, popular naturalist thinkers are often scientific experts.

As in the larger culture, both naturalists and behaviorists associate women with the body. They believe women are closer than men to "nature." Because naturalists see parenting as a natural human activity, and because women are understood to be closer to nature than men, naturalists understand women to be *the* natural parent. Naturalists argue that women instinctively know how to mother. In other words, naturalists essentialize women.

Behaviorists and naturalists are fundamentally split, however, over their views about human development. Behaviorists understand the development into an independent individual as the most important human development goal. They value separation from other human beings. By contrast, naturalists focus on human relationships. Naturalists hope to raise children who are attached to others and who are also centered in themselves individually. In this focus on relationship, naturalists have an anti-materialist bent. Indeed, in one of its slogans, naturalist La Leche League International argues: "People before things."

This study examines explicit naturalist and behaviorist thinking about adult–child touch, as well as implicit thinking about child sexual abuse and incest. Behaviorist thought contains an underlying fear of the body's potential sexuality-run-amok and of adults (particularly women) being sexual with children. This anxiety goaded behaviorists in the first half of the twentieth century to explicitly argue against the touching of children. In the later part of the twentieth century, they were more typically implicitly anxious, as suggested by arguments that each person should have his or her own room, bed, and physical space. They were unspoken, if not overt, proponents of the bottle and the crib. Through mechanisms such as cribs and bottles, behaviorists hope to prevent the body from behaving savagely and from losing control.

Naturalists likewise associate the body with women. For them, though, the body is pure, beautiful, and trustworthy. It is also often frankly asexual.[35]

These two frameworks represent the Madonna/whore complex or, in racialized terms, the "noble savage" versus the "dirty Indian." In both, the woman and the native are associated with the body and the so-called natural world. On one side of the split, women are pure, natural beings, as native people are noble "primitives" of the wild. On the other side, women and native people are dirty and out of control. For naturalists, women are mothers, "pure," and "natural." Their touch, too, is pure, natural, and asexual.

These two parallel schools, the behaviorist and the naturalist, are intertwined by the mind–body split, the central dichotomy in the history of Western thought. Where behaviorists abhor and fear the body, naturalists glorify it. *Both* understand the body and the mind as separate parts that together make up the person. Behaviorists understand incest and child sexual abuse as cultural markers or signs of the body run amok. The potential for incest means the potential for the body to lose control, the way many people think of weight gain or binge eating. Underlying the fear of incest is fear of the body. Behaviorists take on the task of containing, controlling, and shaping the body. By contrast, naturalists glorify the "natural" body in the same way the noble savage stereotype does. Naturalists settle the issue of child sexual abuse/incest by considering, as one of my interviewees argued, that "it really never happens."

Implications

Besides linking ideologies of touch to power structures, this book addresses the implications for mainstream thinking about adult–child sexuality. Whether or not a touch is sexual or abusive is a question that bubbles up again and again. For example, certain schools of thought consider breastfeeding after a child reaches a certain age to be sexual and thus abusive. Other schools of child rearing advocate breastfeeding until the child initiates weaning. They call this "natural" or "child-led" weaning. For them, extended breastfeeding is good for children—and never sexual—even for children as old as five or six years.

I feel this tension around breastfeeding in my own mothering, especially because it is fed by my history of childhood sexual abuse. Before having Isaiah, I felt extremely uncomfortable around women who breastfed their older children. I don't even mean children who were walking and talking; I felt uncomfortable around women who breastfed infants of ten or eleven months. I thought it would be a struggle for me to breastfeed beyond six months, and did not plan to continue past twelve months. Yet I am now practicing extended breastfeeding and child-led weaning with my four-year-old son. The more I read on extended breastfeeding, while working on this book, the more convinced I became that it was a good idea. It wasn't just the reading, though. Isaiah wanted to continue breastfeeding, and still does. Or at least he "wanted" to as best I could divine his wants. Was it really my wanting, my need for closeness displaced onto my child? At any rate, we kept on breastfeeding, and kept on, and on. In my mind's eye, looking ahead at the child he will be in one year, he inevitably seems too old for nursing. This was as true when I imagined him at eighteen months as it is now, as I imagine him at six years. Yet, right now, as I have *only* known him breastfeeding, and he has always wanted to breastfeed, breastfeeding *seems* like the most "natural," most "normal" thing to do. Making him stop *seems* like unnecessarily pushing him to do something he is not ready to do.

On the other hand, I am acutely aware of the cultural judgments around me. I know that most people in my social world think it is very strange to breastfeed a child Isaiah's age. And ironically, given my own history, I know that many people believe breastfeeding a four-year-old is more than weird; it might be seen as abusive, sexually abusive. I hide us, as I did in our first-floor Pennsylvania apartment, carefully putting down the shades of our windows when Isaiah asked to nurse.

Indeed, in recent years women have lost their children over extended breastfeeding. Documentarian Alyssa R. Bennett explores this issue along with the territory between sexual and nonsexual touching of children in her 1994 documentary *Touching Children.* Bennett argues that we have become deeply paranoid about our children's sexuality and about our own sexual feelings toward them. Bennett interviews Denise Perrigo, a white single mother of one who was arrested on charges of sexually abusing her child and had her two-year-old daughter taken away from her and put in foster care for a year. The charge: "mouth-to-breast contact."

Perrigo practiced extended breastfeeding, although she says in the interview that she and her daughter Cherilyn were "working on weaning" when the arrest happened. One day while nursing Cherilyn, Perrigo experienced sexual arousal. This alarmed her, and so she called a community volunteer center and asked to be put in touch with La Leche League International, as it is an organization that strongly advocates breastfeeding and works to support breastfeeding mothers. When the volunteers heard "sexual arousal," they directed her to a rape crisis center instead of La Leche League. The counselor at the rape crisis center heard Perrigo's story and believed it to be "child sexual abuse." She told Perrigo that because the situation involved a child she had to get her supervisor. When the counselor explained the situation to her supervisor, she told her it was a case of child sexual abuse. The supervisor got on the telephone believing Perrigo to be sexually abusing her child as they spoke. Perrigo says that everything the supervisor heard fit, in her mind, as "proof" of child sexual abuse. For example, she asked Perrigo where her daughter was right then. Perrigo said that Cherilyn was in her bed. Although Perrigo, speaking on the telephone, was in a different room than Cherilyn, who was in bed, the supervisor wrote down that Perrigo was in bed with her daughter.

While she was on the telephone arguing with the rape crisis center supervisor, the supervisor contacted the sexual abuse "hotline," which sent local police to arrest Perrigo. She was taken into custody and interviewed by the police for five straight hours. Perrigo claims that the police tried everything to get her to "admit" to sexually abusing her daughter. The police made clear their ignorance about breastfeeding, telling Perrigo that it was not possible to breastfeed a two-year-old. Even though the criminal charges were eventually dropped, social services filed charges of sexual abuse and neglect with the family court, and Perrigo was allowed only biweekly supervised visits with her daughter for nearly a year.[36]

The Perrigo case happened because many scientific experts are wary about touching children. Their anxiety springs from the ever-present possibility of sexuality involved in physical contact. However, as an indicator of the confusions of dualistic thought, other scientific experts hold the opposite view.

David Finkelhor, in his book *Childhood Sexual Abuse: New Theory and Research*, argues that child sexual abuse is *more* likely to happen in homes with little physical contact.[37] Noelle Oxenhandler concurs, writing that "when there is an absence of healthy, affectionate touch, children are actually at greater risk of becoming both the victims and the eventual perpetrators of abusive touch, whether violent or sexual."[38]

How did we get to this place where women risk losing their children for breastfeeding beyond a prescribed cultural norm of twelve months—a norm that is *not* the norm in most of the global community? I will explore this issue. But first, I briefly locate my work in the scholarly literature and describe my methodology.

Scholarly Debates on Child-Rearing Advice and Practice

Some of the many texts written on child rearing in recent years examine the history of American child-rearing advice. Julia Grant's *Raising Baby by the Book: The Education of American Mothers* considers child-rearing literature's impact on mothering practices and ideologies across diverse classes and ethnicities, from the early nineteenth through the twentieth century. She explores the medicalization of mothering, the interaction of experts and mothers, and mothers' responses to scientific advice. Grant claims that mothers have both increasingly sought expert advice and simultaneously been critical consumers of it, choosing to use some or all of it, depending on their circumstances. Another recent history of twentieth-century child-rearing advice by Ann Hulbert, *Raising America: Experts, Parents, and a Century of Advice about Children,* examines the "flood of child-rearing guides that had by now inundated Spock-marked middle-class parents." She investigates why and how popular child-rearing experts came to be "so numerous and contentious."[39] Hulbert argues that the advice has not eased the intense and somewhat unique American anxiety about parenting. Yet she claims that the experts do offer a window into the twentieth-century United States. She claims that they reflect "American confusions about children's natures and futures, and about mothers' missions, during a disorienting century."[40]

My book explores some of the same practices, experts, and themes as those of Hulbert and Grant. However, unlike those researchers, I focus on beliefs about touching children. My book investigates adult–child touch in terms of the underlying ideologies that I argue are dualistic and reproduce social power. Child-rearing advice is only one, albeit important, element in my story about how the mainstream United States regards adult–child touch.

Other books on particular types of child-rearing practices have come out in the past few years. Chris Bobel's *The Paradox of Natural Mothering*, for example, discusses naturalism. Bobel writes about "a population of mothers who embrace values that many would consider old-fashioned, even backwards."[41] She argues that these mothers behave in a contradictory way because they both rationalize "women's inferior social position" and simultaneously resist "certain capitalist and technological structures and attempt to wrest control from institutions and 'experts' they perceive as threatening to the best interests of American families."[42] Bobel describes the "natural mother" as one who

> gives birth to her babies at home; she homeschools her children; she grows much of her family's produce and sews many of their clothes. She seems at first glance an anachronism, recalling a time when women derived their identities from raising their large families and excelling at the domestic arts. But unlike the women of the past, whose domestic lives were responsive to society's dictates, today's "natural mother" resists convention. While her contemporaries take advantage of daycare, babysitters, and bottle feeding, the natural mother rejects almost everything that facilitates mother-child separation. She believes that consumerism, technology, and detachment from nature are social ills that mothers can and should oppose.[43]

In another book focusing on a child-rearing practice, *At the Breast: Ideologies of Breastfeeding and Motherhood in the Contemporary United States,* sociologist Linda M. Blum looks at breastfeeding practice and ideology. She argues that breastfeeding is a public matter that "provides a lens with which to sharpen our focus on the conflicts shaping and dividing women's lives."[44] From her interviews with white middle-class, white working-class, and Black working-class mothers about their breastfeeding experiences, Blum concludes that views vary greatly depending on race and class. She also criticizes scientific and other expert demands on mothers, arguing that they neglect these class and racial differences and histories. In other words, experts ignore the question of social power in mothers' lives.

My book is distinct from Bobel's and Blum's in several ways. First, it focuses on ideologies rather than practices. It also moves outside of the realm of child rearing to examine how popular social movements address adult–child touch, how the issue is represented in mass media, and the views of famous thinkers like Alfred C. Kinsey and Harry F. Harlow. Further, unlike Bobel, who only looks at naturalism, I also examine scientific ideologies. And unlike Blum, who focuses on breastfeeding, I investigate three forms of adult–child touch via three case studies: breastfeeding versus bottle-feeding; "sharing sleep" with parents—in other words, infants and children sleeping in the same bed with their parents—versus using cribs and separate beds; and, finally, child sexual abuse. My book discusses these issues in the context of changing ideological patterns of thought, which I understand as normalizing belief systems. I show how these ideological patterns reveal and reproduce mainstream structures of gender, race/ethnicity, and class.

In an important book, *Mother's Milk: Breastfeeding Controversies in American Culture,* feminist scholar Bernice L. Hausman develops the themes Blum addresses. But instead of focusing on refuting the influences of the medical and scientific community, Hausman argues for the "biological benefits of breast-feeding over artificial infant feeding."[45] I argue that Hausman replicates the naturalist's approach to breastfeeding in popular child-rearing literature. Like the naturalists, Hausman uses contemporary scientific information to argue strongly for breastfeeding over bottle-feeding. This contrasts with mainstream medical advice that, even with all of its ideological and problematic commitments, does not push for breastfeeding to the same extent as the naturalists do. Hausman, like the naturalists, uses science and biomedical information to argue that breastfeeding is *the* way to feed human infants.

I find Hausman's argument compelling on a personal level because I've chosen to practice attachment parenting, with its extended breastfeeding and other implications. And I certainly want all the information about breastfeeding and its benefits, among other care practices, to be available to all women. Yet politically, it does not make sense to me to press women to enact a particular practice, given class, race, and sexuality differences, and given that, as Blum argues, the body is "always historically, politically, and culturally shaped."[46]

In response to Hausman, I wonder how we as feminist scholars can argue for a particular mothering practice—no matter how personally compelling—by using biomedical claims, given the diverse and contradictory mothering practices science has pushed over the past century. Indeed, to promote one mothering practice for all women is to replicate dualistic mainstream ideologies of touch. We cannot erase history but, rather than joining the naturalist movement and taking part in its breastfeeding advocacy, I prefer to support movements that support mothers in making their own (albeit always culturally situated and power-bound) choices and in getting all mothers access to the resources they need to live well and truly be able to make choices.

I agree with Hausman that it is important to make breastfeeding and other information available to all women. But perhaps we might also focus on the struggle for a social and political world where women and children have access to decent and affordable child care, housing, health care and nutrition, freedom from violence, high-quality schooling, and good jobs. For most of human history, most mothers have breastfed their infants. That is probably a good thing. Yet with decent alternatives like clean water and infant formula, and for all kinds of sociohistorical reasons, some women have chosen not to breastfeed. And those choices can make sense too.[47]

My project aims to help open the possibility for women to think *why* they feel they must touch or not touch, continue breastfeeding or wean, or sleep with their infant or use a crib. I hope this engenders a freedom that will dissolve the reified identities and practices women have and engage in.

Methodology

Overview

I employ both interpretative and historical arguments[48] and a variety of data sources with a focus on prescriptive child-rearing literature as evidence of the different ways people have thought about the touching of children. I order my study chronologically, and through the use of case studies. The frameworks used by Foucault and Bordo lie beneath all of my work. Foucault's thinking on power, discipline, and normalization informs my analysis regarding the formation of subjectivity of mothers and children and orientations concerning touch. From Bordo, I take the centrality of dualistic thought, particularly in reference to gender, sex, and sexuality. From both, I look to a perspective that moves away from binary thinking; not a "complete" (impossible) freedom from powers that constrain, but an understanding of power that helps to enable critical thought about who "we are."

In chapter 2, I set forth a sociocultural history of ideas about adult–child touch, exploring ideologies from the first half of the twentieth century, when social scientists were the most prominent ideological voices on adult–child touch. I examine the prominent behaviorist ideologies of the time, early "naturalist" experts such as Dr. Benjamin Spock, and mainstream thinking as represented in child-rearing literature. In this chapter I primarily draw on the methods of historical sociology, analyzing a series of texts to divine their differing ideological frameworks.

Among the texts I examine, because of their authority in mainstream thought in the United States, are: Luther Emmett Holt's *The Care and Feeding of Children: A Catechism for the Use of Mothers and Children's Nurses* (1901); John B. Watson's *Psychological Care of Infant and Child* (1928); Benjamin Spock's *The Common Sense Book of Baby and Child Care* (1945); Alfred C. Kinsey's *Sexual*

Behavior in the Human Male (1948) and *Sexual Behavior in the Human Female* (1953); and Harry F. Harlow's "The Nature of Love," which appeared in *American Psychologist* (1958).

Chapters 3 and 4 explore touch ideology in terms of feeding and sleep. Chapter 3 investigates the contemporary behaviorist and "naturalist" schools of thought on breastfeeding versus bottle-feeding and adult–child touch. Chapter 4 explores the thinking of these two schools about sharing sleep space versus using the crib.[49] In these chapters I analyze ways the mass media has portrayed adult–child touch, especially in the popular child-rearing books that were sprouting by the 1960s.[50] Because of time constraints, I examine only a limited number of the most popular child-rearing texts published between the 1950s and the present. I chose the texts in the following way: for the first half of the century through the 1980s, I read all the secondary sources on child-rearing literature and expert advice to women that I could locate via library searches. I read all the child-rearing texts to which the secondary sources referred. I then used the child-rearing texts to lead me to more texts. Whenever they referred to another expert or text, I read that as well. The texts that came up numerous times, such as those by Luther Emmett Holt and John B. Watson, became the focus of this study. To confirm that these were the most popular texts, I combed through the complete century in the *Reader's Guide to Periodical Literature.* I counted the number of articles by and about the authors I had found. Those that were never mentioned were dropped from the study.

Over a three-year period from 1999 to 2002, I bought and read all of the popular child-rearing books recommended to me by women that I interviewed and by those in parent groups that I took part in. I also read all of the popular books prominently displayed in the child-rearing sections of major bookstores in the urban area where I live. Finally, I read the books recommended by each of these books.

To get a better sense of the issues contemporary parents face, and to find out which texts were most influencing their approach to touch, I participated in parenting groups and subscribed to popular parenting magazines. These did not provide the focal evidence of my study. Rather, they helped me to grasp the issues parents face today and to track down the most central child-rearing literature.

After Isaiah was born in February 2000, I made use of my tiny new research assistant as a partner—literally—in arms. For a year I sat in on two weekly, almost uniformly white and middle-class, mother–infant groups. (Although the groups were open to men, to my knowledge, none ever attended.) The late Arlene Eisenberg, who wrote the popular *What to Expect* series with her two daughters, led one group. Often, after the meeting, some of the women would gather at a nearby coffee shop (as one might imagine, all the single people quickly packed up and left as around ten women with small babies descended upon the café). In informal conversation, I told the women about my study and discussed the issues involved with them.

I also conducted in-depth interviews with six white middle-class American mothers ranging in age from twenty-eight to seventy-three. These women represented a range of generations and child-rearing philosophies. All of these women had recently been in or were currently in heterosexual relationships.

In 2000, I subscribed to two of the most popular, and tellingly named, middle-class parenting magazines, the behaviorist-leaning *Parenting* and the solidly naturalist *Mothering,* and read the work of many experts cited there. As a result, in chapter 3 I examine the thinking on breastfeeding of the popular organization La Leche League International and of the mainstream American Academy of Pediatrics, and in chapter 4, I examine the advice of two extremely popular contemporary child-rearing specialists, Richard Ferber and William Sears, who are on opposite sides of the debates about sharing sleep versus using the crib. I therefore discuss Ferber's *Solve Your Child's Sleep Problems* (1985) and Sears's *Nighttime Parenting: How to Get Your Baby and Child to Sleep* (1985). Ferber is an advocate of what is now known as "Ferberizing" your child, under which, through a series of behavioral treatments, the child learns to sleep alone and through the night without waking. Sears, by contrast, is an advocate of a popular movement called "attachment parenting." He argues for sleeping with children, or what he calls "sleep sharing" in the "family bed." One reason Sears recommends "sleep sharing" is that it allows for more touching of the child. Even though their seminal texts were written twenty years ago, the Sears and Ferber approaches to child sleep crystallize the two key strains of thought on the subject today.

Chapter 5 focuses on the sociohistorical moment when adult–child touch, particularly sexual touch, became an issue of social power for the radical feminist movement of the 1960s and 1970s and the 1980s conservative backlash to feminism. The radical feminist movement raised the question of violence against women and girls. One of its primary concerns was "violent" touch. Under the rubric of violence, the radical feminists included father–daughter incest and child sexual abuse. In raising the issues of incest and child sexual abuse, radical feminists implicitly challenged the dominant ideologies of adult–child touch. And although feminists opposed the mainstream thinking on touch, they did not fully break away from its binary thinking. I look at the conceptualization of adult–child touch as violent and at its links to power in radical feminist literature. I explore the convergence of social scientific ideology, so prominent in the first half of the century, with the feminist ideology of the 1960s and 1970s, and then examine political thinking about adult–child touch from the late 1970s to the early 1990s. I conclude chapter 5 with an examination of how the ideas of radical feminism were exploited by conservatives and an exploration of the conservative focus on child sexual abuse, including the day-care scandals of the 1980s and the anti-feminist "backlash."[51]

Prescriptive Literature

My primary sources are prescriptive writings on child rearing. In particular, I review the most popular child-rearing books in the United States during the twentieth century. As the texts advise parents about child rearing, they counsel them on the "appropriate" touching of children by adults.

I realize that the use of prescriptive texts in sociohistorical work is problematic.[52] Foremost among the concerns are that we, first, cannot be sure who bought and read the literature and, second, know how seriously the advice was taken or if it actually influenced anyone's behavior. Clearly, the relationship between the ideologies expressed in the prescriptive literature and the behaviors of real people is problematic; there may be limits to what these books can tell us about how people truly lived. I don't argue, however, that parents followed any particular child-rearing advice. Indeed, I don't focus on the behavior of parents, but rather on the ideological milieu in which they lived. By noting the changes in prescriptive literature, I track the shifts and movement of the ideologies surrounding adult–child touch through the twentieth century.

For the purposes of my study, prescriptive texts also hold a distinct advantage. I am particularly interested in mainstream ideologies of adult–child touch. As noted by other social historians, the majority of prescriptive literature has a strong class bias. In her social history on advice to women, Maxine L. Margolis writes, "Most child-care manuals and household guides were written by, and intended for, the white urban middle class."[53] It must be noted that child-rearing advice was also meant for those who aspired to *become* middle class. Indeed, child-rearing expert advice was one medium for the Americanization campaigns "conducted by middle-class, largely Protestant reformers to usher immigrants into mainstream society."[54] Because of this class bias, prescriptive writings are a particularly good place to find mainstream or normative ideological thought.[55]

Mainstream White, Middle-Class Ideologies

I focus on white middle-class ideologies in the twentieth-century United States in part because I lacked the time and resources to examine other places and groups. Yet more than that, the mainstream white (and this was predominately Anglo-Saxon until the middle of the twentieth century) middle class has often been a norm-setting group in the United States, although not the only one. Indeed, I am interested in *ideological* norms rather than particular behaviors.

In *The Way We Never Were: American Families and the Nostalgia Trap*, sociologist Stephanie Coontz also focuses on the white middle class and its beliefs or "myths" because, as she argues, the white middle class is the predominant mythmaker in our society, and because the "media tends to project fragments of the white, middle-class experience into universal 'trends' or 'facts.'" Similar to Coontz, I am interested in mainstream ideologies because they are normative. And, like her, I argue that these ideologies "distort the diverse experiences of other groups in America and . . . they don't even describe most white, middle-class families accurately."[56]

Of course, race as a descriptive category must always be historically situated because it's a social construction rather than a biological reality. What it means to be "white" has changed over time in the United States. Early in the century, whiteness primarily described Anglo-Saxon middle- and upper-class Americans. As other ethnic groups with white skin, such as the Irish, Italians, and Greeks, sought membership—and were pushed to assimilate—they too over time "became white." As sociologist Scott Sernau argues, "whiteness is not so much about origins as it is about privilege."[57] As new racial lines were drawn, many groups with light skin entered this privileged category; others with darker skin were perpetually excluded. I argue that to become white in the early twentieth century, new immigrants and other light-skinned members of the working class assimilated by taking on Anglo-Saxon middle-class cultural norms such as those involved in child rearing.

Of special use to my work is sociologist Arlene Skolnick's explanation of her focus on the middle-class family in *Embattled Paradise: The American Family in an Age of Uncertainty* (1991). Skolnick writes that she's not unaware of the ways American families vary by race, class, region, religion, and gender preference, but says she focuses on the middle class because "the mainstream middle-class family has defined the norms of family life in America."[58] During the twentieth century, deviations from middle-class norms, such as single parenthood, have been considered deeply problematic digressions. Indeed, a cause of the current feeling of crisis is that "the middle class has been engaging in practices formerly considered deviant. Mothers work outside the home, unmarried couples live together, single women give birth or adopt children."[59] Ironically, the middle class has also been "America's most revolutionary class insofar as the family is concerned. Our major periods of family crisis have occurred when the middle class has redefined the meaning of the family."[60]

To begin my exploration of mainstream ideologies of adult–child touch and the connection of these ways of thinking to the meanings of family and other cultural phenomena, I now turn to the first half of the twentieth century.

TWO

The Rise of the Expert,
the Fall of the Mother

Most of us probably remember Dr. Spock, one of the earliest "scientific" experts offering popular child-rearing advice, who continues years after his death to instruct us. But he and all those others who glut today's marketplace with their recommendations and warnings are relatively new phenomena. In part, this is because of Spock's new at the time pro-touch leanings. Until the 1940s, most child-rearing experts were adamantly opposed to the intimate touching of children. Many advised against breastfeeding, and they were certainly against children sleeping in bed with their parents. Of central importance in this anti-touching period are the mind–body split and the dominant culture's general fear of the body and, in particular, of touching the body.

Yet, starting at the beginning of the twentieth century, child-rearing experts in general were a relatively new form of authority. Their influence took hold simultaneous to industrialization. With industrialization and modern science came new ideals about what it meant to be modern parents.[1] Increasingly, and in particular for the Anglo-American middle class, being "modern" meant turning to science to learn how to live. Further, science and modernity were associated with the modern principles of masculinity; this encompassed being male, rational, controlled/ing, strong, and, as one might imagine, heterosexual, middle-class Anglo-Saxon Protestant. Finally, being masculine meant an avoidance of emotion, physicality, and physical contact.

These ideologies expose underlying dualistic patterns of thought. Because many dualisms are embedded in and born from the fundamental Western mind–body split, in this chapter I address several of these binary variants, including the science versus nature dichotomy, the bad mother–good mother split, and the masculinist versus relational dualism.

In Western history for centuries, the body has been associated with that which is "savage" and the mind with that which is "godly" and "rational." The body also became associated with that which is not male, not middle class, and not white. Bordo argues that the "scheme is frequently gendered, with woman cast in the role of the body, 'weighed down,' in Beauvoir's words, 'by everything peculiar to it.'" In contrast, man casts himself as the "inevitable, like a pure idea, like the One, the All, the Absolute Spirit."[2] To touch the animalistic body, one risked awakening its ostensibly out-of-control passions. And thus, for a period of time in Anglo-American middle-class ideology, touching, including mothers touching their children, became taboo.

In the first half of the century, scientific experts on child rearing came largely from the fields of mainstream medicine and psychology and, in particular, the new behaviorist school of thought. Thus, I briefly examine the thinking on adult–child touch of the following experts: medical doctor Luther Emmett Holt, behaviorist psychologist John B. Watson, pediatrician and psychoanalyst Benjamin Spock, biologist Alfred C. Kinsey, and psychologist Harry F. Harlow. I also succinctly consider the challenge offered the experts by early popular health/back-to-nature movements.

Sociohistorical Context

Scientific Experts and Mothers

Well into the nineteenth century, many if not most parents in the United States sought parenting advice from the Bible and religion and from the families and communities in which they lived. With the advent of the twentieth century and the effects of industrialization, urbanization, and the growing power of technology, the prestige of science increasingly competed with religion in offering guidance to people on how to live in the modern age. Eventually, science, as well as the scientific expert, became the new god and authority on almost everything, including the newly recognized "work" of child rearing. The middle class, especially, looked to the scientific expert to learn how to raise their children.[3] And scientific experts in turn disseminated their special knowledge via the mass-mediated written word in books and magazines.

The rise of the scientific expert parallels the decline of the large family. Whereas in the past, religion, supported by the economic imperatives of farm life, sanctioned large families, now children were an expense rather than an asset. Given this, smaller families were increasingly common. As Robert S. Lynd and Helen Merrell Lynd wrote in their 1920s study done in Muncie, Indiana, *Middletown: A Study in Modern American Culture,* "families of six to fourteen children, upon which the grandparents of the present generation prided themselves, are considered as somehow not as 'nice' as families of two, three, or four children." They continued, "in this urban life of alluring alternate choices . . . children are mouths instead of productive hands." The Lynds claimed, "With increasing regulation of the size of the family, emphasis has shifted somewhat from child-bearing to child rearing."[4] This new focus on child rearing opened up a special place for the advice of scientific experts.

Prior to the advent of industrialization in the early 1800s, women worked alongside men in and around the home. Female and male adults, along with their children, took part in the productive labor necessary to live, as most people did, at a subsistence level. Work and life happened in the same place. This did not mean that each person was valued equally, or that all were accorded the same rights. In fact, until the mid-1800s, married women had no right to own property. Women entered marriage as dependents of their husbands. The fruits of free women's work legally belonged to their husbands; free men owned the products of their free wives' and children's labor. And, except for the enslaved, fathers had complete legal custody of their children. They could marry off or apprentice their children without the mother's approval.

With industrialization in the nineteenth century, the new cash economy spread. More and more men, and some women, began to work for wages. However, most women still worked and lived primarily in the barter economy of the home and family. Slowly, "work" became synonymous with the labor done by men for a wage. And usually this work was done in the public "workplace" or factory away from the private sphere of the home. Economics journalist Ann Crittenden argues, "The stage was set for the assumption—still with us—that men 'supported' their wives at home, as if unpaid work were not productive and not part of the 'real' economy." Crittenden continues, "One of the first appearances of the monetary definition of 'productive' is in Alexander Hamilton's 1791 *Report on Manufactures,* an argument for national investment in manufacturing industries. Only goods that could be sold to create revenue were included in Hamilton's definition of 'the total produce' of society. He attributed a 'superiority' of . . . productiveness to labor whose product was geared for exchange outside the household."[5] In contrast to "productive" labor, reproductive labor was, and remains, unpaid. Needless to say, both forms of labor were and remain inextricably bound with cultural categories of gender, sex, and (hetero)sexuality.

As women's work in the home sphere lost status as "labor," it gained a new kind of sentimental status as that which upholds private morality and love in a cold and calculating world. Crittenden writes, "The emerging ideology of 'separate spheres' thus served a dual purpose: it discouraged women from demanding greater participation in public and economic life, and it gave mothers license—and the moral authority—to rear their children as they saw fit. It ratified the withdrawal of fathers from the home and the expansion of mothers' responsibilities within it. Women's new assignment brought with it a significant strengthening of their domestic position."[6] The new emphasis on motherhood worked to keep women out of the mainstream public sphere. As Alexis de Tocqueville noted, "American women never manage the outward concerns of the family or conduct a business or take part in political life. . . . Nor have the Americans ever supposed that one consequence of democratic principles is the subversion of marital power."[7]

Yet the new focus on motherhood did not only keep women out of public life. Intensive mothering—and the huge investments of time increasingly deemed mandatory for child rearing—was believed necessary to the developing of the capitalist economy and to the growing middle class's survival within it. "By the late eighteenth century, the countries with the most dynamic economies of the day, the rising bourgeoisie understood that their children would have to become educated, motivated little achievers if they were going to improve or even maintain their station in life."[8]

In a subsistence agrarian economy, even very young children supply valuable help in the family enterprise. People need not and cannot spend limited resources, including emotions and time, on their children. Rather, their children "spend" themselves on their families. Yet, in the modern United States capitalist economy, children have ceased to provide economic value to their families. Instead, modern children in wealthy capitalist nations are an expense for their parents. This does not mean that children are "useless" for the modern economy. In fact they are—or they will be—essential, when they grow up. Crittenden writes, "As the story of the family is conventionally told, virtually all serious economic activity had left the household by the mid-nineteenth century, as manufacturing migrated from farms into factories. The household evolved from a workplace, where most necessities were produced, into a place of leisure, consumption, and emotional replenishment; a 'haven in a heartless world.' Ostensibly, industrialization put families, and the women in them, 'out of business.'"[9] Of course, the family remained central to the economy. Only the things produced in and the services offered by the home changed. Crittenden writes, "The new domestic product was the intensively raised child."[10]

During the socioeconomic transformation from a preindustrial to an industrial society, United States families changed as labor units. Whereas in the preindustrial society the family had produced food, the industrial family produced educated laborers for the industrial labor market. Children were products-in-process; they were to be the future workers. Women's job was to raise and prepare them for this. However, this was neither women's nor children's only role; both women and children were potential consumers as well. And in the early part of the twentieth century, these consumer roles were increasingly important to business.[11]

Of course child rearing, and eventually consumption, were only a part of the work done at home by women. In the increasingly commercial economy, "women by default had to perform what had been men's and even children's domestic work." Men left the home to work and older children left the home to go to school. "The family's unpaid labor force was shrinking down to the adult women, who had to handle chores with animals, gardens, and repairs on top of the traditional work of cooking, cleaning, and child care. The angel of the hearth was increasingly on her own, up to her elbows in coal dust and soapsuds."[12]

Child-rearing expertise coupled with the new "domestic science" played several roles within the middle class. These new "fields" legitimized the work of white middle-class women as they were pushed out of other forms of productive labor and relegated to the private realm of the home. Yet as these areas of scientific study gave prestige to middle-class women's work, they also delegitimized the "traditional" knowledge of women about child bearing and child rearing as unscientific and dangerous. Childbirth and child rearing entered the area of mainstream medicine. They became bodies of scientific knowledge that women must learn about or risk damaging the health and well-being of their children and families.

Indeed, in the early twentieth century, scientific medicine quickly moved from a marginal to central position in many areas of mainstream American culture. As Freund, McGuire, and Podhurst argue, "In the nineteenth century, most medical doctors were barely considered professionals. Their credentials were relatively easy to achieve (or fake), their body of medical knowledge was skimpy . . . and their abilities to heal were not particularly impressive."[13]

However, in the early twentieth century, "medical doctors achieved, within just a few decades, virtually total professional dominance. Subsequently, they successfully eliminated, co-opted, or subordinated all competing health professionals."[14] Via the process of medicalization, child rearing was just one of many areas that "previously were not defined as properly 'mèdical' matters but, through the medical profession's influence were redefined as needing doctors' attention."[15]

Along with its role in the middle-class social construction of gender, child-rearing expertise played a part in the "Americanization project" of the white Protestant middle class. This was at a time when massive numbers of immigrants from Europe were surging into the United States. Furthermore, early in the twentieth century there was extensive working-class resistance to industrial capitalism. Both of these factors played a role in making the middle class extremely nervous about the growing and noncompliant working class and the new immigrants particularly. Through their Americanization project, the middle class took on the task of turning the strange immigrant cultures and the resistant working class into "civilized"—scientific—peoples. Raising one's children in a scientific manner, according to the advice of child-rearing experts, became a way of delineating class. "Scientific" meant "civilized." "Civilized" meant "American." And "American" meant middle class.[16]

Mothers, Marriage, and the "Traditional" Family

At the end of the nineteenth century, most American women lived what sociologist Arlene Skolnick calls the "marriage plot" story line. The marriage plot is one of the two basic narratives commonly found in modern Western culture. The other is the male story of adventure and heroism.[17] In the marriage plot, the heroine looks for and finds heterosexual love, marries, has children, and lives "happily ever after" caring for her children and husband. In nineteenth-century Western culture, the marriage plot describes the reality of most women's lives (with or without the love and happiness). In 1900, only 6 percent of married women worked outside the home.[18] These 6 percent were mostly poor, immigrant, and African American women. Marginalized from white middle-class society already, these women working outside the home and thus rupturing mainstream norms garnered little attention.

The early stages of modernization helped to develop the marriage plot story as a cultural ideal. The "traditional" family of the marriage plot consists of a mother who stays home and cares for her husband and children, and a father who works outside the home as the family "breadwinner." This traditional marriage plot family might also be called the traditional "breadwinner" family, where it is husbands, not wives, who are employed outside the home. Women stay at home and men work in the public sphere for a wage with which they—more or less—support their families. When conservative politicians and religious figures speak about "family values" and the "traditional family," this is the family structure to which they refer.

Yet as sociologist Kingsley Davis argues, this traditional breadwinner family is an "aberration that arose in a particular stage of development and tends to recur in countries now undergoing development."[19] Many look to the 1950s for an example of the traditional family in the midst of its heyday and before its supposed decline began. Yet in reality, the 1950s were an oddity in the twentieth century. Over the course of the whole century, people have come to marry later and later in life, birth rates have dropped, and divorce rates have risen. In fact, divorce rates have been rising in a steady pattern since the mid-nineteenth century. Only one decade, the 1950s, diverged from this trend. Further, during the twentieth century, women have been increasingly leaving home to work for a wage. The increase of women in the workforce continued even during the 1950s, albeit at a slower rate.

The 1950s were a strange moment in the middle of fairly consistent patterns in the surrounding decades. In other words, the marriage plot cultural ideal is just that—an ideal. The so-called traditional family is actually not very "traditional." And we have no authentic enchanted-family past to look back upon.

The breadwinner family developed in the early stages of the Industrial Revolution. Before that, work had been centered in the home with all members of the family taking part. With the Industrial Revolution and ensuing modernization, the workplace shifted to the new and separate public industrial sphere. Simultaneously, the private sphere, made up of women and children in the home, arose. This new breadwinner family slowly spread with the process of modernization until it reached its apex in 1890.[20]

Yet, as Skolnick argues, "the early stages of modernization helped to create the breadwinner/housewife family, [and] the later stages helped to undo it."[21] Again, during the course of the twentieth century, more and more women left the home and entered the separate public sphere of the workplace. Nonetheless, in child-rearing literature throughout the century, and still today, most experts assume that women do not work outside of the home and that the 1950s enchanted-family ideal was and is reality. With this background, I now turn to the early scientific experts and their child-rearing advice.

Luther Emmett Holt

One of the earliest and most popular child-rearing experts was Dr. Luther Emmett Holt—indeed, Dr. Spock's own mother used Holt's advice in raising her
son. Holt offered his readers a new, modern scientific ethos in his once-famous
book, *The Care and Feeding of Children,* originally published in 1894, with multiple later editions including a second revised and enlarged edition in 1901. It
was a stiff-backed book that castigated touch between parent and child.

Holt tipped his hat to the religious "experts" of the past by subtitling his
book *A Catechism for the Use of Mothers and Children's Nurses.* Against ancient
wisdoms, Holt argued the cause of science. He warned his readers that mothers' knowledge was limited and that they should look to science for guidance
rather than relying on misleading "motherly instincts."

> If a man wishes to raise the best grain or vegetables, or the finest cattle or
> horses, all admit that he must study the conditions under which alone
> such things are possible. If he is in doubt regarding these matters he may
> apply to the Agriculture Department at Washington, and be furnished
> with the reports of the best scientific work on these subjects by experts
> who make these matters their study under government supervision. But
> instinct and maternal love are too often assumed to be a sufficient guide
> for a mother.[22]

No longer were women seen as having an innate or "instinctual" ability to
mother. Nor did they learn about the rearing of children from their parents
and extended families. Women were told to turn to science rather than "intuition"—or other women—to learn about mothering.

Holt's text represented the beginning of decades of scientific experts telling
women how to raise their children. Yet Holt offered no evidence or studies to
back his claims. Indeed, the only scientific evidence readers received was on
the title page where Holt's name was shown. Here readers saw the following
credentials: "By L. Emmett Holt, M.D." and "Professor of diseases of children
in the New York Polyclinic; attending physician to the Babies' Hospital and
The Nursery and Child's Hospital, New York."[23] Holt himself was trained as a
scientist and this seemed to be all the scientific proof Holt needed; at any rate,
it was all he offered. His lack of scientific grounds for his supposedly scientific
conclusions is itself evidence of the ideological nature of his thinking.

Nonetheless, people increasingly wanted to learn from science how to
rear their children. Indeed, the Lynds found that in both working-class and
middle-class families there was an "attitude that child rearing is something

not to be taken for granted but to be studied." They claimed, "One cannot talk with Middletown mothers without being continually impressed by the eagerness of many to lay hold of every available resource for help in training their children."[24] Along with women's magazines, many women looked to such "'baby books' as Holt's *Care and Feeding of Infants*" which was "supplanting the family 'recipe book' of 1890."[25] The Lynds found that although families were now smaller, nonetheless, many parents were overwhelmed by the plethora of scientific child-rearing information. One woman they interviewed claimed, "Life was simpler for my mother. . . . In those days one did not realize that there was so much to be known about the care of children."[26]

This new scientific approach to child rearing sprang in part from the larger movement of modernity into people's everyday lives. The modern and its scientific approach to life were both frightening and exciting. The unfamiliarity of modern science engendered confusion. Yet it also brought hope. People understood science as offering them the possibility of freedom from the age-old terrifying human problems of hunger and disease. This mixture of anxiety and hope was the emotional backdrop for many of the child-rearing ideologies of the early twentieth century.

Avoiding disease through sanitary environments and through controlling even the most mundane details of children's behavior was a core component of turn-of-the-century child-rearing advice to the middle class. The fear of disease was not an idle anxiety. In fact, disease lurked as a deadly reality for everyone. Women in particular shared special vulnerabilities. Women across the social classes repeatedly risked death, and often died, in childbirth. The first year that national statistics are available is 1915, and in that year, "61 women died for every 10,000 live babies born" (compared to 2 per 10,000 in more recent decades).[27] In all likelihood, this is already an improvement from prior years. And this number does not even account for women's lives lost during childbirth when the baby did not survive. Tuberculosis—TB or the "white plague"—presented another special threat to women, especially young women. In the mid-nineteenth century, tuberculosis spread at epidemic rates, and it continued to be a major problem affecting everyone well into the twentieth century. Young women were particularly vulnerable and often died "at rates twice as high as men of their own age groups."[28] And, of course, poor women especially succumbed to the hazards of childbearing and tuberculosis. Contagious diseases have almost always attacked the poor hardest of all; further, poor women contended with the dangers and diseases of industrial work as well.

Given the omnipresence of disease, it makes sense that science became a kind of religion. Yet as Ehrenreich and English, among others, argue, scientism, or science worship, grew from something more than just pragmatics. Scientific ideology held and engendered special qualities that were very appealing in the early twentieth-century United States and Europe. Science appeared to be "tough and yet transcendent—hardheaded and masculine, yet at the same time able to 'soar above' commercial reality."[29] In other words, scientific ideology fulfilled and reinforced a larger modern Western masculine social ideal. Science, like the model man, was understood to have willpower, honor, and courage; it never shrank from the Truth.[30] Much like perfected masculinity, science had an image of "uncompromising disinterestedness and objectivity."[31] This masculine aura gave "science its great moral force in the mind of the public."[32] And this very association between masculinity and science both promoted and reinforced the deep misogyny of early twentieth-century child-rearing advice.[33]

At the turn of the twentieth century, the development of domestic science as an area of expertise coincided with that of "germ theory," the new bacteriologists' theory that diseases were spread through contagious bacteria germs, and also with the arrival of immense numbers of immigrants into the United States. "Germ Theory, which became known to the public in the eighteen nineties . . . set off a wave of public anxiety about contagion."[34] Fear of disease was not unrelated to middle-class fears of "contagion" from the "lower orders." For example, an author warned readers in her household hygiene book, *Women, Plumbers and Doctors, or Household Sanitation,* "A man may live on the splendid 'avenue,' in a mansion plumbed in the latest and costliest style, but if, half a mile away, in range with his open window, there is a 'slum,' or even a neglected tenement house, the zephyrs will come along and pick up the disease germs and bear them onward, distributing them to whomsoever it meets, whether he be a millionaire or a shillingaire."[35] And, as Ehrenreich and English argue, "When domestic science leaders . . . spoke of the endangered home, their first concern was with the middle-class home. It had to be rationalized, sanitized, and, above all, stabilized through the efforts of its resident domestic 'scientist,' the scientific homemaker."[36] "But," Ehrenreich and English continue with an edge of sarcasm, "anyone with a minimum of social awareness could see that the gravest threat to the home, and hence to 'civilization,' lay in the urban slums."[37] Immigrants, along with African Americans and other people of color, were seen as deeply threatening to the white middle class. Not only were they believed to carry "germs," they also threatened what was understood to be the very nature of middle-class Americans. The middle class was invested in "converting" or Americanizing those who could be converted—those with white skin—and drawing strict boundaries between themselves and the rest.

Expert advice was informed by and reproduced both a fear of disease and the Americanization project. Holt argued implicitly against touching children, although he never explicitly addressed touch per se. At that time, middle-class people's positive belief in breastfeeding was only beginning to shift. According to Holt, even when being fed from a bottle or taken out for a walk, a baby should not be carried in arms; it should be placed in its carriage. No Snugglies for Dr. Holt. In fact, he argued that babies should not be played with or held at all but kept still and alone in their cribs. To the question as to what age playing with babies might begin, Holt answered, "Never until four months, and better not until six months. The less of it at any time the better for the infant."[38] Playing with infants makes them "nervous and irritable, sleep badly, and suffer in other respects."[39] Finally, he did not waver about whether or not a child should sleep in the same bed with its mother or nurse: "Under no circumstances. . . . Very young infants have often been smothered by their mothers, by overlying during sleep. If the infant sleeps with the mother, there is always the temptation to frequent nursing at night, which is injurious to both mother and child."[40] It is interesting that Holt uses the same still-unsubstantiated reason employed today for keeping babies out of adult beds—anxiety about smothering the baby.

All this reasoned advice of Holt's comes out of a particular way of viewing daily life: a middle-class bias. Holt assumed that his readers had the resources to organize their child rearing according to his dictates. Of course, many did not. He made this bias clear when he claimed that not only should children sleep apart from adults but also each child should have his or her own bed. "Older children also should, if possible, have separate beds; many contagious diseases and bad habits are contracted by children sleeping together."[41]

Holt focused on the development of "good habits"—white middle-class habits—rather than messing about with children's emotional issues. He argued that children should be trained quickly and without fuss to use the toilet, wean, sleep through the night, and feed efficiently on a schedule. For example, infants who cry "from habit" or out "of indulgence" should be trained to stop. About such children Holt wrote, "This is often heard even in very young infants, who cry to be rocked, to be carried about, sometimes for a light in the room, for a bottle to suck, or for the continuance of any other bad habit which has been acquired."[42] By no means should infants be comforted when crying. They should be fed on schedule and changed when wet. "If all these matters are properly adjusted and the child simply crying to be taken up, it should not be further interfered with. . . . It should simply be allowed to cry it out."[43] Holt argued that in very little time, the infant will learn to be quiet. "A second struggle will be shorter and a third rarely necessary."[44]

Holt had two special obsessions: thumb-sucking and regular bowel movements. He insisted that a child may "be trained to be regular in its bowels . . . by endeavoring to have them move at exactly the same time every day."[45] By what age should an infant be using the potty? "Usually by the second month if training is begun early."[46] Holt described his training method in detail. He suggested twice a day, at the same hour, immediately following the morning and afternoon feedings, placing the infant over a "small chamber, about the size of a pint bowl." At first, he explained, "there may be necessary some local irritation, like that produced by tickling the anus or introducing just inside the rectum a small cone of oiled paper or a piece of soap, as a suggestion of the purpose for which the baby is placed upon the chamber; but in a surprisingly short time the position is all that is required. With most infants, after a few weeks the bowels will move as soon as the infant is placed on the chamber."[47]

Holt's thinking was part of a broader white middle-class attempt to control children through the definition of "acceptable" touching. In other words, tolerable touching entailed adults touching children for the purpose of managing them. The aim was to be in charge of even the child's most mundane behavior. This attitude swept through the United States and affected behavior as minor as thumb-sucking. Medical professionals went to great lengths to stop an infant from sucking her or his thumb, an activity believed to cause disease. Doctors and nurses regularly insisted that parents put white cloth mitts on the baby's hands or apply bad-tasting glue or iodine to the thumb. About this "bad habit," Holt wrote, "In the case of sucking or nail-biting, confining the hands to the sides during sleep or the wearing of mittens will often succeed if persisted in. The application of pasteboard splints to the elbows makes it impossible for the child to get his hand to his mouth. On no account should the habit of sucking be allowed as a means of putting children to sleep or of quieting them while restless or suffering from indigestion."[48] If the baby persisted in thumb-sucking, the behavior had to be forcibly stopped by tying the baby's wrists to the sides of the crib.

John B. Watson

This was an era in which touch not meant to control children was essentially unacceptable. The middle class felt that children were not to be touched—or allowed to touch themselves—else they risked harm both to their physical well-being and to their character development. Indeed, two women I interviewed, Laura and Jeanette, both in their early seventies, told stories about their childhoods filled with controlling touch and void of other physical contact.

For example, Jeanette had a younger brother who was fed by bottle in his crib. Her mother did not even hold the bottle but propped it up while he drank. Jeanette explained that the only noninvasive touch he received was while being burped and bathed. There was, however, a lot of invasive touch. This included enemas and years of forced feeding. Laura herself was regularly force-fed until she was three years old. And Laura had a cousin who was force-fed for many years. Seemingly in response to the force-feeding, this child began spontaneously vomiting. She would often vomit after eating, or at other times too, such as when her mother would arrive to pick her up from a visit to Laura's home. Jeanette claimed that children "had no say" about food intake, defecation, or clothing. Their bodies were, quite literally, not their own. And, as Holt demanded, children were even controlled in how they touched themselves.

This anti-touch ethos only increased in the decades following Holt. By the 1920s, psychologist John B. Watson had invented behaviorism, a system that thoroughly incorporated how, when, and where to touch children into its methods. Watson's *Psychological Care of Infant and Child* (1928) complemented Holt's more practical guide. Both Jeanette and Laura were raised in the 1930s on Watson's behaviorist principles.

Watson himself explained his expertise in reference to Holt: "Ever since my first glimpse of Dr. Holt's 'The Care and Feeding of Children,' I hoped some day to be able to write a book on the psychological care of the infant. I believed then that psychological care was just as necessary as physiological care. Today I believe it is in some ways more important."[49]

Unlike Holt, Watson did refer to his own scientific research as the basis for his claim to being "scientific." Indeed, he began his book with the following acknowledgments: "The scientific material, upon which the convictions set forth in this small book are based, has been gathered in the Maternity Ward of the Johns Hopkins Hospital, the Harriet Lane Home for Crippled Children, at the Heckscher Foundation, and in many private homes."[50] Further, Watson devoted a full chapter to discussing "How the behaviorist studies infants and children."[51] However, as one might imagine, Watson made giant leaps between his behavioral scientific evidence garnered in laboratory studies of infants and children and his anti-touching theories. Often while reading Watson's famous book, I struggled to find any connection at all between the studies he described and the child-rearing practice he promoted.

Watson explicitly focused on *touching* as a locus of parental—and in particular motherly—harm to children. "Never hug and kiss them, never let them sit in your lap," he advised. "If you must, kiss them once on the forehead when they say good night. Shake hands with them in the morning."[52] He argued that children do not love naturally or instinctively—they love in response to being touched: "Our laboratory studies show that we can bring out a love response in a new born child by just one stimulus—*by stroking its skin*. The more sensitive the skin area, the more marked the response."[53] He considered this a deeply dangerous phenomenon: "Love reactions soon dominate the child. It requires no instinct, no 'intelligence,' no 'reasoning' on the child's part for such responses to grow up."[54]

Indeed, Watson believed there were no intrinsic human instincts. Children, he argued, become who they become purely as a result of their parental upbringing and childhood environment. "There are no instincts. We build in at an early age everything that is later to appear."[55] Watson represents one of two major ideological strands about child rearing running through the twentieth century, "behaviorism." The behaviorists believed children should be systematically trained to enter the human community. For them, nurture, not nature, was everything. Through training, children become useful members of society. The behaviorists argued that *only* they, in their role as scientific experts, could tell women how to raise their children and mother. The behaviorists claimed that if women were left to their own inclinations, they would harm their children. In particular, women caused harm through touching their offspring.

The consequences of too much touching show themselves in, interestingly, nonmasculine traits such as whining, sickness, and frailty—"invalidism." And it wasn't just any touch that worried Watson. What really threatened children was feminine touch and female bodies. Mothers were dangerous. Watson asked his readers, "Won't you then remember when you are tempted to pet your child that mother love is a dangerous instrument? An instrument which may inflict a never healing wound, a wound which may make infancy unhappy, adolescence a nightmare, an instrument which may wreck your adult son or daughter's vocational future and their chances for marital happiness."[56] Indeed, in the 1920s, Americans generally began to think that mothers were hazardous to your health. They were bad at mothering unless proven otherwise.

Watson argued that "mother love" ran a high risk of being irrational. He never felt compelled to define what he meant by "mother love," yet when he referred to it, he clearly described it as women touching their children. Nothing could be more detrimental both to the individual child and to society at large. One complete chapter of his book was devoted to this menace: "Chapter three: The danger of too much mother love." In it he wrote, "It may tear the heart strings a bit, this thought of stopping the tender outward demonstration of love for your children or of their love for you. But if you are convinced that this is best for the child, aren't you willing to stifle a few pangs? Mothers just don't know, when they kiss their children and pick them up and rock them, caress them and jiggle them upon their knee, that they are slowly building up a human being totally unable to cope with the world it must later live in."[57]

Whereas Watson particularly feared the danger presented by women, his fear was not unusual. Anxieties about women, feminization, and homosexuality were ongoing themes of modernity. These fears counteracted the modern celebration of the masculine and heteronormative culture. Much as women represented "femininity," religion, and the traditional past, men represented masculinity, science, and the modern future. Historian George L. Mosse writes, "the male body . . . was thought to symbolize society's need for order and progress, as well as middle-class virtues such as self-control and moderation. Woman as a public symbol was a reminder of the past, of innocence and chastity."[58] Indeed, modern masculinity played a central part in upholding the sharp boundary between men and women that is so essential to modernity, and the masculine ideal was itself supported by that boundary.

Mosse claims, "At the beginning of the nineteenth century women lost whatever small gains they had made during the eighteenth century Enlightenment and were confined to a sphere clearly distinct from that assigned to men; their task was governing the household and educating the children. . . . Women as individuals had no place in public life."[59] This did not mean that men were superior to women so much as that each had different social roles. People believed that women and men complemented one another. "This difference was all-important in the construction of modern masculinity, which . . . defined itself against a countertype but also in connection with the differences between the sexes. For example, the word *effeminate* came into general usage during the eighteenth century indicating an unmanly softness and delicacy."[60] This "unmanly softness and delicacy" was, of course, also linked in people's minds with the impending "threat" of male homosexuality. Ultimately, the gendered separation between men and women, and the separation's meaning for the support of modern masculinity and heteronormativity, have remained firmly in place through the twentieth century to the present.

Mosse argues about the masculine ideal, "The ideal of masculinity was invoked on all sides as a symbol of personal and national regeneration, but also as basic to the self-definition of modern society. Manliness was supposed to safeguard the existing order against the perils of modernity, but it was also regarded as an indispensable attribute of those who wanted change. Indeed, the exhortation 'to be a man' became commonplace . . . during the nineteenth century or the first half of the twentieth."[61] Mosse claims that although it was a unique historical occurrence, modern masculinity was inextricably connected to the development of the modern social world and its ensuing anxieties and desires. Mosse writes, "Examining the manly ideal means dealing [with] . . . the ideals and functions of normative society."[62]

Watson had a solution to the mother problem: children should be reared away from home and parents. About this, he wrote, "It is a serious question in my mind whether there should be individual homes for children—or even whether children should know their own parents. There are undoubtedly much more scientific ways of bringing up children which will probably mean finer and happier children."[63] Being the scientist he was, he recognized reality: the home was "inevitably and inexorably with us. Even though it is proven unsuccessful, we shall always have it."[64] So he focused on getting mothers to do a better job—in other words, to stop touching their offspring. Because they lacked expertise in mothering, mothers had to scrupulously follow the instruction of the experts.

One answer to the problem of "mother love" never occurred to Watson. Sending mothers to the workplace full time would have certainly cut back on their "excessive" touching of their children. It would keep their female—dangerous—bodies under control. But in the 1920s, experts felt that the only women who could safely pursue careers were those who had no children. Married women with children were permitted to have hobbies, as long as they were not too serious and did not take up too much time, but their place was in the home, with their hands off their children.

Not surprisingly, all this advice was addressed to middle-class women. Married working-class or poor women couldn't afford to live by such guidance. Even so, those who bucked the experts and went to work comprised only 12 percent of married women in 1930. It was not until the 1960s feminist movement that the assumption that women must stay home to rear their children began to be challenged.

Being a man, Watson, of course, did not stay home. Indeed, he was deeply embedded in the highly restrictive "masculine" world of science and industry—so embedded that he was actually an industrial psychologist who worked for early big-business public-relations projects. The overlap between Watson's worlds was clear. His behaviorist method of child rearing held that raising children ought to be done much like a scientific experiment. Children were to be reared in a very controlled time- and cost-effective manner. This was the era of the behavioral "scientific management" of workers—a highly detailed system designed to maximize production that broke down even the most trivial actions of the worker, such as raising the shovel, digging in the dirt, lifting the dirt, and so on, in order to increase efficiency. The behaviorist method of child rearing was part of scientific management's domestic counterpart called, not coincidentally, "domestic science."

It was a strategy that made sense to a country deep into industrialization and assembly-line production. In fact, it was so pervasive, even housewives looked for ways to incorporate it into their routines. So, for middle-class women, time-efficient mothering became an all-consuming job, leaving no time for outside employment. Indeed, this was the historical moment when women's work in the home first began to be understood as *work*. Indirectly, this may be Watson's greatest contribution to American life. In this schema, women were seen as *workers,* or even managers, of the household. And what they did was no longer merely an issue of what was "best" for the child, but rather what was best for American capitalism. Running a household involved consuming mass-produced goods and making decisions about how money was spent in the home. This was big business.

Watson struggled to incorporate rigidly firm schedules into American households. Everything—everything—should be set to, and kept to, clock time. Watson wrote, "Modern training calls always for an orderly life."[65] He offered the ideal daily schedule, beginning first thing in the morning with plans for waking, orange juice, urination, brief quiet play, and an orderly bowel movement.

> Usually from 1 year of age to 3 pediatricians specify that orange juice shall be given when the child wakes up in the morning. Children who sleep properly awaken on a schedule. The waking time can easily be set for 6:30. The orange juice should then be given regularly at that hour every morning, the child put on the toilet for the relief of the bladder (only). Put the child back to bed and allow it to sit up in bed and play quietly alone with one or two chosen toys. It should be taken up at 7 o'clock, sponged lightly, dressed and given its breakfast at 7:30; then allowed to romp until 8, then put on the toilet for 20 minutes or less (until the bowel movement is complete).[66]

As he acknowledges, much of Watson's thinking picks up where Holt leaves off. He does not challenge Holt but further develops Holt's child-rearing advice to incorporate human psychology. Holt argued for a highly scheduled home. Watson made that schedule more detailed; his program incorporates nearly every minute of the day. Watson also offered the behaviorist *psychological* reason for the schedule. For example, Watson commenced with Holt's potty-training advice in which newborn infants are trained to use the toilet regularly by two months. He developed this advice, arguing that by eight months the baby should be using the toilet alone (once strapped to it). "The infant from 8 months of age onward should have a special toilet seat into which he can be safely strapped. *The child should be left in the bathroom without toys and with the door closed.* Under no circumstances should the door be left open or the mother or nurse stay with the child. This is a rule which seems to be almost universally broken. When broken it leads to dawdling, loud conversation, in general to unsocial and dependent behavior."[67] It is interesting to note that according to Watson, neglecting his advice resulted in "unsocial and dependent" children. Indeed, to be "dependent" seems to mean "unsocial" for Watson. This anxiety about dependency runs through the twentieth century to the present in behaviorist thought.

For Watson, nothing seemed to legitimate challenging his strict program. Even the endless crying of a small infant was not a reason to alter the schedule. In her famous novel about a set of middle- and upper-class young white women in 1930s, *The Group* (1954), Mary McCarthy's character Priss struggles with listening to her baby cry, and cry, and cry, on his feeding schedule. Yet, as was the custom, hungry or not, the baby Stephen had to wait until feeding time. "He was in the nursery now, behind the plate-glass window at the end of the corridor—roaring his head off; his feeding time was at six o'clock."[68] Priss's mother comments on Stephen's crying, "'That's Stephen again,' said Mrs. Hartshorn. 'I recognize his voice. He yells louder than any other baby in the nursery.'" Priss's husband responds to her with his belief in another of Holt's and Watson's ideas—that babies cry for exercise.

> "Shows he's a healthy young fellow," replied Sloan. "Time to worry if he didn't cry for his dinner. Eh, Priss?" Priss smiled wanly. "Sloan says it's good for his lungs," she said, grimacing. "Develops them," agreed Sloan. "Like a bellows." He drew air into his chest and released it.
>   Mrs. Hartshorn looked at her watch. "Can't the nurse bring him in now?" she wondered. "It's quarter of six." "The *schedule,* Mother!" cried Priss. "The reason babies in your time had colic [was] . . . because they were picked up at all sorts of irregular times and fed whenever they cried. The point is to have a schedule and stick to it absolutely!"[69]

In spite of her conviction when speaking with her mother, Stephen's crying between feedings was very difficult for Priss. The most awful was when he woke up hungry and distraught right after having been fed; then, he had a long wait in front of him before he would be fed again. The nurses gave him water to tide him over but no milk. "If he woke shortly after a feeding, it was horrible; after an hour's cry, he would get his water, sleep, wake up and cry again without stopping—his record, so far, was two hours and three-quarters. . . . The nights were the worst. There were nights when, hearing him start at three or four in the morning, she would have welcomed anything that would let him stop and rest—paregoric, a sugar-tit, any of those wicked things."[70] Further, in true Watson-like form, holding or touching babies to calm them was strictly forbidden. McCarthy writes, "It was against the rules for the nurses to pick him up; they were allowed to change him and give him a drink of water, and that was all. The babies were not supposed to be 'handled.'"[71]

Watson spoke primarily—and intentionally—to a middle-class audience. He wrote, "I have written principally to mothers who have leisure to devote to the study of their children." He hoped that "some day the importance of the first two years of infancy will be fully realized. When it is faced, every woman will seriously question whether she is in a proper situation to have a child. . . . No mother has a right to have a child who cannot give it a room to itself for the first two years of infancy. I would make this a *conditio sine qua non.*"[72]

He was supremely confident he would be listened to. For by this time in the United States, part of what it meant to be middle class was to look to science for advice, even in everyday matters like raising one's children. No longer did women go to their mothers and grandmothers or female friends for advice. Nor were they told to trust their own bodily common sense or "intuition." To be "civilized"—that is, to be middle class—meant being rational, of the mind and scientific.

Holt's and Watson's focus on the middle class and, in turn, the middle-class fascination with science is not unrelated to the eugenics movement of the early twentieth century. Eugenicists believed that "character (including moral traits as well as intelligence) is inherited"[73] and that human beings should be bred to maximize their intelligence and good character. Of course, the Anglo-American middle class believed themselves to represent the very best, to date, in human genes. Yet they felt deeply threatened by the degenerative others—such as the immigrants, African Americans, and working class more generally—all around them. In the United States, the science of eugenics justified both miscegenation laws that restricted interracial marriage and compulsory sterilization of the "mentally unfit" through the middle of the twentieth century.[74] From the beginning of the movement to bring child rearing into the scientific fold, eugenics influenced child-rearing experts and interested mothers. Indeed, "child study" organizations such as the National Congress of Mothers (later to be renamed the Parent–Teacher Association, or PTA) "put the rhetoric of eugenics in the service of educational and environmental reform."[75] At their 1905 annual meeting, a conference speaker deplored "the unpropitious conditions which environ much of the childhood of the race, and from which only a dwarfed humanity can come forth."[76] Other middle-class organizations interested in questions of child rearing and "child welfare" were also drawn to eugenics. For instance, in 1919, the "Women's Christian Temperance Union appropriated $10,000 annually for five years"—not an insignificant sum—to the study of eugenics in the hope of improving scientific knowledge of "normal" child development.[77]

The new domestic science did not only have a white middle-class bias, it was also extremely hostile toward women. It took away contemporary middle-class women's last vestige of expertise. No longer were women the "natural" keepers of home and children. They had to be suspicious of their mothers' and grandmothers' knowledge and of their own "instincts." What was women's intuition to science? Not only was the ethos of the movement implicitly misogynist, certain practitioners were explicitly so. Watson himself made no attempt to veil his negative feelings about women, dedicating his child-rearing book to "the first mother who brings up a happy child."[78] An odd child-rearing expert from our vantage point, Watson thought women were incapable of raising happy children.

Benjamin Spock

Happiness aside, my own grandmother, an Irish American from a family of working-class immigrants hoping to become "white," hoping to become "civilized," raised her children according to Watson's dictates. She told my mother how hard it was to listen to her first baby cry and cry from his cradle and not be able to pick him up. By the time my mother arrived, the times were finally beginning to change. Unfortunately, my grandmother herself was slow to transform, so the new—touching—culture probably did not help my mother much, but it certainly influenced how my mother raised us, her three children. She read Dr. Spock.

In fact, most people see the touch tide turning with Benjamin Spock. And Spock was indeed a challenge to experts like Watson on every level. After decades of being dangerous, women's bodies were beginning to be seen as potentially nurturing and good. Spock focused on the importance of "nurturance"; although he never concentrated on "touch" in particular, he did not—like Watson or Holt—refer to touching as dangerous and something to be avoided.

Spock represented the beginning of the other twentieth-century ideology of child-rearing experts. These experts were the so-called permissivists or naturalists, and they believed children arrive ready to take part in human culture. In this, the naturalists offered a—albeit limited—challenge to scientific hegemony. Instead of science or the premodern god, the naturalists believed in "nature." The naturalists argued that children have "natural" inclinations that will direct them to behave well in the world. If loved and cared for adequately, human beings are naturally "good." Parents—mothers—must trust in their children to know what they need, when, and how. And to the extent that children cannot or do not express themselves clearly, mothers must listen to their *own* instincts. Women are "natural" parents and by trusting their "instincts," their intuition, they will know how to parent well. About the behaviorist and naturalist (or permissive) schools of thought, Ehrenreich and English write, "The behaviorists had seen the child as a piece of raw material to be hammered into shape. Its natural impulses—to eat when and what it liked, to play, etc.—had to be suppressed as firmly as bed-wetting and thumb-sucking. On the contrary, the permissivist proclaimed that the child's spontaneous impulses were good and sensible and that the child, instead of being a *tabula rasa*, actually *knew*, in some sense, what was right for itself."[79]

The still-popular naturalist child-rearing expert Dr. Spock was raised on behaviorist child-rearing advice. And when he entered medical school to become a pediatrician in the 1920s, he and other students were trained in the thinking of scientists like Holt and Watson. The touching of children at this time was almost taboo. In his training, Spock faithfully followed the behaviorist dictates. Yet, simultaneously, he began to question the underlying premises of these scientific methods of child rearing. He slowly realized that many of the scientific beliefs were based on unproven assumptions. For example, "the practice of tying up a baby's wrists to stop thumb-sucking remained unquestioned by doctors and nurses, mainly because experts like Holt and Watson assured them that thumb-sucking was wrong. 'Nobody had proved it was a bad habit, it was just a general assumption,'" Spock told his biographer Thomas Maier.[80]

Along with the unproven assumptions that Spock questioned, he also began to realize that doctoring children involved more than caring for mere physical needs. As he started to explore ways of getting psychological training in pediatrics, he discovered that in the early 1930s it did not exist. Consequently, Spock became the first pediatrician to have dual training in pediatrics and psychiatry. At that time, much like today, psychoanalysis existed at the fringes of United States medicine. Spock, however, found himself increasingly interested in Sigmund Freud's methods. Eventually, Spock went on to be trained in psychoanalysis, including attending seminars and entering into his own psychoanalysis. By the time Spock wrote his famous book, *The Common Sense Book of Baby and Child Care,* first published in 1945, he was a thorough believer in the thinking of Sigmund Freud. In fact, some scholars argue that it was Spock's book that first successfully popularized Freud for the American public. Maier writes, "In many ways, the book's embrace of Freudian theory was extraordinarily radical, eventually pushing American family life in a whole new direction, but his manual remained so neighborly and reasonable that readers never felt threatened."[81]

Freud aside, Spock himself is one of the—if not *the*—most famous child-rearing expert to date. His book is probably the best-known child-rearing text ever written. Indeed, inside the front cover of the seventh and final edition of his book, which came out the same year he died, 1998, is the impressive claim that *"Dr. Spock's Baby and Child Care* has been translated into thirty-nine languages and has sold fifty million copies worldwide since its first publication in 1946 [referring to the paperback edition]."[82] Yet Spock's popularity and fame took him beyond the private realm of child-rearing expertise. For much of his life he was deeply involved in the public world of political activism and politics, and he knew innumerable famous figures of his day including such legendary Americans as John F. and Jacqueline Kennedy, Lyndon Baines Johnson, and Martin Luther King Jr. Among his various honors, in 1990 *Life* magazine named Spock one of the hundred most important people of the century.[83]

Spock was not only a famous and popular figure; like Watson before him, Spock was also an established scientific researcher of child development and behavior. His career included working at the most prestigious scientific institutions of his time. In fact, shortly after his book came out, Spock became the first consultant in child psychiatry at the Mayo Clinic, which was considered one of the most esteemed medical establishments in the United States.[84] Additionally, he taught at its school of medicine, which was affiliated with the University of Minnesota. And in 1949, Spock became codirector of the institute. For his work there, among other places, Spock would eventually be "recognized by the medical community for pioneering the subspecialty of 'behavioral pediatrics.'"[85]

In contrast to child-rearing specialists like Holt and Watson, Spock's book made a sharp turn on the issue of touch. Spock focused on the issue and importance of "nurturance." Although he never concentrated on "touch" in particular, unlike Watson and Holt, he did not refer to touching as dangerous or something to be avoided. In fact, Spock went as far as to argue that each "baby needs to be smiled at, talked to, played with, *fondled*—gently and lovingly—just as much as he needs vitamins and calories, and the baby who doesn't get any loving will grow up cold and unresponsive."[86] In a section entitled "Kissing and Germs," Spock wrote, "Don't be afraid to kiss your baby when you feel like it." Nonetheless, Spock was influenced by the decades of middle-class fear of germs, for he also claimed, "It's better not to kiss him on the mouth or blow in his face."[87]

Furthermore, a central component of his book is his pioneering discussion of breastfeeding, where Spock indirectly addressed touch as a positive need of children. In the 1940s and 1950s, breastfeeding was considered old-fashioned and vulgar by the mainstream white middle-class culture. Looking back from the first decade of the twenty-first century, Spock is often credited with initiating the contemporary middle-class trend back to breastfeeding.[88]

In line with the naturalist school, Spock "gave prominence to the 'natural' benefits of breastfeeding."[89] Spock wrote, "Breast feeding is natural. On general principle, it's safer to do things the natural way unless you are absolutely sure you have a better way."[90] Along with its "naturalness," in *The Common Sense Book of Baby and Child Care*, Spock gave several other reasons for breastfeeding.

> Breast feeding has definite advantages that we know of, and it may have others that we aren't smart enough to see. It helps the mother physically. When the baby nurses, the muscle wall of the uterus contracts vigorously. This hastens its return to normal size and position. From the psychological point of view, it makes the mother feel close to her baby; she knows that she's giving him something real, something that no one else can give him. This feeling is good for her and for her relationship to the baby. Breast feeding probably gives the baby a feeling of closeness and security, too.[91]

Spock helped start a resurgence in the white middle class back to breastfeeding.[92] However, unlike the more strident naturalists to come, Spock did not see breastfeeding as necessarily more intimate than bottle-feeding. Later naturalists argued that breastfeeding—in other words, mouth-to-breast contact—somehow brought a mother closer to her baby than did holding a baby in a similar manner yet feeding the child with a bottle. In contrast, in his 1945 child-rearing manual, Spock wrote,

> Suppose you want to breastfeed your baby, but don't succeed. Will the baby suffer, physically or emotionally? No, you can't put it that strongly. If you make the formula carefully, and if you keep closely in touch with the doctor when the formula doesn't agree, the chances are great that the baby will prosper from a bodily point of view. And if, when you give him his bottle, you cuddle him in your arms, he will be nourished spiritually,

much as if he were at the breast. Mothers who have read what psychologists and psychiatrists say about the importance of breast feeding sometimes get the idea that it has been shown that bottle-fed babies turn out to be less happy than breastfed babies. Nobody has proved that.[93]

It is interesting to note that in this quote, Spock reiterated the cultural belief in the mind–body split. Spock indicated that the baby will "prosper from a bodily point of view" through formula and "spiritually" through being held. However, in contrast to later naturalists, Spock saw touching—being cuddled in the mother's arms—as promoting only of the baby's "spirit." Later naturalists who also took for granted the mind–body split, such as La Leche League International and William Sears (discussed in chapters 3 and 4), argue that touching aids in both components of the dualism, the child's mind and body.

Spock was fundamentally pro-touch. In this, he made a radical break from the earlier child-rearing behaviorist experts who were explicitly anti-touching. Indeed, this pro- versus anti-touch split is at the core of the differences between behaviorists and naturalists. And, whereas Watson founded behaviorism, Spock is known as the father of the "permissive" or naturalist school of child rearing. Interestingly, a political analogy also exists here. Although Watson and behaviorism tended to be proponents of the political right and big business, Spock challenged right-wing values, grounding himself firmly on the left. Indeed, because of the popular understanding of Spock as "permissive," many people blamed his child-rearing methods for starting the youth movements of the sixties and seventies. The thinking here was that children were spoiled by "permissive" child rearing, and so they became rebellious. "Critics called the youthful rebels the 'Spock-marked generation,' as if they had been inflicted in infancy with a disfiguring disease."[94] To fuel conservative suspicions about Spock, he was very involved in the anti-war movement and was a much-loved figure for the sixties youth activists. Further, before Martin Luther King Jr., was assassinated, King and Spock were considered for candidacy for a presidential election with Spock running for vice president.

Even today, many people maintain this belief that permissive—pro-touch—child rearing caused the radical movements of the sixties and seventies. Wade Horn, a well-known clinical child psychologist and the first President George Bush's assistant secretary for family support at the Department of Health and Human Services, who continues to work hard to challenge feminist efforts, ban gay marriage, and end social spending on the poor, is quoted in *Time* magazine as claiming that there are "good reasons" why the baby boomers are called the

"Me Generation." He states, "They spent the 1950s being spoiled [by Spock-inspired child rearing], spent the 1960s having a decade-long temper tantrum because the world was not precisely as they wanted it to be, spent the 1970s having the best sex and drugs they could find, the 1980s acquiring things and the 1990s trying to have the most perfect children. And not because they felt an obligation to the next generation to rear them to be healthy, well-adjusted adults, but because they wanted to have bragging rights."[95] Here "permissive" (or what I call "naturalist") child rearing produced "spoiled" children; in other words, children who challenge the system.

In spite of the Wade Horns of the world, Ben Spock and "permissive" or naturalist child rearing quickly became very popular. And although there has been a resurgence of behaviorist child rearing, naturalist theories of child rearing continue to be extremely common. With this new naturalist style, children were no longer to have their "natural" inclinations crushed, but were to be given free rein. Children were not to wait for their feedings until the proper time on the schedule. Mothers were told to feed their babies on demand and to let them sleep when the babies seemed tired. Moreover, women were not only to follow the "natural" inclinations of their children; Spock said women should listen to their own "instincts" as well. Here, he challenged the misogyny of earlier experts such as Watson. He advised women to trust themselves.

However, Spock's pro-women turn in popular child-rearing advice was limited. As the second-wave feminists were to eventually point out, Spock—like Holt and Watson before him—was still sexist. For one, Spock admonished women to heed their "instincts" only insofar as they *also* read up on and followed the advice of the experts. Spock told mothers to "take the anxiety out of child care by following their own instincts. . . . But maternal instincts could only go so far, and herein lay a mixed message in Spock's advice. He gave mothers quite limited autonomy and, in fact, advised them to consult often with their pediatricians about even the most minor problems of child care."[96] For example, before giving any instructions on feeding, Spock indicated that it is always best to consult a doctor before taking any steps. His instructions were to be followed only "if it's impossible to consult a doctor."[97] It was the doctor who should be making not only the concrete decisions such as what kind of formula to use, but also the intimate decisions—including those involving the mother's body—such as "how much nursing the mother's nipples can stand."[98] Spock was fairly up front about his faith in the scientific expert. Early in his book, in a section entitled "Trust Yourself," Spock wrote, "Don't be afraid to trust your own common sense. Bringing up your child won't be a complicated job if you take it easy, trust your own instincts, *and follow the directions that your doctor gives you.*"[99]

Further, Spock's instructions were often so detailed and simplistic, they made a mockery out of his maxim that mothers should follow their own common sense. For example, in explaining to mothers how to give their baby a bath, Spock wrote,

> Test the temperature with your elbow or wrist. It should feel comfortably warm. You can use any kind of mild soap. Use only a small amount of water at first, until you get the knack of holding the baby securely. . . . Wash his face first, with a soft washcloth, without soap. The scalp needs to be soaped only once or twice a week, if the baby doesn't spit up too much. Then soap and rinse the rest of the body. If you feel nervous at first about dropping him in the water, you can do all the first part of the washing while he is in your lap or on a table. If so, do it quickly, so that he won't get cold. Then rinse him off in the tub, holding him securely with both hands. Use a soft bath towel for drying him.[100]

Of course, Spock as a pediatrician was a scientific expert. He believed himself to be an authority to be trusted. His advice to trust yourself could be trusted because an expert told you to do so. And the rest of Spock's advice was so simplistic that it left no room for mothers to make their own decisions. Essentially, Spock told mothers to follow the directions of their doctor. Then if the doctor was not available, follow the directions of Spock's book. And only then, if there were further questions and a doctor could still not be reached, trust yourself.

Not only were women to trust the experts before all else; they were to trust themselves in a way that essentialized women, attaching what it meant to be women to biological understandings of femaleness. Much like the attachment-parenting popular health movement that was to start in the 1950s, Spock believed in women's "motherly instincts." For Spock, women were "natural" mothers, and thus parents were naturally women. Spock's book was almost entirely addressed to women, and to middle-class women at that. And as the "natural" parent, Spock believed proper parenting/mothering entailed a full-time commitment from women, which was often financially difficult for working-class and poor women to do. Middle-class women—good mothers—were to make their children the center of their lives. The ideal Spockean mother was fulfilled by doing all the small and, often, dull tasks of child care. Her satisfaction came "naturally" from her maternal instinct. She had few interests outside her motherly realm, the home.

Spock believed that decent mothers would not seriously consider working away from their babies. He did acknowledge that mothering could be difficult. However, he advised mothers who got depressed to "go to a movie or to the beauty parlor, or to get yourself a new hat or dress."[101] Employment was not a solution to maternal melancholy. Here Spock wrote,

> What about the mothers who don't absolutely have to work but would prefer to, either to supplement the family income, or because they think they will be more satisfied themselves and therefore get along better at home? . . . The important thing for a mother to realize is that the younger the child the more necessary it is for him to have a steady, loving person taking care of him. In most cases, the mother is the best one to give him this feeling of "belonging," safely and surely. She doesn't quit on the job, she doesn't turn against him, she isn't indifferent to him, she takes care of him always in the same familiar house. If a mother realizes clearly how vital this kind of care is to a small child, it may make it easier for her to decide that the extra money she might earn, or the satisfaction she might receive from an outside job, is not so important after all.[102]

Understandably, this thinking led second-wave feminists to critique Spock for his sexism, and feminists and others to critique him for his middle-class bias.

Among the critics, Nancy Pottishman Weiss argued that Spock's child-rearing manual embodied a "world view" that was "free of dissonance or conflict, or the recognition of poverty or cultural difference. Such a world has invented a motherhood that excludes the experiences of many mothers."[103] Along with denying the cultural differences and the poverty in countless women's lives, feminists argued that Spock covered up many middle-class women's misery with the general assumption of their happiness. However, to his great credit, and unlike many other child-rearing experts, Spock listened to his critics, took them seriously, and attempted to challenge his own thinking. In a November 1971 issue of the *New York Times Magazine,* Spock wrote an apologetic essay entitled "Male Chauvinist Spock Recants—Well, Almost." Here and in other articles, interviews, and speeches, Spock apologized for the "underlying sexism" in his work and he "talked about his change of heart on traditional matters of sex and child rearing."[104]

Alfred C. Kinsey

Spock was only one figure in the mid-century turn to touch. Another extremely important person, although not typically recognized in terms of child rearing or adult–child touch, was Alfred C. Kinsey. Contra Holt and Watson, Kinsey argued that all bodies, including children's bodies, were *meant* to be touched. For Kinsey, the body side of the mind–body split was to be celebrated and enjoyed.

As with Spock and the soon-to-arrive attachment-parenting movement, Kinsey believed in the "natural." In a sense, Kinsey's work advocated letting the body go, uncontrolled, to fill its "natural" desires. Not only was controlling them *not* necessary, it was impossible. Furthermore, Kinsey believed in a continuum of normal behaviors. Some behaviors may happen more or less often than others, but no behavior is "abnormal" in the sense of morally bad. Kinsey's thinking radically challenged heteronormative culture. Indeed, this is largely why there was such a profoundly critical response to his work. Allowing for no morally wrong behavior, Kinsey's thinking was particularly interesting, and potentially problematic, when considering adult–child sexual touch.

Kinsey researched American sexuality in the 1930s and 1940s. His study explored sex just after what some call the cultural revolution of the twentieth century—the 1920s. During the 1920s, mainstream United States culture witnessed an earth-shattering break with Victorian sexual customs and gender roles. Divorce rates offered one sure sign of massive social change—in the first decades of the twentieth century, they rose rapidly. In fact, the total went from "7,000 in 1860 to 56, 000 in 1900, to 100,000 in 1914."[105] Yet along with increasing divorce rates, there were many other indicators of substantial transformation. In 1920, women had finally won the right to vote. The middle class was growing rapidly. A vast array of amazing new inventions, such as the radio, the automobile, the bicycle, electricity, X-rays, anesthesia, the telegraph, the telephone, and the movies, was dislocating the previous familiar tools of everyday existence. The new seemed to be pushing the old out of every aspect of modern life.[106]

The 1920s was a time to challenge older ways of understanding human sexuality. This was especially true for women. Not only were women divorcing and being divorced from their marriages; not only were they newly enfranchised; women were also beginning to explore their sexuality and to understand themselves as sexual beings. The famous "flapper" of the 1920s was the symbol of this new sexual woman.

However, women were not the only ones giving new attention to sex. Men were too. And particularly young men and women were increasingly interested, even obsessed, with their emerging sexuality.[107] The latest way of understanding sex involved believing it essential to personal happiness. And with this new meaning, thinking about sexuality began to be separated from reproduction.

Kinsey's research happened at the end of this sexual revolution. Not only his data but also his very questions exhibit colossal cultural transformation.

Kinsey's work on the touching of children not only presented an important variation from the earlier, extremely popular thought of Holt and Watson, but it also differed sharply from other well-known thinkers such as Sigmund Freud. A point on which Kinsey diverged markedly from both Freud and popular thought was the issue of adult–child sexual interaction, or what would later be called "child sexual abuse" by the 1960s feminist movement. In his study, Kinsey found that one in four women reported childhood sexual contact with an adult. Unlike Freud, who came to believe that the majority of such claims were actually women's repressed childhood sexual desire for their fathers, Kinsey believed that these sexual interactions literally happened. Yet he minimized the importance of the interaction. Kinsey believed, as did Freud, that children—like all humans—are sexual, embodied beings. And in sharp contrast to mainstream thought at the time, Kinsey felt strongly that there is nothing morally or physiologically wrong with children's sexuality. Kinsey argued that children are sexual from a very early age and that this is completely normal and appropriate. Yet unlike Freud, Kinsey claimed that if the child does not suffer physical injury, adult sexual interaction with children is not harmful. He wrote, "It is difficult to understand why a child, except for its cultural conditioning, should be disturbed at having its genitalia touched, or disturbed at seeing the genitalia of other persons, or disturbed at even more specific sexual contacts."[108]

Indeed, in terms of adult–child touch, Kinsey believed that sexual attraction not only brought adults together, but it was responsible for the connection between women and their children as well. "Labeling the mammalian breast 'a sex organ,'" he described how "the nerves in that breast are continuous with the nerves of the reproductive organs, and stimulation of that breast by the feeding babe brings a sexual response which is the basis of the thing that the poet calls 'mother love.'"[109]

Indeed, recent research seems to confirm the connections Kinsey made decades earlier between women's breasts and their sexual responses. Of course, it is more questionable whether, as Kinsey argued, that sexual response accounts for women's love of and connection to their children. Nonetheless, it is fascinating that Kinsey claimed that a sexual—incestuous—connection is responsible for parental love. From the other end of the anti- to pro-touch continuum, Kinsey made an argument not dissimilar from that made by Watson—Watson *also* argued that touching brings about a "love response." However, Watson focused on children loving their mothers because they, children, are touched by them; in reverse, Kinsey focused on mothers loving their children because they, mothers, are touched by their children in the mouth-to-breast contact of breastfeeding. And, of course, whereas for Watson this was a dangerous and worrisome event, for Kinsey, it was a right, good, or "natural" event.

Kinsey argued that mothers love their children because they are touched by them; in return, Kinsey believed that parents were responsible for teaching their children to enjoy sex and to feel good about their bodies. In Kinsey's framework, clearly, bodies are good things. He believed that children should be taught that it is as appropriate to touch the genitalia as any other part of the body. With his own children, Kinsey taught by example. In order to impart a positive outlook about the human body and sexuality, he both exercised and advocated nudity in his household. His daughter, Joan, recalled many mornings as a child when she would watch her father as he shaved in the bathroom. "She would sit on the toilet seat, and he would stand naked before the mirror, making up 'silly sing-song rhymes' to entertain her while he shaved."[110] The family often bathed together or hung around together naked on vacations and at home.

Kinsey directly referred to his thinking on adult–child sex. He wrote, "Older persons are the teachers of younger people in all matters, including the sexual."[111] Strangely, it was not until the 1970s that Kinsey was criticized for his thinking on adult–child sexual interactions. The first to comment on this aspect of Kinsey's ideas were second-wave feminists such as psychiatrist and scholar Judith Lewis Herman. She pointed to—and challenged—Kinsey's conviction in his *Sexual Behavior in the Human Female* (1953) that adult–child sexual contact may not be as harmful as is typically thought.[112]

Herman focused on Kinsey's chapter "Pre-Adolescent Sexual Development" in his 1953 book on the human female. He had a similar chapter in his book on the human male; however, interestingly, in the female book's version of this chapter he has a subsection specifically focused on "Pre-Adolescent Contacts with Adult Males." In this section in *Sexual Behavior in the Human Female,* Kinsey broke down the data into the following smaller subsections: "Incidence and Frequency of Contacts with Adults"; "Nature of Contacts with Adults"; and "Significance of Adult Contacts."[113] In particular, under the "Significance of Adult Contacts," Kinsey made clear his thinking about adult–child sexual contact. Kinsey wrote, "There is a growing concern in our culture over the sexual contacts that pre-adolescent children sometimes have with adults. Most persons feel that all such contacts are undesirable because of the immediate disturbance they may cause the child, and because of the conditioning and possibly traumatic effects which they may have on the child's socio-sexual development and subsequent sexual adjustments in marriage."[114] Kinsey noted, "there has hitherto been no opportunity to know what proportion of all children is ever involved." And he continued, "We have data from 4441 of our female subjects which allow us to determine the incidence of pre-adolescent sexual contacts with adult males, and the frequency of such contacts. . . . We find that some 24 per cent (1075) of the females in the sample had been approached while they were pre-adolescent by adult males who appeared to be making sexual advances, or who had made sexual contacts with the child. Three-fourths of the females (76 per cent) had not recognized any such approach."[115] And about the significance of adult–child sexual contacts, Kinsey argued, "If a child were not culturally conditioned, it is doubtful if it would be disturbed by sexual approaches of the sort which had usually been involved in these histories."[116] Indeed, as Herman commented, "Kinsey himself, though he never denied the reality of child sexual abuse, did as much as he could to minimize its importance."[117]

Kinsey passionately wished to free society from its Victorian restraints, which he saw as deeply damaging. He was pro-touch and pro-sex of almost any and every kind. And by the end of his career, when he wrote his book about female sexual behavior, Kinsey had come to believe that even adult–child sexuality was not problematic, abusive, or morally wrong. For Kinsey, the fact that some adults enjoy being sexual with children was fine. And he believed that, in a sense, adult–child sex benefited the children, who learned about sexuality through such contact. He thought that not only did the adults involved enjoy the sexual contact, but often the children did as well. In Kinsey's thinking, perhaps the only way in which a child could be harmed through such sexual contact with an adult is, insofar as adult–child sexuality is socially taboo, society conditions children to be bothered or upset by it. Thus, it is the conditioning—the Victorianism—that is harmful, rather than the adult–child sexual contact.

Kinsey did not merely write about adult–child sexual contact. He relied heavily on a pedophile for his data on child sexuality. And all the while, he seemed to do nothing to ensure that the pedophile was no longer active in his extensive sexual encounters with children. Perhaps most strange of all was that no one seemed to notice, much less critique, this component of Kinsey's work.

Kinsey came to know this pedophile—and data source—through one of his many contact people, Robert Latou Dickinson, a retired New York gynecologist and pioneering sex researcher. While Margaret Sanger was working to make contraception acceptable and available to the American public, Dickinson crusaded to convince physicians to offer birth control to their patients. Dickinson worked hard to advance Kinsey's research. During his extensive career as a sex researcher, Dickinson had come to know many noteworthy eccentrics with a diverse array of sexual histories that he passed onto Kinsey. Among these was the pedophile whom Kinsey's biographer, James H. Jones, refers to as "Mr. X."[118] Mr. X's sexual behavior was a family legacy. The product of a family full of cross-generational incest, Jones claims "he had sex with his grandmother when he was still a young child, as well as with his father."[119]

> In the years that followed, the boy had sexual relations with seventeen of the thirty-three relatives with whom he had contact. And this was just the beginning. After he reached adulthood, Mr. X was obsessed with sex, a walking id with polymorphous erotic tastes. By the time Dickinson brought him to Kinsey's attention, wrote Pomeroy, "This man had had homosexual relations with 600 preadolescent males, heterosexual relations with 200 preadolescent females, intercourse with countless adults of both sexes, with animals of many species, and besides had employed elaborate techniques of masturbation."[120]

Mr. X also had collected a sizable number of erotic photographs. And, as a pop scientist in his own right, he had made extensive notes on all of his sexual activities, keeping track of not only his behavior and reactions but also those of his partners/victims. These notes included a rich and full record of his life as voyeur.[121]

Kinsey was intrigued by and admiring of Mr. X's elaborate sexual history. In fact, at one point in March 1945, Kinsey even tried to hire Mr. X. He offered to pay Mr. X's salary if Mr. X would take a leave from his job with the government to organize his sexual records and other "materials." Although Mr. X declined this offer, over time Kinsey obtained vast amounts of data from Mr. X, and Kinsey even roped Mr. X into reading and criticizing those parts of his book that dealt with preadolescent development and behavior. Kinsey could never acknowledge Mr. X's contribution publicly because of the illegal nature of his behavior, yet he wrote Mr. X that he wished he could.[122] Indeed, Jones argues that Kinsey was very enthusiastic about his relationship with Mr. X, though, at least in part, Kinsey's enthusiasm was probably a way to gain Mr. X's assistance with Kinsey's research.

In his 1948 book, *Sexual Behavior in the Human Male*, Kinsey reported Mr. X's "data" in a forthright fashion. He indicated that the boys being discussed ranged in age from two-month-old infants to fifteen-year-old adolescents.

He claimed that the data came from adults being questioned about their own childhood and from "older subjects who have had sexual contacts with younger boys."[123] Kinsey had data concerning infants less than twelve months old, toddlers, and young children who were sexually stimulated and observed for hours. He wrote, "The record includes some cases of pre-adolescent boys involved in sexual contacts with adult females, and still more cases of pre-adolescent boys involved with adult males. Data on this point were not systematically gathered from all histories, and consequently the frequency of contacts with adults cannot be calculated with precision."[124]

Kinsey almost bragged of his vast amounts of data, saying that although other studies offer little to nothing in terms of data on the occurrence of the first ejaculation in boys, he has a quite a record.[125] He wrote, "This material is now augmented by a considerable record based on the memory of persons who have contributed to the present study, and on an important body of data from certain of our subjects who have observed first ejaculation in a list of several hundred boys."[126] This "subject" is, with little doubt, Mr. X.[127]

Kinsey described the six types of reactions Mr. X observed boys to experience when having an orgasm. In today's mainstream ethos of dread and fascination with what we call "child sexual abuse," it is hard to imagine these six types not garnering extensive attention, particularly given their suspiciously violent nature. For example, type three entails extreme tension with violent convulsions. Kinsey described this type of reaction by male children as including a "gradual, and sometimes prolonged, build-up to orgasm, which involves still more violent convulsions of the whole body; heavy breathing, groaning, sobbing, or more violent cries, sometimes with an abundance of tears (especially among younger children), the orgasm or ejaculation often extended, in some individuals involving several minutes (in one case up to five minutes) of recurrent spasm."[128] About his reaction type five, Kinsey wrote that it culminates "in extreme trembling, collapse, loss of color, and sometimes fainting of subject." And in Kinsey's reaction type six, the child was "pained or frightened at approach of orgasm." Here Kinsey continued,

> The genitalia of many adult males become hypersensitive immediately at and after orgasm, and some males suffer excruciating pain and may scream if movement is continued or the penis even touched. The males in the present group become similarly hypersensitive before the arrival of actual orgasm, will fight away from the partner and may make violent attempts to avoid climax, although they derive definite pleasure from the situation. About 8 percent of the younger boys are involved here, but it is

a smaller percentage of older boys and adults which continues these reactions throughout life.[129]

In a world where child molesters are the contemporary version of Salem witches, Kinsey used one of the most practiced child molesters imaginable to write significant chunks of his book, a book that is still considered our most important resource concerning human sexuality. And nobody questioned it.

Indeed, this is truly fascinating: no one questioned or even seemed to notice Kinsey's data source, even though Kinsey's book was *heavily* criticized. Critiques include his poor use of statistics, his lack of "objectivity," his exposing the public to morally harmful information, and his use of "science" and scientific funding to examine "morally harmful" populations and behaviors such as homosexuals and sexually active single women. Given that his book was criticized in almost every possible way, one wonders how it could be that no one scrutinized his use of Mr. X's "data."

Throughout the twentieth century, one finds a strange gap between the mainstream reality of adult–child touch—the actual ways children are touched—and the ideologies of adult–child touch. Often the areas of biggest concern involving touch, the areas experts and others spend extensive time addressing, mirror not what actually happens so much as our dominant cultural ways of thinking and living social power. When Watson worried that women were dangerous, his worry did not reflect real danger on the part of women. Instead his "worry" reflected a reality where women were deeply controlled and their lives and choices fundamentally limited. Further, his anxiety and thinking reinforced and helped produce that reality of women's oppression.

Oddly, Kinsey's work tells the truth, in a sense, about what was actually happening to children. In other words, his work reflected children's reality, although his interpretation of that reality was deeply problematic. Yet no one bothered, or was able to see, what he exposed. Instead, it is only while looking back that we recognize the social power embedded in adult–child relations as the reflected, unacknowledged reality of Kinsey's research and thinking.

Controversy surrounded Kinsey's work at the time of its publication in 1948, yet almost nothing was said about his chapter "Early Sexual Growth and Activity" that gives detailed descriptions of child orgasms—clearly in the context of an adult being sexual with a child—that sound very much like our contemporary definitions of child sexual abuse. I argue that this lack of response to a very questionable part of Kinsey's work was because of the then-taken-for-granted way of thinking about children and children's bodies. Children had long been understood as, quite literally, belonging to adults.

Their bodies were adult property. This way of thinking about children as adult territory was so unquestioned that no one bothered—or, rather, realized to bother—to focus on this chapter.

Kinsey's work came out just as the tide was beginning to turn from a deeply anti-touch ideological ethos to one more accepting and even enthusiastic about the touching of children. Controlling children was the other side of the anti-touch ethos: adults touched young children so as to tie their wrists to the sides of their crib to prevent them from masturbating or sucking their thumbs, and adults touched newborn infants to insert objects in their rectum so as to induce a bowel movement at a desired time. Kinsey's data reflected this pro-control ethos. Although probably few people *consciously* supported adult–child sex, exercising detailed control over children and their bodies was nonetheless acceptable. If this control, and often what might now be called violation, involved adult–child sexual touch that in some way benefited the adult, then so be it. In other words, people did not criticize Kinsey's data source because people did not notice it as anything unusual. This was not because there was widespread acceptance of adult–child sexual contact so much as there was widespread acceptance of adult ownership and control over children's bodies. People took adult control over children for granted, so much so that they did not pay attention to the *sexual* way adults were controlling children in Kinsey's data. There may also have been an element of readers actually not seeing what they were reading because of the taboo nature of adult–child sexual contact. At any rate, it is fascinating that according to Jones (1997), no one to date, even the radical feminists in the 1960s and 1970s who criticized Kinsey's *thinking* on adult–child sexual contact, has ever discussed or taken issue with this aspect of Kinsey's work and data.

Along with Kinsey's unnoted use of a pedophile for data, in terms of adult–child touch, Kinsey's research raised other relevant issues. Is adult–child touch dangerous as Watson indicated or something to celebrate as Kinsey implicitly argued? What about sexual touch between adults and children? Is it possible to fully separate nonsexual from sexual touch, and, if not, is that problematic? In mainstream American culture, experts have argued strongly for their own positions in term of adult–child touch. Yet, in spite of the strong positions taken by the various experts after Kinsey, it seemed less clear than anyone willingly acknowledged wherein lies the truth vis-à-vis touching children.

Harry F. Harlow

Around the same time Kinsey was publishing his extensive studies on human sexuality, another researcher, University of Wisconsin psychologist Harry F. Harlow, was exploring the issue of touch in child development. With Harlow, science took another big step in the pro-touching direction. That children may actually *need* to be touched by adults had become a concern of scientific inquiry. In terms of my focus on dominant ideological thought, Harlow's research represented mainstream thinking insofar as his research was and continues to be taken very seriously by a broad audience. For example, it is hard to find an Introduction to Psychology college course that does not address Harlow's work. Given this, Harlow's work—the very questions Harlow decided to ask—point to a variation in dominant ideologies of adult–child touch. Harlow explored the positive importance, even the necessity, of adults touching children.

Harlow began his famous 1958 paper on touch, "The Nature of Love," with philosophical musings about love, and the lack of love, so to speak, in psychological research. Harlow's outlook was deeply modernist. For Harlow, love was an important piece of human life. He argued that it was the job of science, and in particular psychology, to study each and every element of human existence and to know all there was to be known about it. Harlow wrote,

> Love is a wondrous state, deep, tender, and rewarding. Because of its intimate and personal nature it is regarded by some as an improper topic for experimental research. But, whatever our personal feelings may be, our assigned mission as psychologists is to analyze all facets of human and animal behavior into their component variables. So far as love or affection is concerned, psychologists have failed in this mission. The little we know about love does not transcend simple observation, and the little we write about it has been written better by poets and novelists. But of great concern is the fact that psychologists tend to give progressively less attention to a motive which pervades our entire lives.[130]

The "children" Harlow worked with were baby rhesus monkeys. Like Kinsey, Harlow was not a child-rearing expert but a scientific researcher. Harlow wanted to better understand how love, attachment, and sexual activity develop, and he explored the behavior of monkeys in hope of explaining these phenomena among human beings. Importantly, Harlow, like both Watson and Kinsey, equated "love" with touching; in other words, when Harlow looked for evidence of monkey "love," he looked for physical contact. Given the immense importance of social interaction and touching (love) to normal development in primates, Harlow came up with a set of experiments to examine just what social interaction and touching or love teaches monkeys.

Harlow's studies were extensive and took numerous forms. In one, he separated baby monkeys from their mothers—and from all possibly of bodily or other contact—while meeting all of the monkeys' physical needs for food and shelter. Harlow studied the effect of isolation on the infants. The monkey's cage was a "blank space equipped with a one-way mirror. The scientists could look in but the monkey inside could not see out. He had no company but himself." Harlow raised some monkeys from birth to thirty days in this complete isolation. "When the monkeys were moved, they were so 'enormously disturbed' that two of them refused to eat and starved themselves to death." Indeed, the scientists began to force-feed the "monkeys coming out of isolation to make sure the animals stayed alive." Later, Harlow kept the infants in isolation for six months and then for a year. "If the researchers kept a monkey in isolation for twelve months, they ended up with a rhesus macaque entirely new in the natural world, an animal who didn't explore, didn't play, barely moved, appeared alive only by the thud of its heart and the sigh of its lungs."[131]

When, upon adulthood, these monkeys were forcibly impregnated, as they were "incapable of having normal sexual relations," they exhibited little capacity to parent. At best, many ignored their babies. At worst, one "held her infant's face to the floor and chewed off his feet and fingers. Another took her baby's head in her mouth and crushed it."[132]

In another study, Harlow gave motherless monkeys two kinds of mother-substitutes. One substitute the baby monkeys received was a wire mother that gave milk through a nipple, but had no place for the monkeys to cling and touch. In other words, this "mother" fed her baby, but did not touch and could not be touched by it. The other substitute was a terrycloth mother to which the baby monkeys could cling and touch but receive no milk. As one undergraduate psychology textbook puts it, "History was made when the babies spent far more time with the soft mother-substitute than the fast-food mother. Harlow had demonstrated that monkeys are born with a need for cuddling and closeness."[133] Harlow wrote, "It is apparent that the cloth mother is highly preferred over the wire one, and this differential selectivity is enhanced by age and experience. In this situation, the variable of nursing appears to be of absolutely no importance: the infant consistently seeks the soft mother surrogate regardless of nursing condition."[134]

When monkeys mothered by the cloth surrogate had their "mother" removed, they became visibly upset. Harlow wrote, "Frequently they would freeze in a crouched position. . . . Emotionality indices such as vocalization, crouching, rocking, and sucking increased sharply."[135] Harlow further described some infants' powerful responses to their cloth mother's disappearance: "In the absence of the mother some of the experimental monkeys would rush to the center of the room where the mother was customarily placed and then run rapidly from object to object, screaming and crying all the while.

Continuous, frantic clutching of their bodies was very common, even when not in the crouching position."[136]

Given the monkeys' deep need for physical contact at an early age, Harlow theorized about the development of adult sexual relationships in primates. He argued that monkeys go through three steps before they are ready for adult sexual "love." He claimed that the first two steps have to do with touching between mother and infant, and the third involves physical contact between the young monkey and its peers.

Once again, for Harlow, touch and love were the same thing. The first love happens with the first touch, adult–child touch. And perhaps more important, Harlow found that love/touch are not secondary needs but primary, much like hunger and thirst.

> We were not surprised to discover that contact comfort was an important basic affectional or love variable, but we did not expect it to overshadow so completely the variable of nursing; indeed, the disparity is so great as to suggest that the primary function of nursing as an affectional variable is that of insuring frequent and intimate body contact of the infant with the mother. Certainly, man cannot live by milk alone. Love is an emotion that does not need to be bottle- or spoon-fed, and we may be sure that there is nothing to be gained by giving lip service to love.[137]

Harlow, perhaps like most of us, was himself an odd character. He spent his life's work exploring the nature of love and arguing for children's deep-seated need of physical contact. Yet in his own life, he was a bit of disaster as a parent and spouse. He constantly worked, took terrible care of himself, and drank extensively. As his biographer, Deborah Blum, put it, for a period of his life, "He seemed to exist on coffee, smoke and alcohol."[138] One of Harlow's odd and more endearing habits was his punning. Nearly all his life, Harlow was a passionate punster. He left little notes with rhythms and poems on the desks of students and colleagues, and even fleshed out his academic papers with them.[139] In the middle of his "The Nature of Love" paper, Harlow underlined his argument about adult–child touch with several bizarre little images and a number of his poems.

At one point, Harlow claimed, "We believe that contact comfort has long served the animal kingdom as a motivating agent for affectional responses. Since at the present time we have no experimental data to substantiate this position, we supply information which must be accepted, if at all on the basis of face validity." After this statement, Harlow offered six images, including the following: a photograph seemingly of a mother hippopotamus rubbing her nose against her baby hippopotamus; a photograph of an adult and infant rhinoceros walking together; a sketch of bunches of snakes entangled with each other; and a cartoon image of snakes, cats, dogs, birds, chickens, rabbits, and mice, each with one adult and many babies grouped together. Under five of the images there is a short poem, and under the cartoon image merely the statement "You see, all God's chillun's [sic] got skin."[140] For instance, the Harlow poem under the hippopotamus image stated:

THE HIPPOPOTAMUS

This is the skin some babies feel
Replete with hippo love appeal.
Each contact, cuddle, push, and shove
Elicits tons of baby love.[141]

Harlow finished his paper with theoretical musings. First, he showed his debt to John Bowlby, who will be addressed further in the following chapters. Bowlby argued that children have a near-constant need to be in the physical presence of their mothers. Harlow's acknowledgment of Bowlby aligned Harlow with the extremely pro-touch attachment-parenting movement born with the founding of La Leche League International in the 1950s. However, whereas La Leche League used Bowlby's theories to argue that mothers must physically be with their children as much as possible, Harlow merely made reference to Bowlby's studies of "affectional variables." Then, after acknowledging Bowlby, Harlow veered sharply away from him, putting forth a deeply feminist and potentially anti-breastfeeding, albeit still pro-touch, argument: Harlow claimed that men as well as women can be primary parents.

Harlow acknowledged the reality that because of the current social and economic situation, women had entered the workforce. This meant that our society faced new child-rearing problems. Harlow wrote, "The socioeconomic demands of the present and the threatened socioeconomic demands of the future have led the American woman to displace, or threaten to displace, the American man in science and industry. If this process continues, the problem of proper child-rearing practices faces us with startling clarity."[142] However, Harlow continued by making a radical argument for his time. He claimed that the problem is not so great; if women enter the workforce, thus leaving the home and children, men can step in, into the private world of the home, to fill the child-care gap. "It is cheering in view of this trend to realize that the American male is physically endowed with all the really essential equipment to compete with the American female on equal terms in one essential activity:

the rearing of infants."[143] Harlow strongly believed that human infants need extensive physical contact with their caregiver. However, for Harlow, this crucial touch did not necessarily include breastfeeding. In other words, men could touch—and thus care for—children as well as women. Truly foreseeing the future, Harlow claimed, "We now know that women in the working classes are not needed in the home because of their primary mammalian capabilities; and it is possible that in the foreseeable future neonatal nursing will not be regarded as a necessity, but as a luxury . . . a form of conspicuous consumption limited perhaps to the upper classes."[144]

There is something profoundly moving about Harlow's monkeys. It certainly seems that human infants, among other animals, do *need* to be touched. But, to argue for this need with Harlow's monkey evidence is a far cry from arguing that they need to be touched nearly constantly or always by their *mother,* as later child-rearing experts would claim.

Harlow holds an important place in my story. His work informed the pro-touch movement, and he simultaneously supported the feminist perspective that *men* can touch; in other words, that men can care for children. This component of his thinking had the potential to free women to work outside the home without guilt or social sanction. In direct contradiction to La Leche League International and the soon-to-arrive attachment-parenting movement, Harlow used his pro-touch research analysis to argue that breastfeeding and mothers are less necessary, rather than more. If nothing else, this profound contradiction between thinkers points to the ideological—rather than factual—nature of child-rearing advice. Each made arguments bound up with social ways of understanding what it means to be human, to be worthwhile and successful, to be sexual, male and female, white and of color, and poor and middle class.

A Note about the "Back-to-Nature" Movement

The progress toward pro-touch thinking in the mid-twentieth-century United States was further nourished by a variety of long-standing popular health movements. These took various forms and offered alternatives to the mainstream medical establishment, including alternative medical schools and medicines. Among them, and in sharp contrast to the mainstream medical establishment consistently dominated by white, middle- to upper-middle-class men, women were relatively prominent. Positions filled by women included their roles—ones that were both ancient and common well into the twentieth century—as midwives, healers, and childbirth attendants.

Among the popular health movements were those that advocated a "return" to nature. Women celebrated their "traditional" knowledge, along with their body's capacity to give birth and raise children without the control of institutionalized medicine. These women presented a challenge to the mainstream scientific and medical establishment, particularly around issues of childbirth and child rearing. Yet they are not to be confused with the soon-to-arrive, 1960s—also known as the second-wave—feminist movement. Although the second wave had a women's health movement, many of what I call for lack of a better term the "back-to-nature" women were not explicitly feminist. In fact, often their goals directly clashed with the 1960s feminists' goals. La Leche League International, one important "back-to-nature" group—to be discussed at length in the next chapter—believed that men and women are fundamentally, biologically different.

"Back-to-nature" groups such as La Leche League were largely interested in a celebration of "traditional" women's knowledge and women's domestic role as the bearers and rearers of children. Insofar as they took power back from the mainstream medical establishment, they also essentialized women and women's roles in society. In other words, the "back-to-nature" movement tended to believe that there was something inherent in women that differentiated them and their sociobiological roles from men. For most elements of the "back-to-nature" movement, women were *naturally* meant to live in the domestic realm and care for their children, man, and home. Further, "natural" sexual relationships were always heterosexual.

The "back-to-nature" movements like La Leche League shared theoretical roots with other modern United States movements, including a conservative branch of feminism. These theories shared an outlook about gender sometimes called the gender-difference orientation.[145] And, although the gender-difference orientation garners little attention from contemporary feminism, it continues to be accepted in traditional scholarly fields such as sociology. A primary theme was that women's psychic life was fundamentally different from men's. Gender-difference theorists argued that women are different from men in their interests and values, their manner of making value judgments, their achievement motives, their writing, their sexuality, their identity, and their general consciousness and self-understanding. Gender-difference theorists claimed that the overall makeup of women's and men's relationships and life experiences are different. In this thinking, women relate to their children and others differently than do men. And women experience their own development and aging differently than do men. The gender-difference orientation of feminist thought tended to recommend mutual respect as the "answer" to problems springing from gender difference.[146]

The gender-difference orientation offered various explanations for the differences between men and women. The most conservative and popular explanation was the biological. Here, gender differences are fundamental and unchangeable aspects of being either male or female. In this model, biology is destiny. So for organizations like La Leche League, because women give birth to and have breasts for feeding infants, women are naturally meant to be the central caretakers of children.

THREE

Breasts versus Bottles
and the Sexual Mother

La Leche League International was started in 1957 by seven stay-at-home Catholic, white, middle-class mothers in Illinois. They met through their shared involvement in an ecumenical Christian social action and family organization. These seven women were part of the post–World War II childbirth reform community. Like the larger childbirth reform movement, the seven La Leche League International "Founding Mothers" believed in "natural" childbirth, breastfeeding with child-led weaning, and large families cared for by stay-at-home mothers.

The La Leche League founders wanted to support the few white middle-class women in those days who wished to breastfeed their babies. Previously, breastfeeding had a rocky history in the United States. Early in the century, as middle-class mothers increasingly turned to scientific experts to learn how to parent, adults touching children was considered "dirty" in both senses of the word. With the new scientific awareness of germs, people realized that touching potentially brought about the spread of germs and could be unhealthy. Furthermore, touching involved the body, the always-bordering-on-being-out-of-control, savage/passionate, sexual body. During this time, breastfeeding fell out of favor in the middle class, only to return again in the 1960s and 1970s.

Consequently, throughout the nineteenth and twentieth centuries, there have been enormous pressures on women to breastfeed, not to breastfeed, and then, again, to breastfeed. And throughout, the middle class has been very anxious about the body and its potentially out-of-control sexuality. The anti-touching, anti-breastfeeding ethos of periods in the twentieth century were, in part, a response to this anxiety. And the middle class continues to be at once deeply anxious about and infatuated with the body, but now the question is not whether to breastfeed, but for how long.

The child-rearing texts of the early part of the twentieth century that I examined pay little to no attention to breastfeeding. Holt did claim that breast-feeding—"Mother's milk"—is the best food for infants, but spends only four or so pages discussing breastfeeding before he turns his attention to formula, about which he writes thirty-two pages, carefully describing the making of "formula" from cow's milk, schedules for feeding, and so on.[1] Watson never even mentioned breastfeeding, although he did briefly comment on bottle-feeding, arguing that bottle-fed babies can be weaned from the bottle at six to eight months.[2] This lack of attention to breastfeeding in the early-century child-rearing texts exemplifies the ideological turn away from breastfeeding.

Because my data sources—popular child-rearing books—early in the twen-tieth century focus so little on breastfeeding, I turn to secondary sources for the historical precursor to the contemporary debates on breastfeeding in the United States. Through scholars like sociologist Linda M. Blum[3] and historian Julia Grant,[4] I argue that attitudes toward breastfeeding have shifted over time, sometimes being promoted as central to good mothering and other times dismissed.

Blum argues that in the eighteenth- and nineteenth-century United States, mothers were criticized harshly if they did not breastfeed their young. Blum writes, "Maternal breastfeeding, moreover, became almost an emblem of new democratic ideals, as images of 'nature' were linked with equality, the rejec-tion of decadent, aristocratic 'culture,' and the rising health and wealth of the middle class of the young nation."[5] Nonetheless, some women were unable to carry out this "civic duty."

If a woman was not able or willing to breastfeed, she had two alternatives in feeding her child. One was to have the child breastfed by another lactating woman, and another was "dry nursing" with an artificial food, "usually diluted animal milk or a 'pap' of flour, sugar, milk, water, or tea."[6] People knew that infant mortality was high with either alternative, but more especially with "dry nursing."

At the same time, there were fundamental divisions of race and class be-tween elite families and their wet nurses. In the northern United States, wet nurses were usually poor or working-class immigrants. In the South, they were African American slaves. Given these divisions, wealthy families worried about the "fitness" of the wet nurses they hired. African American women were seen as "naturally" nurturant simultaneous to often being denied their own mother–child bonds. Enslaved women routinely had their children taken from them to be sold. If for a time the woman lived with her child, her time was taken up with working long hours for the slave owner, which left little to no time to care for her own children. Although Black women were understood by elites to be nurturant, they were "also cast as primitively oversexed and thereby polluted. . . . In the North, where the racial placement of European immigrant groups . . . was only later established as 'white,' wet nurses were seen as inferior and suspect."[7] In part because of elite concerns about "pollution," when maternal breastfeeding failed, affluent families increasingly turned to artificial feeding, renamed "scientific infant food" by the turn of the century. This way, they avoided contact with supposedly unclean peoples and simultaneously advanced the cause of science.

In the United States in the early twentieth century, mass immigration greatly increased anxiety in the Anglo-American Protestant middle class. To some extent in response to this anxiety, issues of child care became matters of state policy. Further, Blum writes that the state

> made gendered, raced bodies public issues: the push for military "fitness" targeted white (and potentially white) male bodies, but the improvement of population quality, to be achieved through "higher," "Americanized" mothering, targeted female bodies. . . . State policies of "race betterment" and public health promotion emerged in this nation-building climate, but from an uneasy alliance between eugenics followers, who wanted to control immigrants and non whites and their immutable, biological inferiority, and "race liberals," who wanted to promote their cultural assimilation—at least, those who were potentially "white" and could be reshaped to Anglo-American, middle-class norms.[8]

As Grant argues, it was largely middle-class Protestant reformers who worked with the state to "usher immigrants into mainstream society by teaching them the English language and American principles of citizenship." She writes, "The reformers also strove to disseminate American 'family values' to ensure the acculturation of seemingly unassimilable southeast European immigrants."[9] A simultaneous and connected campaign, the parent-education movement, worked to develop and disseminate expert—scientific—knowledge about child development and child rearing. This movement began around the turn of the century and developed through the first half of the twentieth century. It was committed to an odd mix of scientific motherhood—proposed in the work of Holt and Watson—and the more traditional "maternalism."

The ideology of maternalism held that "women had unique personal *and* civic responsibilities to children and families that were based on their reproductive capacities."[10] The National Congress of Mothers and the American Association of University Women were two important organizations involved in this movement. Many middle-class women, labeled "maternalists" by historians, were deeply engaged in these social welfare and Americanization campaigns. The maternalists used the language of "gender difference," focusing on women as mothers who were to play a national role in "baby saving"; that is, working to lower the rates of infant mortality and sickness. For the most part, maternalists believed that mothers should be home caring for children full time. They argued against women with children working for a wage, and against child labor as well. "In contrast to European welfare states, United States maternalists did not strive for family or maternity allowances, fearing that such provisions, by removing the disciplining effect of the family's dependency on the father, might encourage men to abandon their families (as well as cause labor unrest)." United States materialists only worked to provide public support for poor mothers "in selected, 'worthy' cases of the father-provider's absence: 'deserving' mothers in the early twentieth century were primarily white widows."[11] In spite of these severe limits, the "Mothers' Pension programs never gained sufficient backing to fully fund the domestic ideal. Similar moral eligibility requirements, which disqualified most poor women of color and single or divorced mothers, continued under the enlarged federal New Deal program, Aid to Dependent Children."[12]

Strangely, even though maternalists understood the social causes of poverty, they tended to hold impoverished mothers responsible for their need to do wage work. Despite clear socioeconomic reasons for mothers working outside the home, maternalists believed that poor mothers needed education to be persuaded to stop working for a wage. In other words, if mothers only knew how important it was to stay home with the children, then somehow they would find a way to do it. This thinking imbues similar debates today in the United States. Of course, other nations had a vastly different tactic. In sharp contrast to our individualized approach, European "welfare states provided day nurseries and cash maternity benefits in response to fears of depopulation."[13]

Besides protesting against wage earning, American maternalists focused on infant feeding. They were against artificial feeding and irregular breastfeeding—and they were correct to see feeding as a central concern. "Gastrointestinal ailments, easily prevented by breastfeeding and adequate sanitation, were responsible for as many as one-third of all infant deaths—and this figure was cut nearly in half by the campaign's education efforts."[14] However, here again, the maternalists held the poor women responsible for infant feeding problems. Blum writes that they "regarded healthful breastfeeding as irreconcilable with wage work, in marked contrast to the European model of scheduling nursing breaks during the workday and putting nursing rooms in factories, as endorsed by the International Labor Organization."[15] Blum notes that reformers in the United States Children's Bureau had a list of requirements for nursing that were difficult for even full-time middle-class homemakers, much less wage-working women, to fulfill. They required that mothers sleep at least eight hours at night, along with napping during the day, exercising and spending time outdoors for one hour in the morning and again in the evening, and nursing their infants on a very rigid schedule.

This advice directly addressed adult–child touch. It instructed nursing women to "eat a 'bland,' i.e., American, diet, and to keep a physical distance from her baby." Following the culturally biased advice of the experts, maternalists stressed that mothers "must avoid 'excessive' cuddling."[16] Keeping a physical distance from one's baby made no sense in many immigrant cultures. As Blum argues, Anglo-American Protestant middle-class maternalists raised the issues of who should mother, how mothering should be done, and what resources are required. They fought to keep white poor and working-class women at home with their children full time, without supplying the financial assistance needed to stop their wage work.

In spite of their biases, they did help immigrant families in one important way, with health care. Blum writes, "White-ethnic women did successfully extend preventive health services to many urban dwellers."[17] This made a vast difference because of the enormous problem of child disease and death among white poor and working-class peoples.

Given a history of slavery, vehement white racism, and enduring poverty, the problem of infant mortality was even bigger for African Americans. Access to health care, like most things in the United States, was—and remains—raced. Whereas Anglo-American maternalists claimed to be "saving" all babies, they really worked only for white babies. However, within the small African American middle-class, Black women organized to "save" Black babies. "Such Black maternalists subverted racialized meaning by labeling themselves 'pure mothers for pure children.' And although they had less aversion to wage-earning mothers, their actions were similar to those of white reformers: they set up clinics for children, hygiene classes for mothers, and milk stations to distribute safe, low-cost cow's milk."[18] In contrast to white maternalists, and in spite of their extensive efforts, Black maternalist reformers never gained the bit of state power that the white maternalists had garnered. Indeed, as Blum makes clear, the national baby-saving campaign blamed Black people for their own poverty and suffering. Ironically, one of the few sources of health care for the Black community, African American midwives who delivered most Black babies in the South, were faulted for the high Black infant death rate. And African American mothers were blamed for turning to the Black midwives. The midwives were coded as dirty and "primitive"—the polar opposite of "scientific." At the Southern Medical Association meeting in 1925, Black midwives were described as "filthy and ignorant and not far removed from the jungles of Africa, laden with its atmosphere of weird superstition and vodooism."[19]

In time, national legislation made training and licensing—supervised largely by white public health nurses—mandatory for midwives. Many traditional practices, such as standing or squatting during labor and delivery, now known to be beneficial while birthing, were prohibited. Supervisors regularly inspected the uniforms, bags, and even the homes of midwives. Blum and other scholars suggest that this fanatical attention to Black midwives' personal appearance indicates their being symbolically "cleansed" of their race and sexuality. Yet the national legislation regulating midwives was also born from the efforts of the new medical establishment to eliminate its competition. The growing medical profession focused not only on midwives, but also on many other health practitioners. Freund, McGuire, and Podhurst write, "Some professional competitors, such as homeopaths and osteopaths, were coopted; others, such as pharmacists, nurses, anesthetists, and X-ray technicians, were subordinated" into the medical profession. Yet they argue that midwives, and others such as clergy and barber-surgeons, were eventually "driven from legitimate practice outright."[20]

Blum argues that Anglo-American maternalist reformers seemed to want to clean sexuality from poor mothers as well as Black midwives with their instructions against cuddling and sensual, on-demand, infant feeding. To be qualified for the Mothers' Pension meant abstaining from sexual relations. "Since eligibility for the Mothers' Pensions depended on the absence of a male breadwinner, recipients were required to refrain from sexual relationships, which were considered immoral by definition."[21] The enlarged program, Aid to Dependent Children, with its "man in the house" regulations, "justified such practices as midnight home 'visits' and other invasions of privacy."[22] These practices disciplined maternal bodies—particularly poor mothers' bodies.

By 1930, Black and white maternalists contributed to big drops in infant death and disease rates. "And despite medical models nearly impossible to emulate, most mothers in all groups continued to breastfeed their infants. Although national statistics were not collected, those available from limited community studies indicate that between 85 and 90 percent of mothers breast-fed their babies at birth in the first three decades of the century." Blum writes, "Rural women were slightly more likely to nurse than urban women, and, while all mothers were nursing for shorter durations, urban mothers weaned earliest."[23] The limited records available indicate that before 1950, and in sharp contrast to the present, African American women were much more likely to breastfeed than white women.[24]

In spite of the ongoing association of breastfeeding with good mother-ing, there was a period in United States history when breastfeeding fell out of fashion. During the first half of the twentieth century, particularly from the 1930s to the 1950s, artificial feeding became popular among Anglo-American Protestant middle-class women and other women striving to enter the white middle class. These mothers increasingly opted for the sterile, measurable, "civilized," and scientific feeding method; that is, "formula" via the bottle. The very word "formula" speaks of a culture infatuated with science.

Coincident with this shift to artificial infant food, a new understanding of human breasts developed. Breasts have not always been sexualized in Western culture, and are not sexualized in many parts of the world today. Social mean-ings surrounding the body shift and change in different cultural and historical contexts. As breasts have been eroticized in modern Western cultures, they have become dangerous, dirty, threatening, and something to hide away. In the early-twentieth-century American middle class, offering one's breast to the hungry mouth of an infant became taboo, something done by "savage" or as-yet uncivilized people.

With this sexualization of "natural" infant feeding practices, and with the middle-class shift to "scientific" methods, new authorities in child rearing developed. Medical practitioners had become the new experts for the private realm. Middle-class mothers came to believe that healthy babies required the watchful eye of science. This included frequent visits to the doctor. Within this new schema, doctors' interests were complicated. On the one hand, doctors colluded with the rapidly growing formula industry. By the 1930s, formula producers regularly funded pediatric research. At the same time, like the ma-ternalist reformers, doctors held humanitarian concerns for women. They responded to the needs that women articulated. Blum argues, women "wanted freedom from the control biology extended over their lives, including pain-free, safe childbirth and birth control." To some extent, middle-class women "saw medical science as an ally."[25]

Not later than 1930, as middle-class women increasingly turned to formula, this kind of feeding became safer with new discoveries in bacteriology, physiology, and nutrition. The proliferation of refrigeration in the first half of the century also played a central role in the spread of formula-feeding. Before adequate refrigeration, cow's milk (formula) quickly went bad. "Even if milk was bought in bottles, there was no way to keep it cold—in the summer it would go bad by mid-morning."[26] This was especially problematic for working-class and poor mothers. "Most immigrant mothers had small iceboxes that had to be supplied with ice bought daily from the iceman. Since a small amount of ice cost between five and ten cents, few women could afford to buy more than small quantities."[27] With refrigeration, cow's milk could be kept safely for a matter of days, making formula a much less dangerous alternative than it had been before refrigeration.

Slowly, doctors took over the supervision of infant feeding, turning it into a central and very profitable component of pediatric and family medicine. Not only bottle-feeding, but breastfeeding as well, became thoroughly regulated. And in turn, this undermined the success of individuals who breastfed with the medical recommendation of feeding on a strict schedule, weighing infants before and after feeding, and supplementing with formula. Even hospitals—organized according to the findings of sponsored research—"sabotaged breastfeeding: They relied on strict feeding schedules, separated mothers and babies for long intervals, and regularly gave supplemental bottles."[28]

The Mainstream Medical Model

To a lesser extent, the medical regulation of infant feeding is still a problem today. In 2000, I gave birth in an urban hospital rated as one of the top ten hospitals for labor and delivery in the United States. We went home from the hospital the "normal"—as mandated by health insurance companies—two days after delivery. The next day, my infant son was—unnecessarily, it turns out—hospitalized. He was three days old. My breast milk was slow to come in, my baby become mildly dehydrated, and we had an unfortunate telephone encounter with a young, overanxious pediatrician. Once back in the hospital, the medical model took over and put my son through an immense number of unnecessary tests, pinpricks, weighings, and other invasive examinations. The young pediatrician who had admitted my son refused to give his approval to let my son go home for three days, during which he tested and monitored my new baby. And to make matters worse, hospital policy did not recognize my son and me as a unit; he was admitted, I was not. All three days, along with the numerous and assorted tests, turned out to be completely uncalled for. Those three unnecessary days of separation nearly cost us my breast milk.

Ironically, I did need to be hospitalized. I had lost an immense amount of blood during the delivery. Yet, as most new mothers are quick to find out, once the baby is delivered, the focus shifts from her, the mere container, to the new life. It took several days of my mother's persistent telephone calls to my obstetrician, my primary physician, and various other doctors, administrators, and bureaucrats in my health maintenance organization for me to be readmitted to the hospital for a blood transfusion. Meanwhile my family took turns spending days and nights with my son at the hospital. I was in no condition to stay with him myself. Because no adult was admitted with my son, staying with him meant sleeping in a chair in his hospital room. My family reported back to me that the hospital staff insisted my son be fed on a strict schedule. He was fed—much the same as in the early twentieth century—every four hours. If he was asleep, he was woken for a feeding. If he was crying and seemingly hungry, he had to wait for the schedule to catch up with his need. At one point, my sister sneaked him a leftover bottle from the last feed. She was caught by an angry nurse who slapped one hand against the other several times, saying, "The schedule! The schedule! The schedule!"

In the first half of the century, most doctors did not—and many still do not—understand that a woman's breast milk supply is produced in response to a baby's sucking, or demand.[29] Human milk is much more easily digested than cow's milk, so breastfed babies are usually hungry more frequently. Supplemental bottles of formula fill babies up so that they suck at the breast less, starting a cycle of decline in the amount of breast milk. Indeed, when my infant son was hospitalized, my partner expressed fear that the formula fed to him there would result in my breast milk drying up. The pediatric-ward doctor to whom he addressed this concern told him this was needless worry and merely a myth of "politicized midwives." Of course, the doctor could speak with confidence. He spoke from the perspective of science, free from ideology—in other words, the Truth. To him, the *midwives*, because of their grounding in political ideology (myth), were busy spreading falsehoods.

When women's milk did dry up as a result of the medical model and its practice of separating mothers and infants, offering supplemental formula bottles, and feeding on strict schedules, doctors blamed the women. Blum writes, "Not surprisingly, 'insufficient milk' quickly became the most prevalent reason for breastfeeding failure."[30] Middle-class women's "failure" at breastfeeding surprised no one. Physicians, who worked primarily with a middle-class clientele, worried that their patients, "'civilized' women who lived under unnatural strains and had 'highly developed nervous system[s]'" were not fit for nursing.[31] Physicians thought that, in contrast to "primitive" mothers who were "natural" breastfeeders, white middle-class women's bodies were not reliable. Although they were told that breast milk was best for babies, they were also told that their bodies were unlikely to be dependable. The mainstream medical establishment told women that bottle-feeding was very nearly as good as the breast. By 1950, a bottle-fed baby was not an object of pity—"and as L. Emmett Holt Jr. wrote (in the revised edition of his father's manual): 'a bottle mother may still be a perfect mother.'"[32]

The formula industry played a central role in the middle-class move to bottle-feeding. Formula was and continues to be a very lucrative business. "U.S. infant formula sales reached approximately $2.59 billion in 1993 representing a six percent increase over 1992. Since 1989, when formula companies lifted their previous voluntary ban on marketing directly to consumers, the market has grown by 54 percent. The average bottle-feeding family in the United States spends between $800 and $2,000 per year on infant formula."[33] Formula companies target doctors and hospitals as well as individual consumers.

> Almost all American hospitals with maternity services have a contract with one or another of the infant formula manufacturers through which the facility receives free infant formula, "educational grants" (seminars and literature in which hospital staff receive lactation science training from . . . employees of the formula company), and even cash gifts in return for the formula company's exclusive right to market directly to that hospital's patients. . . . Nurses or doctors who formula-feed their own children can depend on their sales rep to provide them with a year's supply of infant formula at absolutely no charge. Additionally, formula manufacturers routinely host lavish parties and receptions for pediatricians at AAP functions.[34]

Upon giving birth, women often receive as much as an entire case of infant formula delivered to their home, compliments of a formula company. Because of the finely tuned supply-and-demand nature of breastfeeding, using even small amounts of the formula can bring about a slow, at best—or quick, at worst—end to breastfeeding. The formula industry is highly aware of this and even more aware that breastfeeding is their biggest competition. Formula companies spend millions of dollars every year on advertising and product giveaways. From their perspective, it is money well spent. Their own research "has clearly demonstrated that advertising, 'educational literature,' and especially product giveaways all make it statistically less likely that women will breastfeed without formula supplementation—or breastfeed at all."[35]

"Every time a woman chooses to breastfeed instead of bottle-feed her baby, the formula [companies] lose *at least* one thousand dollars in sales."[36] Breastfeeding advocate Katie Allison Granju argues, "Because pharmaceutical companies which produce formula also develop and market medications and medical supplies, you can be sure that they are acutely aware that the better health enjoyed by breastfed infants and their mothers as a group also impacts their bottom line, possibly even more than the sale of the formula itself."[37]

Yet, the success of formula and the medical establishment's intervention in infant feeding was not due only to greed or the desire to control and contain women's bodies. The medical enterprise also acted in answer to women's voiced wishes. The maternalists and other elite women worked to advance medicalization. They understood medicine as offering women some freedom from the dictates of nature. The medical world presented women with birth control and increased safety and relief from pain during childbirth. With the option of artificial infant feeding, and the newly available refrigeration that made formula a longer-lasting, safer alternative, women gained more independence. In other words, formula did not merely benefit the companies selling it. As artificial feeding methods and formula became safer for babies, the bottle gradually became a symbol of progress and modernity. Advice literature implied this, encouraging mothers "to give 'relief' bottles to relax and enjoy 'freedom' from the 'very confining duties of nursing.'"[38]

Among the middle class, a kind of anti-breastfeeding ethos took hold in the 1930s and lasted well into the 1950s. Even a contemporary popular medical manual for parents recognizes this pro-bottle-feeding period in United States history. In *Taking Care of Your Child: A Parent's Guide to Medical Care* (1990), the three doctors who author it write, "It is unfortunate that fashion is often responsible for making a mother feel she should choose one particular method. Bottle feeding became popular 50 years ago. The society at the time wanted to do everything 'scientifically,' women wanted to be free to leave the home, and the female breast was shifting from being a nursing object to being a sexual object." Here it is important to note that, in the 1940s, "scientifically" meant bottle-feeding; in contrast, today, "scientifically" means breastfeeding. Clearly, science discourages and encourages breastfeeding at different socio-historical moments as mainstream ideologies of touch shift and change. The authors continue, "Fortunately, social attitudes are constantly in movement. Currently, there is widespread acceptance of mothers nursing in public. Breast feeding is now gaining in popularity and is currently considered to have many 'scientific advantages.'"[39]

Although many women would contest the doctors' claim that "currently, there is widespread acceptance of mothers nursing in public,"[40] nonetheless, breastfeeding has more than "gained in popularity."[41] In the white middle class today there is a cultural imperative to breastfeed. This shift from the bottle back to the breast began around the time Dr. Benjamin Spock's famous child-rearing book first came out in 1945. That it encouraged women to breastfeed was one of the revolutionary things about Spock's book. Subsequently, over the next two decades, white middle-class women did slowly return to the breast as the optimum way both to feed and to nourish an infant. By the 1970s, "earlier sentiments in favor of 'natural' mothering had resurged."[42]

There are few, if any, places in the contemporary United States where women are told *not* to breastfeed. Of course, this does not mean that all women breastfeed. Some do very little, if they breastfeed at all. In general, most American women do not breastfeed exclusively or for very long. Various contemporary studies have found that white middle-class women are among the most likely to breastfeed their children. In contrast, African American working-class women are among the least likely to breastfeed.[43] In a recent policy statement on breastfeeding, the American Academy of Pediatrics (AAP) data show that among women who initiate *any* breastfeeding at birth, albeit not necessarily exclusively, many of those also feed their infants formula—72 percent of white women, 73 percent of Latinas, and only 53 percent of Black women initiate some breastfeeding (the AAP had no data on Asian or other groups of women). By six months, no group seems to be doing a lot of breastfeeding, with only 34 percent of white women, 33 percent of Latinas, and 22 percent of Black women doing any breastfeeding (with or without supplemental formula). At one year, only 18 percent of white women and Latinas and 12 percent of Black women are still doing any breastfeeding.[44]

This is a flip from the first half of the century when Black women were more likely to breastfeed and white women less likely. "Hospital birth records from 1948 show the Southeast, where most Blacks still resided, with the highest rates of maternal breastfeeding . . . and retrospective surveys confirm that more Black mothers breastfed in the 1940s and 1950s."[45]

There are many good reasons why Black women today tend not to breastfeed exclusively or for long, if at all. In a history of racism and slavery, African American women's bodies were owned and used for sexual exploitation, and their oppression was often justified by their supposed closeness to nature. Enslaved women's "breasts, which sometimes suckled white babies, were examined like part of the livestock at auctions."[46] Based on her in-depth interviews, Blum argues that one of the reasons why African American working-class mothers rejected breastfeeding was the "exposure of sexuality and the physicality or animal-like qualities it represented to them."[47] And like other working-class mothers, Black working-class women also "shared the stressful life circumstances that can make breastfeeding overwhelmingly burdensome or exhausting."[48] It is interesting—and I would argue, admirable—that the African American mothers in Blum's study were "much less likely to be pained by guilt or regret about their bottlefeeding than the white mothers" that she interviewed.[49]

In contrast, for the white middle class in particular, the question is no longer whether or not to breastfeed. Instead, the problem is *how long*. Without taking socioeconomic class into account, the American Academy of Pediatrics claims that 72 percent of white women breastfeed their babies and 53 percent breastfeed exclusively at birth.[50] Studies such as Blum's[51] point out that if the Department of Health and Human Services had broken this statistic down by class, the number would have increased significantly for the white middle class. Being in the white middle class in the United States means listening to expert advice, and today, child-rearing experts all argue for breastfeeding. Popular health movements, organizations such as La Leche League International, and mainstream medical associations like the AAP all argue that "breast is best" for human infants. The reasons given vary depending on the source, from the superior nutritional value of breast milk compared with infant artificial formula to the intimacy—in other words, mother–child touching—in breastfeeding. For example, the AAP claims,

> Extensive research using improved epidemiologic methods and modern laboratory techniques documents diverse and compelling advantages for infants, mothers, families, and society from breastfeeding and use of human milk for infant feeding. These advantages include health, nutritional, immunologic, developmental, psychologic, social, economic, and environmental benefits. . . . Human milk is species-specific, and all substitute feeding preparations differ markedly from it, making human milk uniquely superior for infant feeding. Exclusive breastfeeding is the reference or normative model against which all alternative feeding methods must be measured with regard to growth, health, development, and all other short- and long-term outcomes.[52]

The AAP is today's equivalent of the John B. Watsons of the 1920s and 1930s. This is not to say that the AAP speaks as one voice or that it is solidly behaviorist. It has behaviorist leanings, yet more important for the purposes of this study, the AAP is solidly grounded in the middle class. It is one very prominent voice of mainstream culture. Today, doctors commonly advise new mothers to breastfeed their infants for the first year. Indeed, the AAP recommends that breastfeeding continue for "at least the first year of life and beyond for as long as mutually desired by mother and child."[53] Interestingly, adult–child touch is not among the AAP's long list of reasons to breastfeed, nor does it cite the advantages of added intimacy. This contrasts sharply with the broad attachment-parenting movement where adult–child touch is a central—if not the central—reason to breastfeed. The AAP's numerous reasons focus on health benefits to the infant.

> Research in developed and developing countries of the world, including middle-class populations in developed countries, provides strong evidence that human milk feeding decreases the incidence and/or severity of a wide range of infectious diseases including bacterial meningitis, bacteremia, diarrhea, respiratory tract infection, necrotizing enterocolitis, otitis media, urinary tract infection, and late-onset sepsis in preterm infants. In addition, postneonatal infant mortality rates in the United States are reduced by 21% in breastfed infants. . . . Some studies suggest decreased rates of sudden infant death syndrome in the first year of life and reduction in incidence of insulin-dependent (type 1) and non-insulin-dependent (type 2) diabetes mellitus, lymphoma, leukemia, and Hodgkin's disease, overweight and obesity, hypercholesterolemia, and asthma in older children and adults who were breastfed, compared with individuals who were not breastfed. . . . Breastfeeding has been associated with slightly enhanced performance on tests of cognitive development.[54]

The AAP also gives possible health benefits for mothers as further reasons to breastfeed. Breastfeeding increases levels of oxytocin in women, resulting in less postpartum bleeding and faster uterine involution. Breastfeeding postpones the return of women's menstrual cycle. This delay, called lactational amenorrhea, means a delay in ovulation and increased child spacing. Research demonstrates that lactating women have a quicker return to prepregnancy weight, advanced bone remineralization postpartum with less hip fractures in the postmenopausal period. Women who breastfeed have a reduced risk of ovarian cancer and of premenopausal breast cancer.[55]

In addition to individual health benefits, the AAP argues that "breastfeeding provides significant social and economic benefits to the nation, including reduced health care costs and reduced employee absenteeism for care attributable to child illness."[56] Further, "The significantly lower incidence of illness in the breastfed infant allows the parents more time for attention to siblings and other family duties and reduces parental absence from work and lost income."[57] The AAP points out that there are significant direct economic benefits to the family and to the nation. They claim that the 1993 cost of purchasing infant formula for the first year after birth was estimated at $855.[58] And they argue that increased national rates of breastfeeding offer the "potential for decreased annual health care costs of $3.6 billion in the United States; decreased costs for public health programs such as the Special Supplemental Nutrition Program for Women, Infants, and Children (WIC); [and] decreased parental employee absenteeism and associated loss of family income."[59]

Although the AAP gives many persuasive reasons to breastfeed, nowhere does it discuss adult–child touch. This "neutral" approach to touch resonates with the AAP's history. The AAP is a central component of mainstream medicine in the United States. I argue the that AAP, mainstream medicine, and science generally are suspicious of touch because the dominant medical establishment is suspicious of "the body." And more than the body, scientific thought entails suspicion of "nature." Scientific ideology understands the body, and nature, as instruments to be used or misused. From the scientific vantage point, we can study the body and understand it better. Through understanding it, we increase our ability to control it. Through controlling the body, we foster our capacity to use it. This instrumental ideological framework has no place for enjoying the body as intrinsically valuable. At best, the body is to be used in life. Minimally, one uses the body to get through or survive life; maximally, to gain the goods of life and to live a "successful" life. The body "itself" is neutral mass or, at the worst, dangerous, savage, and out of control.

La Leche League International

In sharp contrast to mainstream medicine, La Leche League International and the larger attachment-parenting movement do discuss touch, and they discuss it a lot. La Leche League values the body. Further, La Leche League values the present moment, the *now,* more than mainstream medicine; it is both less future oriented and less instrumentally focused than mainstream medicine, or much of mainstream United States culture. Touching, bodies, children, relationships all matter in the present. And children matter for who they are now—rather than only for the future independent adult one's child is supposed to become. In this orientation, La Leche League offers a powerful challenge to mainstream culture.

La Leche League and the attachment-parenting movement also challenge mainstream medicine and culture through their championing women's expertise over scientific experts in parenting. On the other hand, La Leche League demands women who mother, do *nothing* but mother. Women who have to, much less want to, work outside the home are disparaged by the attachment-parenting movement.

Attachment-parenting philosophy reinforces the larger culture's mind-body split, although they reverse the valuation. In sharp contrast to behaviorist child-rearing experts, attachment parents cherish the body. And they cherish it—and the "natural"—for itself; for attachment parents, "being with" the "natural" body through touching is one of the most important components of parenting. Sleeping and feeding are not merely means to maintain the growing infant body. The mother body sleeping and feeding *with* the infant body is purely valuable beyond any other particular usefulness.

The attachment-parenting movement and the largest organization representing this movement, La Leche League International, believe that breast-feeding is fundamentally important. However, unlike contemporary mainstream scientific ideology, where there is some room for mothers to choose *not* to breastfeed, La Leche League offers no alternative to breastfeeding. For instance, coming from the mainstream medical perspective, the three doctors who wrote *Taking Care of Your Child: A Parent's Guide to Medical Care* claim, "Breast feeding is best for some mothers, whereas others will prefer bottle feeding. Either choice is fully acceptable and will be guided by *individual* circumstances."[60] In contrast, for La Leche League, there is no real choice. Good parents—that is, good mothers—breastfeed. Although La Leche League focuses on biological mothers and biological/"natural" mother–child connections, even adoptive mothers are encouraged to breastfeed using a special mechanism called a nursing supplementer. And again, setting themselves apart from mainstream medicine and the AAP, the attachment-parenting movement and La Leche League International believes breastfeeding to be important largely because it involves adult–child touch. For the attachment-parenting movement, adult–child touch is central to—perhaps *the* central component of—good parenting. And because touch and the intimacy that springs from touch is so important, they argue that children should be breastfed indefinitely, until the child is ready to wean itself. They call this "natural weaning" or "child-led weaning."

In the 1950s, when La Leche League International was founded, not only did white middle-class women tend to bottle-feed their infants, but it was also considered inappropriate to even talk about breastfeeding. So the seven La Leche League founders "had to come up with a name that would allow them to discreetly discuss their activities, as well as list their meetings in the local newspaper. . . . The idea for the fledgling organization's name came from a statue."[61] La Leche League International explains in their manual, "The name of our organization was inspired by a shrine in St. Augustine, Florida, dedicated to the Mother of Christ under the title 'Nuestra Senora de la Leche y Buen Parto,' which translates freely, 'Our Lady of Happy Delivery and Plentiful Milk.'"[62] It is telling that the La Leche League name—like its founders—has Christian roots.

Within a traditional and Christian framework of women living and working in the home, these women wanted to take the rearing of children back from the scientific experts and return it to the sphere of women, women's "instincts," and women's "natural" expertise. According to La Leche League, a mother can achieve natural mothering by listening to her instincts. La Leche League offers this challenge to the mainstream medical establishment—including people like Holt and Watson—that insists on telling women how to raise their children. For La Leche League, women do not need science to tell them about child rearing. Women naturally know how to be mothers. On the other hand, La Leche League does not challenge traditional Christian mainstream gender roles. This philosophy maintains that women *should* stay home and raise their children. This is what women are "meant" to do and this is what women "naturally" do best. In this way, La Leche League International was and continues to be both empowering and disempowering for women.

According to La Leche League, women trusting their own intuition or instincts will be led to a number of clear outcomes: One, mothers who heed their instincts will breastfeed their infants. Two, in sharp contrast to Watson, intuitive mothers will respond to their babies' cries quickly. Three, intuitive mothers will *touch* their babies and children a lot. Pointedly diverging from the 1950s medical model, La Leche League maintained—and still maintains today—that the physical contact of adult with child is one of the most important elements of raising a child. And it cannot be just any adult. La Leche League argues that babies need extensive physical contact with their *mothers*.

One woman I interviewed, Myra, an active La Leche League International member, made clear her and La Leche League's focus on the mother. Fathers are secondary parents during the child's first three years. Myra talked about a basic biological link between the mother and child that is developed and maintained through breastfeeding. According to Myra, mothers should be prepared to focus primarily on their baby for the first three years of its life. When asked about the sacrifices in terms of women's careers and other interests and activities, Myra made the traditional argument: True, it is a sacrifice, but a worthwhile one. Mothers are *meant* to be with their babies. And, she added, nothing could be more important than raising a child.

Myra granted that this practice excludes fathers, but she believes that, biologically, that is what is "meant" to happen. In other words, in their very nature, fathers are not meant to be central to a child's life for the first three years. Myra implied that after the first three years, fathers can become a more equal partner in child rearing. Myra was vague as to whether this meant equal but different roles for fathers. In their literature, La Leche League implies that after the first three years, the role of fathers is still less important, or at least less central, than that of mothers. And like most child-rearing literature, La Leche League reproduces heteronormativity. It does not consider the possibility of single mothers, gay or lesbian parents, or other increasingly common diverse forms of family in the United States. In their popular manual, *The Womanly Art of Breastfeeding: Seventh Revised Edition* (2004), in a section titled "Dads Can Help," La Leche League offers a fairly traditionally gendered place to fathers. He can "help" when he is not at work. And his way of helping mostly entails roughhousing.

> An understanding husband is one of a nursing mother's most treasured assets. He can step in to provide you with a welcome respite when he is home, and your older one will thrive on the extra attention.
>
> Dads are often masters at keeping toddler minds and hands busy when mother needs some time alone with the baby, or when she decides to take advantage of baby's nap time for a relaxing bath or some much needed rest. Father and toddler will both enjoy toddler-size roughhousing, and who but daddy can add such excitement to stories by putting in all of those low, rumbling noises?[63]

One way of fathers "helping" does not occur to La Leche League (or for that matter, any of the mainstream advice givers). In her popular book of nonfictional stories about breastfeeding, *Fresh Milk: The Secret Life of Breasts,* Fiona Giles discusses the numerous claims she encountered in her research about men who breastfeed, or "milkmen." One man she contacted "lactated sufficiently to help his wife breastfeed their second child."[64] Another man told about breastfeeding his third child, Miyuki, on a regular basis at times when the mother, Naomi, returned home late from work. It started one day when the infant was hungry and upset, and her father had already given her all of the expressed breast milk. This man writes, "Miyuki was frantic, so I was cuddling her, and patting her, and trying to get her to stop crying. . . . I was almost beside myself. She was throwing her head from side to side, then at one point she brushed against my nipple, and latched on."[65] He described the infant as initially confused but then soothed. And he found it "a little painful" and "strange," yet "better than her crying. . . . So it became a common thing. If Naomi was going to be late, I knew that there was always something there. If I'd run out of Naomi's milk, and Miyuki wouldn't suck on a piece of apple in a stocking or play with an ice cube, there was always my breast."[66]

Laura Shanley also writes about male lactation in her Internet article, "Milkmen: Fathers Who Breastfeed." Indeed, because they were "intrigued with the idea," she claims that her own husband, David, induced lactation. About their experience, she writes, "We had just had our first unassisted home-birth and were excited about applying our positive thinking techniques to other aspects of our lives. . . . Perhaps, we thought, David could do it [begin to lactate] simply through suggestion. He began telling himself that he would lactate, and within a week, one of his breasts swelled up and milk began dripping out."[67] Among other examples she offers of men lactating and breastfeeding, Shanley quotes from a friend's letter telling about a man in a gay relationship nursing their baby. Shanley quotes the letter about this milkman, "He used an SNS (supplemental nursing system) after she was born, with donated milk from several friends who were nursing. He was making milk but not a full supply. By the time the baby was 12 weeks old he was making a full milk supply! He stayed home with the baby . . . and nursed her exclusively until she was 8 months old. . . . I don't think many people outside their intimate circle knew about it, I'm sure folks would have had a fit if they'd known."[68]

Granted, La Leche League is not alone in neglecting to address male lactation. But the fact that it is not addressed by La Leche League or any of the mainstream advice literature points to our culture's profound unwillingness to think outside of our binary system in terms of male/female gender roles. Nonetheless, La Leche League offers a more extreme example of binary thinking. For them, men and women have biologically predetermined positions in society. These positions dictate what they do and how they parent in almost every aspect of life.

Initially, La Leche League drew on London psychiatrist John Bowlby's "attachment theory." Bowlby, like La Leche League, sharply differentiated his thinking from that of behaviorists like Watson. Throughout his writing, he aligned himself with the naturalists and their general tendency to both propagate psychoanalytic thinking—as in the case of Benjamin Spock—and to strongly challenge the behaviorists. For example, Bowlby interjected clear criticism of the behaviorists in his discussion of cases of maternal deprivation ranging from the institutionalization of a child to the common practice of leaving a child to "cry it out." Clearly referring to Watson's prominent book, *Psychological Care of Infant and Child* (1928), he wrote, "Naturally cases [of maternal deprivation] . . . are very numerous and of all degrees of severity from the child whose mother leaves him to scream for many hours because the baby-books tell her to do so to infants whose mothers wholly reject them."[69]

In his famous text, *Maternal Care and Mental Health,* originally published in the *Bulletin of the World Health Organization,* Bowlby argued that any separation of the young child from its mother brings lasting harm. He believed that the absence of working mothers from their children was a form of maternal deprivation that caused deep and extensive psychological damage. Bowlby likened this form of "deprivation"—mothers working away from home—to the experience of orphaned children during wartime. In a chapter titled "Causes of Family Failure in Western Communities, with Special Reference to Psychiatric Factors," Bowlby listed three primary causes of what he calls the "natural home group"—the nuclear family—failing. With "social calamity—war, famine" and "death of a parent," Bowlby included "full-time employment of mother." He claimed, "Any family suffering from one or more of these conditions must be regarded as a potential source of deprived children."[70] Bowlby offered a detailed and tragic description of a deprived child. A twenty-four-month-old boy, Bobby, was sent to a residential nursery in Hampstead, England, to live during World War II. At the time of this description, Bobby had been living in the institution seemingly for months, and, up to this point, without a visit from his mother.

> He became listless, often sat in a corner sucking and dreaming, at other times he was very aggressive. He almost completely stopped talking. He was dirty and wet continually, so that we had to put nappies on him. He sat in front of his plate eating very little, without pleasure, and started smearing his food over the table. At this time the nurse who had been looking after him fell ill, and Bobby did not make friends with anyone else. . . . A few days later he had tonsillitis and went to the sickroom. . . . He hardly ever said a word, had entirely lost his bladder and bowel control, sucked a great deal. On his return to the nursery he looked very pale and tired. . . . He did not seem to recognize the nurse who had looked after him at first.[71]

It is difficult to understand how Bowlby made the leap from this painful story of an institutionalized child to children whose mothers work full time. Nonetheless, components of Bowlby's work continue to dominate developmental psychology in the United States. In the United Kingdom, "Bowlbyism" was a term used to talk about state policies meant to keep mothers at home and away from the workplace.[72] And Bowlby's work clearly continues to influence the contemporary thinking of La Leche League.

Yet along with his sexist demand that mothers remain home with their children, Bowlby made an argument practically unheard of in the United States. Bowlby spent extensive time in his book arguing that the state must financially support mothers so that they can stay home and care for their children. From the conservatives to La Leche League International, plenty of thinkers through the twentieth century until today have argued that women should—indeed, that "good mothers" *must*—stay home full time with their children for the well-being of the children and society at large. Yet none of them believe society has any financial responsibility to mothers, making it practically impossible for the vast majority to stay home. In sharp contrast, Bowlby addressed a chapter, "Prevention of Family Failure," to the need for "socio-economic" and "socio-medical" aid to families. For example, Bowlby argued, "Husbandless mothers of children under five, and especially those under three . . . have the greatest difficulty in most countries in both making a living and caring for the children—activities which are incompatible when the children are very young. . . . Direct assistance to the mother is commonly meager. . . . Until the child has reached [the age of three], direct economic assistance should be given to the mother."[73] Further Bowlby continued, "Essential though socio-economic aid frequently is, it is often useless unless help of a socio-medical kind is given as well. In many cases there would be no economic problem at all if it were not for physical or mental illness."[74]

It is fascinating—and one might add a tragic example of La Leche League failing mothers—that for all of its time and energy spent advocating for breastfeeding and mothers devoting themselves to their babies, La Leche League never discusses the social and political context that might make their demands possible. Indeed, this leaves the majority of women who simply cannot afford to stay home with their children blamed—and blaming themselves—for social circumstances far beyond their control.

From its inception, La Leche League grew quickly in size and popularity. By 1991, the organization claimed to be second in size only to Alcoholics Anonymous among United States self-help groups. The group's manual, *The Womanly Art of Breastfeeding,* was first published as a book in 1958 and sold 17,000 copies. The second edition sold over one million copies between 1963 and 1981, and by 2004, the manual had sold three million copies. It is now available in nine languages. By 1981, La Leche League had a central office with paid staff, around 4,000 active groups, and approximately 60,000 subscribers to their bimonthly newsletter. By 2004, La Leche League International was truly international with groups in over sixty countries.[75]

La Leche League challenges mainstream science and, at the same time, depends on scientific experts to make and support its case. In telling the history of the League, its founders include experts as central players.

> It was at a church picnic that Mary White and Marian Tompson decided there had to be a way to help their friends who wanted to breastfeed their babies but found only frustration and failure when they tried. . . . We had no grandiose plans about how to go about helping our friends, but we were willing to try. Two local physicians, Drs. Herbert Ratner and Gregory White, advised us on those aspects of breastfeeding and mothering that were commonly associated with the medical community and gave us the benefit of their wisdom and insights into human nature.[76]

And in their dedication, the League founders write, "This book could not have been written and the basic principles underlying the work of La Leche League would not have withstood the test of time, had it not been for the unfailing counsel of Doctors Herbert Ratner and Gregory White, who have wholeheartedly supported us from the earliest days of the League."[77]

La Leche League argues that breastfeeding is good for infants because it involves touching. La Leche League advises mothers to breastfeed their infants while both mother and baby are nude to allow for maximum skin-to-skin contact. For La Leche League, breastfeeding—and the touching it entails—is the centerpiece of a healthy mother–child relationship. Because of the centrality of breastfeeding in their philosophy, La Leche League has always advocated what it calls "complete" breastfeeding, "a relational process, and one in which the mother and baby take their cues and habits reciprocally, from each other rather than from outside experts."[78] And they have pushed for breastfeeding on demand with "child-led weaning," arguing that children know what they need. Breastfeeding on demand and child-led weaning allowed for as much breastfeeding and touching as the child needed. La Leche League also advocates mothers "sharing sleep" with their babies. Bringing one's baby to bed allowed for extensive nighttime breastfeeding and ongoing physical contact between mother and child. "Complete breastfeeding therefore includes minimal separation from the baby, few supplemental bottles (if any), and feeding on the baby's demand, even if very frequent and/or irregular. Ideally, from this point of view, mothers should rely as little as possible on substitutes for the bodily comfort they provide—this includes bottles and pacifiers, but also playpens and carriages, as League mothers prefer slings and carriers that keep the baby on the mother's body and at or near the breast."[79]

La Leche League International, and the attachment-parenting movement in general, have been the foremost United States proponents of what they call "natural" or "child-led weaning." In her recent book, La Leche League leader and author Diane Bengson defines this form of weaning as allowing the child "to outgrow nursing on his own timetable."[80] In other words, the child nurses as long as she needs. When she is ready, she will wean "naturally." In her book, *How Weaning Happens,* Bengson argues that there are numerous advantages to natural weaning. She claims that these involve health advantages for both the mother and child. "Illness, including ear infections and diarrhea, is greatly reduced in breastfeeding children." Breastfeeding women "have elevated levels of prolactin . . . [which] produced the feelings of relaxation that women associate with nursing. A recent study showed that lactation reduces the body's chemical reaction to stress."[81] Unfortunately, like many popular child-rearing books, Bengson does not back up any of her references to "studies" with citations.

Along with the health benefits, natural weaning advocates such as Bengson and La Leche League argue that breastfeeding—and in particular breastfeeding on the child's "timetable"—offers an intimacy unavailable in other feeding options. Bengson does not explain why she believes breastfeeding to be more intimate than bottle-feeding. She simply states, "Extending nursing helps to make a child confident and people-oriented. . . . Nursing teaches a child to build close relationships and to trust intimacy and commitment to other people."[82]

In regard to adult–child touch, Bengson explicitly discusses the need for touching, and she always refers to touching in terms of *mothers,* not fathers, touching their children. She believes touching to be so important for the mother–child relationship that it must be replaced with a new form of touching between mother and child as the child weans. During weaning, mothers must find "new ways to touch your child." She continues, "[Some] mothers find the child is happy to substitute touching mama's breast for nursing while going to sleep, or he may put his mouth on the breast but not suck."[83] Implicit in this is Bengson's belief that *touching* makes breastfeeding intimate. And it is a specific touch—the touch between a child's mouth and her or his mother's breasts—that seems to do the trick, according to Bengson and other La Leche League members.

The touch involved in holding a child and giving him or her a bottle is, somehow, not sufficient. Oddly, this very touch—mouth to breast—is a touch considered "sexual" in the modern Western world. And insofar as it is sexual, it is also threatening at best, "bad" at worst. "Breastfeeding involves breasts—which in modern America are usually seen more as sexual organs, designed for men to play with, than as nutritive ones, designed for babies."[84]

That breasts are understood to be sexual and so, like one's genitals, must be kept hidden is reflected in American public decency laws. In 1999, Blum writes that only fourteen states had "passed legislation to specifically make public breastfeeding 'decent.' When proposed, such legislation is often met with hostility and ridicule, as it was recently in New Hampshire where it died in committee."[85] Women who breastfeed in public risk being harassed for their supposed indecency.[86] Indeed in 2006, Emily Gillette was asked to leave a Delta/Freedom flight in Burlington, Vermont, because she was breastfeeding her baby on the airplane. "Gillette said she was discreetly breastfeeding her 22-month-old daughter on October 13 as the flight prepared to leave Burlington International Airport."[87] One of the flight attendants asked Gillette to cover herself with a blanket, and Gillette refused. So the flight attendant had a ticket agent tell Gillette and her family that they had to get off the airplane. "[Gillette] didn't want to make a scene and complied." About the incident, Gillette said, "It embarrassed me. That was my first reaction, which is a weird reaction for doing something so good for a child."[88] A spokesperson for Freedom, Paul Skellon, said, "A breastfeeding mother is perfectly acceptable on an aircraft, providing she is feeding the child in a discreet way. . . . She was asked to use a blanket just to provide a little more discretion, she was given a blanket, and she refused to use it." According to Gillette, "she was seated by the window in the next-to-last row, her husband was seated between her and the aisle and no part of her breast was showing."[89]

The concern of the "decency-proponents" seems to be that breastfeeding mothers will use breastfeeding as an opportunity to flaunt their breasts. For example, Betsy Hart, writing in the *Jewish World Review,* makes no effort to hide her hostility against public breastfeeding:

> Yes, breastfeeding is natural and even wonderful. But so are a lot of bodily functions one doesn't draw attention to in public. Nevertheless, according to a recent report in the Associated Press, the activists continue to push lawsuits in many states that would guarantee all moms the "right" to nurse anytime, anywhere. . . . Such legislation is unnecessary for those moms who simply want to nourish their infants as unnoticeably [sic] and without making a public statement. . . . These laws are for women who think that personal really is the political, who want to use such laws to flagrantly display their "rights"—and often way too much of their breasts.[90]

Women, and the body-ness that women represent, must be contained and monitored; for like all things natural, they threaten to run out of control.

Of course, breasts are not "naturally" sexual any more than are other parts of the human body. Any part of the body is up for grabs, so to speak, when it comes to being sexual. Certain parts become more sexualized, and others less so, in different cultures. For instance, women in Mwanza, Tanzania, where I lived in 1993, seemed to understand breasts in an asexual and public way, much as United States women might understand their ankles. Whereas United States women keep their breasts carefully hidden in public, women in Mwanza exposed their breasts in the midst of a busy shopping area either to feed a child or to try on a modern Western bra. My Tanzanian friend tells me that he has helped women fit bras over their bare breasts as they shop at his parents' market shop. Women in Mwanza did, however, keep their legs well covered, and would probably have been embarrassed to be seen in the Western running shorts worn by many women in the United States.

Sexual or not, according to Bengson and others, breastfeeding is essential for the physical and emotional well-being of children. And given this essentiality, weaning should happen according to the child's needs—not the mother's. Bengson quotes one mother who claims, "weaning is not about logic or charts or time. Weaning is about readiness. I only know this because I can see that my baby is not ready to wean." This woman makes clear that although two people are intimately involved in a breastfeeding relationship, it is the baby, not the mother, who should make the important breastfeeding decisions. "She hasn't shown me at all that she is ready to wean, and she is the one person whose opinion on this subject counts."[91]

This attitude, that the baby's "opinion" is the only one that should count, resonates both in and outside the United States. It corresponds with a dominant way of thinking about mothering; that to be good mothers, women must mother selflessly, a view held by all sides in the debate over touch. Women are encouraged to breastfeed even when breastfeeding may be detrimental to their health. Indeed, it is unusual for the issue of potential cost to women's health to be raised when it comes to breastfeeding—or mothering generally, for that matter. Possible examples of this ideological pattern can be found in Third World breastfeeding information. HIV-positive mothers in Third World countries—in contrast to more wealthy and industrialized nations—are encouraged to breastfeed their infants even though they might pass the virus on to their child.[92] In places where finding clean water is a problem, these infants have a better chance of survival breastfeeding in spite of the very limited risk of contracting HIV through the breast milk. Until recently, this information focused on potential risks to the child, not the mother. Still, in common wisdom, women have long known breastfeeding to be, at best, tiring, and, at worst, to withdraw nutrients from the women's body for the infant's milk.

Women of wealthy nations are advised to pay close attention to their own nutrition, but there seems to be little concern over the maternal malnourishment of many women in the Third World. For women whose health is already particularly vulnerable, such as women with HIV, breastfeeding may tap women's resources to an extent that is not healthy for the woman.[93] Recently, a Kenyan study found that "breastfeeding can treble the risk of HIV-infected women dying within two years of giving birth." The researchers randomly selected more than 425 HIV-positive women in Nairobi to either nurse their child or use formula. All the women were "followed up monthly in the first year and quarterly in the second year after birth. ". . . [Researcher]" Nduati and her team discovered that two years after giving birth, 18 of the breastfeeding mothers had died compared to three in the formula group."[94]

About older children, of four, five, and more years, Bengson writes, "Many children wean on their own during this time." Yet "natural weaning is a weaning that happens on your child's individual timetable, when her needs for nursing are fulfilled."[95] In a testimony meant to encourage the exhausted or embarrassed mother of an older nursing child, one woman in Bengson's book wrote that she had promised her worried son, who loved nursing, that he could nurse as long as he wanted. She continued, for "all practical purposes, I suppose Eric weaned at about five or six, but it's not an issue that we have discussed since that day in the pond. Our agreement was that the door would always be open if he really needed it. I sometimes wonder if, years from now, a tall, bearded bank president will walk through my door with a special request for a little old lady."[96]

La Leche League versus Mainstream Medicine: Incest or Abandonment?

Today the question for white middle-class mothers is *how long* to breastfeed, *not* whether to breastfeed. One clear issue springs from our cultural anxiety about incest and child sexual abuse. If one breastfeeds for "too long," defined by the dominant culture as more than one year, one risks being seen as weird or disgusting.[97] The implicit concern is that the transgressing mother is having a kind of sexual exchange with her child. Before twelve months of age, the women is being a good mother and giving her child the "best possible food"—as a popular slogan states, "breast is best"—but nursing beyond twelve months is considered strange by many people in the dominant culture. *New York Times* journalist Tamar Lewin writes, "The same mothers who got kudos from their pediatricians and warm smiles from strangers when they nursed their newborn babies face criticism—and sometimes even formal charges of abuse—for continuing to breastfeed when that sweetly cooing infant becomes a walking, talking schoolchild—a practice not all that uncommon in traditional societies."[98]

Ideas about how long is too long to breastfeed continually change. In the late 1990s and early part of the twenty-first century, the AAP literature commonly stated that the optimal age for breastfeeding is from birth to twelve months, even though this contradicted the recommendations of the World Health Organization (WHO). However, in 2005, the AAP revised their policy statement on breastfeeding. Whereas they still do not go as far as the WHO in recommending that women breastfeed their children for a *minimum* of two years, they now leave open the *possibility* of breastfeeding beyond one year. In their new policy statement, the AAP claims, "There is no upper limit to the duration of breastfeeding and no evidence of psychologic or developmental harm from breastfeeding into the third year of life or longer."[99] This is a fairly radical shift for the AAP.

Nonetheless, even though the AAP now leaves open the possibility of breastfeeding beyond the first year, most popular literature reflecting the mainstream medical perspective continues to encourage women to wean by twelve months. Medical wisdom aside, the global average age of weaning is three years. Katherine Dettwyler, an anthropology professor at Texas A&M University who studies breastfeeding, argues, "Around the world, there are lots of cultures where people nurse three, four or five years on average. . . . All cultures have various ideas about how short is too short and how long is too long."[100] Of course, the American Association of Pediatrics—or the World Health Organization, for that matter—is no more purely "objective" today then it was early in the century when mainstream medicine implicitly, if not explicitly, discouraged breastfeeding. Again, this discrepancy points to the cultural, nonobjective influences in their recommendations.

At one end of the breastfeeding continuum are the "bad mothers" who do not breastfeed at all. They are selfish—one of the worst traits in a mother. Perhaps more than any other characteristic, "good mothers" are giving and selfless. They put their children, and possibly their male spouse, before all else. Bad mothers do not breastfeed. They are more concerned with their own freedom—because breastfeeding ties a woman pretty tightly to her child, or at least to a breast pump—than they are with the well-being of their child.

La Leche League advocates child-led weaning. Of course, this is very hard for working women. Indeed, La Leche League has little room for women who have to work, much less for those who "merely" *want* to work rather than need to work. The manual addressed the "problem" of working mothers in print for the first time in a chapter originally called "Are You Thinking of Going Back to Work?"[101] The chapter, in 2004 renamed "Making a Choice," is filled with not-so-gentle pressure to stay home. La Leche League argues,

> There are many important factors to be considered when you make the decision about returning to work after your baby is born. Let's take a look first at the mother–child relationship. This subject has fascinated the scientific community for a long time. A child's early years hold the clues to his future behavior as an adult. Society stands to gain or lose, depending on the soundness of the mother–baby attachment.
>
> La Leche League is strongly committed to the belief that babies and mothers need to be together in the early years. We are convinced that a baby's need for his mother's loving presence is as basic as his need for food. . . . Scientists hold that the child's initial one-to-one relationship with his mother is the foundation for emotional growth. From the security of the baby's ties to his mother he learns to relate to others.[102]

La Leche League's wording changes slightly from edition to edition, but through their most recent 2004 seventh edition, the meaning remains the same.

In the 1981 edition, the League argues, "Can a baby be 'trained' to accept others and not always expect mother to care of him? Won't this make him more 'independent'? No, say the experts. A baby's need for mother is not a habit; it's biology."[103] And in the 2004 edition, La Leche League claims, "The young child who is separated from his mother exhibits all of the classic symptoms of grief. He may cry unconsolably [*sic*] or withdraw into unnatural quietness."[104] In 2004, in case there is any doubt as to the detrimental effects of mothers working away from their young children, La Leche League makes itself clear by calling on a scientific expert for final validation. La Leche League quotes Humberto Nagera, professor of psychiatry at the University of Montana. Nagera claims, "When the child is confronted with the mother's absence his automatic response is an anxiety state that on many occasions reaches overwhelming proportions. Repeated traumas of this type in especially susceptible children will not fail to have serious consequences for their later development. . . . No other animal species will subject their infants to experience that they are not endowed to cope with, except the human animal."[105]

In each edition, La Leche League is very direct: "The greatest difficulty for you and your baby is the separation from each other that working entails. Being away from mother is a serious disruption in a young child's life. Our pleas to any mother who is thinking about taking an outside job is, 'If at all possible, don't.'"[106] Where does this leave women who want to work, or who *must* work outside the home to survive? Feeling guilty. And, *understood* by La Leche League, as well as other conservative groups, *as guilty*—guilty of bad mothering.

If a woman does decide to bottle-feed, she is told never to "prop" the bottle, but to always feed the baby in her arms while holding the bottle herself. This maximizes the physical contact between mother and child. Even so, breastfeeding proponents worry because the baby will not get the skin-to-skin contact of the mouth on the breast. One informant, a fifty-eight-year-old grandmother named Oma, told me about her good friend, another grandmother, whose daughter became seriously and chronically ill during the first two months of her infant daughter's life. She had been breastfeeding exclusively and then, because of her illness, was forced to abruptly and completely stop. She was deeply concerned about her daughter's missing out on breastfeeding's many benefits. Her first concern was the loss of the benefits of touching her daughter might experience. She convinced her mother, Oma's friend, to "breastfeed" her granddaughter using a nursing supplementer. The supplementer allowed the baby to receive her formula while "nursing" at the breast. The nursing supplementer is a narrow tube taped to each breast that carries formula to the nursing baby from a bottle hanging on a cord around the mother's—or in this case, the grandmother's—neck. The bottle's cap has a valve that prevents milk from flowing until the baby sucks. Some women use this nursing supplementer to "relactate" if they have stopped nursing their baby and decide to start up again. Others use it to induce lactation so that they are able to nurse an adopted child. Oma's friend was probably too old to induce lactation. She did not begin to lactate in the many months that she "nursed" her granddaughter, nor did her breasts adjust to being nursed because she reported that the experience was very painful. However, in spite of her pain, feeding the infant in this way allowed the infant to receive all of the benefits of breastfeeding except for simple nutrition; of course, the baby was receiving formula from the supplementer. The benefits for the infant were in being touched; in particular, the intimate touch of the infant's mouth sucking on the breast. In fact, the mouth-to-breast contact is the *only* difference in terms of touch between bottle and breastfeeding if one holds the infant in arms to bottle-feed.

A central slogan of La Leche League International is "We speak for the babies." According to La Leche League, being touched by the child's mother is what babies want and need most, and this is what babies would tell us if only they could. In sharp contrast to La Leche League and at the other end of the adult–child touching continuum is the dominant culture's deep-seated fear of and fascination with incest and child sexual abuse. Extended breastfeeding elicits this fear.

One very popular series of child-rearing books exemplifies the mainstream's anxiety about extended breastfeeding. The *What to Expect* series includes *What to Expect When You're Expecting, What to Expect the First Year,* and *What to Expect: The Toddler Years.* Arlene Eisenberg and her two daughters, Heidi E. Murkoff and Sandee E. Hathaway, wrote the three books together. In addition, for years before she died in late 2000, Arlene Eisenberg led a weekly, hour-long question-and-answer group for new mothers and their infants at a New York City synagogue. I read her three books and my baby son and I attended her group for nearly one year. Eisenberg in the group, and Eisenberg, Murkoff, and Hathaway in their book, are clearly against extended breastfeeding. (For the purposes of this study, I call a breastfeeding relationship that goes beyond one year "extended.") What is extremely interesting about their advice is that, like much expert advice, it is merely expert *opinion*—or expert bias, expert prejudice, or/and expert musing—masked under the rubric of "truth." In other words, the ideological nature of Eisenberg et al.'s position on breast-feeding is starkly apparent. Of course most, if not all, child-rearing experts espouse ideology in the form of advice. However, usually experts mask their ideology in claims of scientific "proof," or "nature" and "instincts." While on the side of science and the AAP, in their discussion of weaning, Eisenberg et al. present their position as simple "truth" without any reference to scientific evidence.

In chapter 1 of their toddler book, not surprisingly, Eisenberg, Murkoff, and Hathaway discuss weaning at about children's thirteenth month. The section is titled "When to Wean from Breastfeeding." Eisenberg et al. think that for the thirteen-month-old child, *weaning* from breastfeeding is the only thing to be discussed. Each component of the book is framed as a response to a parent's questions. This section is in response to three inquiries. First: "I thought babies were supposed to wean themselves from the breast when they were ready. My daughter is past her first birthday and doesn't seem to be showing any sign of wanting to stop." Without acknowledging diverse opinions about this issue, they write, "If you wait until your daughter decides she's ready to graduate to a more grown-up source of liquid nourishment, you may have a very long wait ahead. Though some babies and toddlers cut back on or discontinue breastfeeding on their own, usually near the end of the first year, others never do. So unless you want to see her rush home from school for a snack at the breast, you should consider initiating the weaning process yourself."[107]

Throughout their book, Eisenberg et al. affiliate themselves with mainstream medicine. Unlike La Leche League International, they do not suggest that parents/mothers listen to their "instincts." They call on the AAP, not on nature, for their "proof." Yet despite having no apparent scientific evidence for the above argument, Eisenberg et al. let their opinion simply stand as "fact."

Another weaning inquiry asks: "I'd really like to continue nursing my son for at least the next year or so. Why should I wean him when neither of us is ready yet?" The only affirmative answer Eisenberg et al. give to this question—or for that matter, the whole issue of extended breastfeeding—is, "Your feelings and those of your toddler are important factors to consider in deciding when to wean." Having stated the only positive reason they can muster for extended breastfeeding, Eisenberg et al. give a page of reasons for weaning. They write, "But other factors merit consideration as well. You will have to weigh these against your own reasons for wanting to continue breastfeeding."[108] Naturally, Eisenberg et al.'s first reason to wean is "Expert Opinion." They claim, with no references or citations, "Most pediatricians and pediatric dentists recommend weaning at a year; their reasons are included in the following list."[109] Then they give a list of nine more reasons to wean, none of which are backed up with a reference to scientific research, a scientific expert, or any other citation. For all their reader knows, Eisenberg et al. pulled this information out of their proverbial hats.

Eisenberg et al.'s reasons to wean early include "Your toddler's age. Weaning at a year is ideal. Nutritionally and emotionally the toddler who has nursed for a year has already gotten the optimum benefit from breastfeeding."[110] This reason may be a good argument *for* nursing at least one year but it is hard to understand why it is an argument for stopping. Another equally peculiar reason is "Your toddler's dietary needs. Both the composition of breast milk and the nutritional needs of the growing child alter by the end of the first year. Breast milk can no longer meet a child's nutritional requirements."[111] Again, this may be a reason to supplement breastfeeding with solid foods but it is no argument for weaning. Eisenberg et al. continue, "In fact, some recent studies indicate that children who are nursed beyond this point may not do as well as those who are weaned. Though more research needs to be done in this area, it does seem clear that there are no nutritional benefits to nursing now."[112] Here Eisenberg et al. directly contradict other "experts" on breastfeeding; even the World Health Organization (WHO) encourages women to breastfeed for *at least* two years.

Eisenberg et al.'s position is especially interesting, not because it is correct or incorrect, but because they are so willing to make statements about very important child-rearing issues without any effort to substantiate them, as though their ideological beliefs are simply true. Right or wrong, Eisenberg et al.'s anti-extended-breastfeeding stance fits well with mainstream medicine's position on touch. Touching is to be avoided, particularly touching like breast-feeding beyond the "necessary" year that is potentially sexual.

Anxiety about incest is at the core of the concern. The extended-breast-feeding relationship, in particular, triggers this incest anxiety, the anxiety that the mother is taking something—something sexual—from the infant. Anthropologist Dettwyler said in a *New York Times* article, "I get one or two calls a month about someone accused of harming a child, even as young as 18 months, by nursing. . . . They claim that the mother is breastfeeding for her own sexual pleasure. It's a logical outgrowth of our society's sexualization of the breast."[113] Sociologist Cindy A. Stearns also addresses this concern in her essay on "Breastfeeding and the Good Maternal Body." Stearns did in-depth interviews with fifty-one women who were currently or had recently breastfed their children. She argues, "The major concern of women is that their breast-feeding is perceived as maternal and not sexual behavior."[114]

Indeed, in informal conversation, several people said to me that women who breastfeed beyond a year are not doing it for the baby. They are doing extended breastfeeding because "they get something out of it." One friend, talking about my study, asked, "Are you going to discuss pathological breast-feeding?" I asked her what she meant by "pathological breastfeeding." She explained that some mothers breastfeed beyond two or three years. She claimed that these mothers are not breastfeeding for the child's sake but to fill some need of their own.

Eisenberg et al. allude to this worry that breastfeeding will cross the line from good maternal to sexual behavior. Their ninth reason to wean at one year of age states the following:

> The effect on your spousal relationship. Breastfeeding that continues well into the second year, especially if it's taking place in your bed, can easily come between you and your spouse. Besides making spousal intimacy in-convenient at best, it may, on a subconscious level satisfy both emotional and physical needs for closeness, diminishing your interest in sex. . . . Re-member, your spouse is yours for life. Your toddler will grow up, leave home, and eventually find a partner of his own. Save some nurturing for your partner.[115]

For Eisenberg et al., it seems that nurturing is a zero-sum game; nurturing for one person takes away from the possible nurturing for another person.

Eisenberg, Murkoff, and Hathaway also allude to the sexually fulfilling potential breastfeeding holds. To be sure, many women *do* experience physical pleasure while breastfeeding. Some even have orgasms. In her paper on "Maternal Experience and the Boundaries of Christian Sexual Ethics," Cristina L. H. Traina describes her own experience of orgasm while breastfeeding.

> One day, as I breastfed my eldest daughter, I decided to practice the Kegel exercises postpartum women use to regain tone in their pelvic floor muscles. Quietly nursing, rocking, contracting, releasing, I felt my vaginal muscles take over: an orgasm. I jolted to attention, shocked that I had experienced a sexual climax while embracing an infant. The connection felt dirty and incestuous. "I'll make sure that I never do that again!" I thought. It was some years before I reflected carefully on the close physiological and emotional connections between my maternity, and my experience of my own sexuality and came to wonder not how I could have permitted myself to have this unsought experience but why the likelihood and even "naturalness" of it had never before occurred to me and why it is so rarely mentioned.[116]

In fact, the physiology of breastfeeding seems to be inextricably connected to orgasm for women. The connection involves a hormone called oxytocin. One of two parts making up the pituitary gland, the posterior pituitary, secretes oxytocin. The pituitary gland is connected to and controlled by the hypothalamus, "a portion of the brain that has centers for body temperature, sleep, sexual activity, and emotional states."[117] Oxytocin causes "milk letdown" during lactation. When a baby nurses or, for many women, when they simply *think* of their baby nursing, a signal is sent to the brain to secrete oxytocin, which in turn causes the mammary glands in the breasts to release milk. Oxytocin also causes the uterus to contract. This is one primary reason mainstream medicine has begun to encourage women to nurse their infant immediately after birth.

This, however, is not all that oxytocin seems to do. "Oxytocin, a hormone that stimulates the smooth muscles and sensitizes the nerves, is produced by sexual arousal—the more you're in the mood, the more oxytocin you'll produce. As you begin to make love, oxytocin is released throughout your body, making your nerves more sensitive to pleasure and giving you that turned-on feeling. As the hormone level builds, oxytocin causes the nerves in your genitals to fire spontaneously, bringing on orgasm and giving you the feeling of losing control."[118] In both men and women, oxytocin activates the physical response in sex. Given this biological reality, it makes sense that women often experience breastfeeding as pleasurable, even sexually so. Of course, women exist as bodies in culture, and this physiological connection between breastfeeding and sex is simply unacceptable in the contemporary mainstream.

Must doing something for the baby only "count" when there is nothing in it for the mother? Ultimately, I argue that according to the dictates of the contemporary dominant culture, to be good mothers *means* "getting nothing back." Getting nothing back is a sign of "love," and good mothers act, purely, out of love. This very justification, mothering as a "labor of love," has grounded the modern capitalist economy in the unpaid labor of women as they reproduce the workforce.

In other words, good mothers do breastfeed, and yet they do not breastfeed for "too long." Ultimately, good mothers do whatever they do *for the child.* They are selfless. "Getting something out of it" herself starts a mother on the slippery slope to bad mothering. And, at the bottom of the slope, mainstream culture understands incest to be one of the worst behaviors a bad mother might ever commit.

While discussing the social stigma against breastfeeding, particularly against breastfeeding beyond the first three months or so, one interviewee, Cara, mentioned that she allows her twenty-two-month-old son, Max, "to touch her breasts." She said that people have a lot of problems with that. She implied that the problems people expressed were because of the potential sexuality of such touch. But she believes the child and mother should have unlimited physical contact.

Clearly there is a very fine line between sexual and nonsexual touch. It may in some ways be a useless line to try to find. Given our cultural context, sexual intercourse or other such clearly sexual behaviors between children and adults does seem deeply abusive of the child. But beyond such obvious sexual behavior, it may be hard to know. The theory behind attachment parenting is that if the child is given lots of loving contact and almost never feels abandoned or alone, the child will be well adjusted and confident as she or he enters the larger world. Indeed, Cara claims that her son, Max, is a very friendly, unafraid, well-adjusted child.

Yet there are many downsides to attachment parenting's demand for near constant mother–child touch. One problem is that, because of the anxiety about incest, it makes it impossible for women to work away from home. Another is that women can lose their children for it. Denise Perrigo, the woman discussed in chapter 1 who was charged with child sexual abuse for nursing a child over one year old, is not alone in her experience. Similar charges take place in the United States regularly. In July 2000, Lynn Stuckey, a mother in Champaign, Illinois, temporarily lost custody of her five-year-old son that she was breastfeeding. After an alarming telephone call from the family's babysitter, child-welfare officials took the boy, charging the mother with child sexual abuse—in other words, breastfeeding. The mother had "planned to wean her son whenever he asked to stop breastfeeding, a practice supported by La Leche League. . . . But Judge Ann Einhorn of the Champaign County Circuit put the boy in foster care with the baby-sitter, saying the extended breastfeeding created a situation with 'enormous potential for emotional harm.'"[119] Journalist Sara Corbett writes, "In interviews with counselors, the boy expressed shame and confusion regarding the situation, and the story went on to grab national headlines, which in turn set off rounds of moralistic clucking over its perceived impropriety."[120]

After an abrupt separation that lasted for six months, Judge Einhorn finally returned legal custody to the mother. The mother had to consent to parenting classes and counseling. Considering the potential harm of unexpectedly removing a young child from his mother for half a year, one wonders if such classes might have done the judge some good. Perhaps most curious, the mother was barred from discussing the matter in public. Whereas the judge did back down on her charge that the mother was sexually abusing her son, Judge Einhorn claimed that the case raised issues about "a parent helping a child to be appropriately independent."[121] In fact, extended-breastfeeding proponents claim healthy independence is one of the primary outcomes of long-term breastfeeding.

A few years ago, two years after the state took her child for six months, and in spite of having been barred from discussing the matter publicly, Stuckey really went public. She appeared with her now-eight-year-old son breastfeeding on national television. Dave McKinney of the *Chicago Sun-Times* writes, "The footage on ABC-TV's "Good Morning America" drew an incredulous reaction from the Champaign County prosecutor who wanted Lynn Stuckey's son placed in foster care. . . . While reading a Harry Potter book, a fully clothed Stuckey was shown briefly nursing her son—something she said occurs once every 10 days to two weeks, even though Stuckey said she is unsure whether she is still producing milk." Stuckey claimed that her son "has not been teased at school or in their Champaign neighborhood." And she denied the "possibility that she is causing him emotional harm by still nursing him."[122]

Stuckey picks up the mainstream's belief about good mothers—they do whatever they do for the child—and uses this thinking to argue for an unusual behavior in contemporary mainstream culture. In the *Chicago Sun-Times*,

Stuckey is quoted, "'I never forced my child to nurse. I did not nurse because I was gaining any sort of sexual pleasure out of this. The state attorney's office and the Department of Children and Family Services are very incorrect and are greatly misstating my motives.'" Stuckey said that her son could continue breastfeeding until "he decides to finish weaning himself." When questioned whether there is an age when it might be inappropriate for breastfeeding, Stuckey said, "Maybe . . . into their teens."[123]

Indeed, breastfeeding advocate and La Leche League International member Elizabeth Baldwin claimed that "it is not unheard of for some mothers to nurse children in private until they are as old as 10." Still, Baldwin "questioned the wisdom of Stuckey allowing her son and herself to be filmed for a national audience." Baldwin said, "I don't believe this is helping the breastfeeding community. I believe it will hurt, and it will hurt herself [sic]. And the only reason I say that is the public's perception."[124] As for Stuckey, she argued that the "greatest harm to befall her son was when Illinois child welfare officials took him from her for six months in 2000 amid allegations she was breastfeeding him against his will and sleeping with him in the nude."[125]

The act of one human being sucking on another's breast contains multiple and significant meanings. Like other forms of adult–child touch, beliefs about breastfeeding have been and continue to exist within contested terrain in the mainstream United States. Yet as compared to other kinds of touching, breastfeeding entails a unique form of touch; breastfeeding involves a sexualized part of the body, and—at least most people believe—it only involves female bodies doing the feeding. Nonetheless, other touching practices are also heavily debated. Stuckey lost her child for six months not only because of her breastfeeding practice but also for her sleeping arrangements. Thus, to proceed from this chapter's exploration of breastfeeding, in the next chapter I explore an adult–child touching practice no less contested, albeit more inclusive of all genders: sleeping alone versus sleeping together.

FOUR

Babies in Bed: To Sleep or Not to Sleep (with Your Baby)

In 1999, a government study caused an uproar among scientific, parenting, and child-rearing experts.[1] The study, by the Federal Consumer Product Safety Commission, argued that parents should never sleep in the same bed with their infants or toddlers, on the basis that parents might, in their sleep, roll on top of their babies, or the babies might suffocate in the parents' blankets. Citing the study's findings that 515 children under the age of two—an average of sixty-four per year—had died as a result of sleeping in adult beds, commission chair Ann Brown argued that "there was no safe way for parents and infants to sleep together."[2] There was dissent. Penelope Leach, a pro-sleep-sharing child-rearing expert and popular writer, angrily cited three other studies, from the United States, New Zealand, and Great Britain, that found sleeping in parents' beds posed no direct risk to babies. "I'm not knocking experts, but I do think we should avoid offering advice until we're absolutely sure that it accounts for every variable," she wrote.[3]

Certainly, how to put—or *get,* as the case may be—children to sleep is a big issue for parents. A 1995 study by Sara Harkness, Charles Super, and Constance Keefer found that "more parents seek advice on how to get their children to sleep than on any other health or behavioral subject."[4] Why does this issue touch such a nerve?

The issue of parents and children sleeping (together or apart) takes place against a backdrop of long-standing ideological and practical debates that are not only about child-rearing and bedtime practices but also about adult–child touching. The disputes are dramatized in the standoff between two experts, William Sears and Richard Ferber, who appear again and again in popular media and forums as the primary contenders in the sleep debates.[5] Sears takes a naturalist and relationship-oriented approach, and Ferber takes a more traditional behaviorist and masculinist-oriented approach. In analyzing the arguments about sleep that have escalated since 1985, the year that both published best-selling self-help books, I focus on their two extremely popular books, Ferber's *Solve Your Child's Sleep Problems* (1985) and Sears's *Nighttime Parenting: How to Get Your Baby and Child to Sleep* (1985), as well as the schools of thought that have evolved around their work.

I examine the split between Sears's relationship orientation, which emphasizes attachment and dependency, and Ferber's masculinist orientation, which focuses on children separating from their parents and siblings and learning to be independent. I show that these two experts place themselves in opposite corners of a matrix of relationship versus individuation and freedom versus restriction in thinking about women's roles in the home and society. Both thinkers have feminist elements, yet ultimately, both are highly problematic. Each fits into and reinforces a larger mainstream heteronormative culture that shapes the discursive boundaries of thinking about touching children in terms of normative ideas regarding gender, sexuality, class, and race.

Ferber and the behaviorists are proponents of masculinist middle-class values. They are against parents sleeping with children and are wary of bodily contact. They believe in the power of science and the rational—isolated—individual. Their goal for the child is individuation, through in part a personal connection to property or things. They value work and support women's work outside the home; there is a pro-liberal-feminist element to the behaviorists because their child-rearing methods offer significantly more freedom for women—more choice—to leave children and work for a wage outside the home.[6] Ultimately, however, Ferber and other masculinists err in defining individuality as abstracted from relationships. They excessively individuate human beings and ignore their relationship-bound context, and they mistakenly characterize individuals as agents of control and power defined by relationships to things rather than people.

Sears and the naturalists, including La Leche League International, take the opposite view. They are strongly for adult–child physical contact, sharing sleep, and the "family bed," as they call it, and have a relationship-oriented understanding of healthy child development. They are explicitly anti-property and anti–consumer culture, as they state in their popular slogan, "People before things." In these orientations, the naturalists offer a profound challenge to mainstream culture. These aspects of Sears's thinking support a left feminist (often an element of socialist feminism) opposition to liberal individualism (and liberal feminism), an individualism that, even if unintentionally, tends to subordinate relationships to personal achievement and striving.[7] Yet embedded in these countercultural beliefs, they are simultaneously deeply anti-feminist. They are proponents of "traditional" gender roles and the sentimental middle-class nuclear family. The naturalists unambiguously believe women (whom they always assume to be heterosexual and married) should stay home with children rather than work for a wage, thus deeply limiting women's choices. And they avoid the political economics of their position, never addressing the contemporary reality that most women cannot afford to stay home full time and forgo wage work. Nor do they validate that many women *want* to work outside the home.

The sleep experts, like other mainstream child-rearing experts, split into the same two recurring and sharply defined positions: if parents support one, they lose what might be useful about the other. These experts make it hard to shape one's own parenting philosophy out of a mix of the different positions. In this, they limit parents' choices. At the same time, both sides reinforce different components of what I call contemporary middle-class ideals. And *neither* recognizes the temporally and culturally bound nature of their claims.

In many parts of the world today (and in most of Europe and the United States until early in the twentieth century), infants and children sleep with their parents.[8] Sharing sleep is expected; it is a norm. Nevertheless, infants' sleeping apart from parents became the fashion among the Anglo-American middle class early in the twentieth century. People believed that sleeping alone, like the avoidance of touch in general, kept infants and older children free from adult germs. However, germs were not the only issue; touch itself was a problem.

Interestingly, there has been a recent resurgence of bed sharing in the United States. The National Institute of Health (NIH) notes that "bed sharing, although common in many cultures, is controversial in this country." Nonetheless, "bed sharing—the practice of letting babies sleep in an adult bed with a parent or caregiver—is increasing."[9] The "National Infant Sleep Position Study (NISP) . . . shows that the proportion of infants usually sharing an adult bed at night increased from 5.5 percent to 12.8 percent between 1993 and 2000. Nearly 50 percent of infants in the study spent at least some time in the past two weeks sleeping in an adult bed at night."[10] And in sharp contrast to contemporary breastfeeding practices, low-income families and families of color are much more likely to share sleep than higher-income families and white families. The NISP study found that "African American infants were four times more likely to bed share as white infants, and Asian/other infants were almost three times more likely to bed share than white infants."[11] Another study funded by the National Institute of Child Health and Human Development (NICHD) and NIH found that "almost 50 percent of mothers in a predominantly low-income, inner city population reported their infant usually shared a bed with a parent or other adult during the infant's first year of life."[12] Both of the above studies "suggest that bed sharing appears to be widespread and strongly influenced by cultural factors."[13]

Albeit increasingly common, sharing sleep continues to raise concerns over what constitutes appropriate touch. In particular, anxieties about incest and child sexual abuse still arise again and again in today's mainstream child-rearing advice about sleep. Depending on one's perspective, Ferber's method is understood to be more "boundaried," leaving the whole family better rested and, thus, the parents better able to parent. For others, Ferber's method entails neglect of the child and, therefore, is tantamount to child abuse. Again, depending on one's beliefs, Sears's method is more loving and leads to a deeper connection with one's child, leaving the whole family better rested and, thus, the parents better able to parent. Or for those on the other, Ferber, side of the debate, Sears's method borders on the incestuous and, therefore, is tantamount to child abuse.

Ferber indirectly cites incest as a reason not to sleep with one's children. Sears and the attachment-parenting experts also address this concern, albeit in an offhand way. Clearly, they understand that this fear about incest is a reason many parents do not sleep with their children. As we have seen in early twentieth-century child-rearing literature and in expert advice on breastfeeding, touching or not touching, bodies touching bodies, connected, or bodies living separately is an issue middle-class American parents worry over a lot. The sleep debate is one place these worries get played out.

The Contemporary Sleep Debate: Richard Ferber

> *The New Age recipe for bringing up baby—carry it about constantly and breastfeed it till it can open beercans with its teeth and have it sleep between you and hubby until it reaches voting age—seems to me to be disastrous for a romantic and happy marriage.*
>
> *The Born Again Cows who advise such a regime may well be responsible for a generation of split families ten years from now. For nothing turns a man off faster than making him feel he is married to a womb rather than a woman.*
>
> —Columnist Julie Burchill, "Smother Love"

Before sharing sleep became an official middle-class child-rearing method, my mother tipped her bed cap to the "Born Again Cow" philosophy, although she did not fully join their league. To be sure, when I was a child, there was nothing I wanted more than to stay with my mother at night in her bed. And when she was between lovers, sometimes she would let me. Richard Ferber, had he known my mother, would have encouraged her to send me back to my room. For Ferber, my desperate desire to stay with my mother at night was a problem, a problem to be confronted, a problem to get through. For Ferber, and the behaviorists generally, given the opportunity, neediness such as mine would only expand. Allowing me to stay with my mother at night only reinforced my need. For Ferber, the thing to do is to meet need head-on by denying its fulfillment.

Even though babies and children often want to sleep with their parents, Ferber argues that parents should not permit it. Ferber uses scientific evidence about sleep to argue for his masculinist child-rearing philosophy that children should not be allowed to sleep in their parents' bed. He claims to offer a way to better health and better parenting—and he has the scientific clout to back up his claims. As his own book notes in the back under the heading "About the Author," "Dr. Richard Ferber is widely recognized as the nation's leading authority in the field of children's sleep problems."[14] At the time his book came out, Ferber was the director of the Sleep Lab and the Center for Pediatric Sleep Disorders at Children's Hospital in Boston (which is Harvard University's pediatric teaching hospital).

Ferber relies on a funny mix of research science and his own opinion, masquerading as science, to back up his claims. His thinking flees from touch, confusing physical contact with incest. It is the child of the patriarchal Watson who worried about the dangers mother love presents to children and who believed working and poor people should not have children. Ferber, like Watson, hides his ideology behind science, which in our culture equals Truth. Ferber assumes that science and scientific experts are authorities to be trusted without question or explanation. Unlike his naturalist opponents, Ferber does not refer to "instincts" or the "natural." Nor does he refer to God or the supernatural, history, "folk" knowledge, or the experiences of other cultures. In fact, he does not mention that there might be other authorities, as though it is obvious that science is the place to turn for answers to parenting questions.

Ferber gives three primary reasons babies and children should not sleep with their parents. Interestingly, given his reliance on science to describe infant sleep and to explain his method, he makes no use of science to back up the "whys" of his argument. In other words, none of Ferber's three reasons are grounded in scientific research. Ferber describes in detail such phenomena as rapid eye movement or REM sleep and non-REM sleep, and the percentage of time babies versus adults spend in REM and non-REM sleep each night. Yet after all his scientific information on sleep, if readers wonder *why* babies and children should never sleep with their parents, they have to trust Ferber's little-discussed opinion on the matter. First, Ferber claims both the child and the parents will not sleep as well and that this is unhealthy. He writes, "Although taking your child into bed with you for a night or two may be reasonable if he is ill or very upset about something, for the most part this is not a good idea." Ferber continues, "We know for a fact that people sleep better alone in bed."[15] This is a "fact" that seems to have eluded many people, including the sharing-sleep proponents and much of the world. That so many people sleep better with someone else does not seem to Ferber to need explaining. He does not explain why untold numbers of people love to sleep with others nearby in bed or where he came up with this "fact." He gives no scientific or other reason he believes this to be true, no reference or footnote connecting this claim to research, and no indication as to whom the "we" is that he refers.

Second, Ferber argues that a child who sleeps with her or his parents will not become independent and individuated. Here again he offers neither hard scientific "proof" nor psychoanalytic or any other theory to back up his thinking on individuation. He merely makes the unsubstantiated claim, "But there are even better reasons for your child to sleep in his own bed. Sleeping alone is an important part of his learning to be able to separate from you without anxiety and to see himself as an independent individual. This process is important to his early psychological development."[16] Ferber directs much of his discussion to the need for parents to have firm boundaries with their children, including establishing individual space, rooms, and, of course, beds; for him, independence rather than interdependence is a primary goal of healthy child development.

Finally, Ferber believes that the child will be overwhelmed by his or her feelings and confused by the situation. Here Ferber seems to be referring, albeit in an unclear manner, to his concern about the possibility of incest. Ferber implies that children sleeping with their parents will experience the situation in a *sexually* stimulating way, and that they will experience confusion related to their own and their parents' sexuality. Ferber writes, "In addition, sleeping in your bed can make your child feel confused and anxious rather than relaxed and reassured. . . . Even a young toddler may find this repeated experience overly stimulating." Ferber concludes, "These feelings may be heightened if only one parent is in the bed."[17] Ferber implies a white middle-class fear of touching and anxiety about the multiple meanings of physical contact, including the suggestion of incest. This ties into mainstream middle-class thinking about close physical contact based on a fear that bodies in close proximity will inevitably run out of control into bad—i.e., sexual—behavior. Bodies must be kept apart from one another so that the rational mind can stay in control.[18]

Interestingly, Ferber is much less explicitly gendered than many child-rearing experts in that he directs his work to both fathers and mothers. Although he does assume heterosexuality, he does not take for granted that fathers will go off to work in the public sphere while mothers stay in the private world of the home, revolving their lives around their husbands and children. Indeed, Ferber's advice has a pro-feminist element in that it offers significantly more freedom for women to leave children and work for a wage. Not only does he not explicitly assume that women stay home; his advice also entails training children to sleep through the night (even if the naturalists would argue that they are not "ready" to do so), and thus frees women—who in our society do most of the parenting[19]—to sleep through the night as well. Finally, he uses gender-neutral language when he talks about or speaks to parents.

In spite of this, and in sharp contrast to the sharing-sleep proponents, Ferber's thinking entails a deeply masculinist way of understanding human development and adult–child touch. Social theorist Roslyn Wallach Bologh argues that a masculine worldview banishes care and nurturance to the private sphere. Through the masculine ideal, one sees the world as a place where "autonomous actors all [strive] to prove their independence and omnipotence. . . . Independent, powerful actors all [contend] to impose their will on the world, a place made up of struggles for power and dominance."[20] Masculine values uphold independence as a central component of healthy human development.[21]

Ferber believes children need to learn to be alone. In Ferber's work, a central focus of child development is the process of individuation. Ferber directs much of his discussion to the need for parents to have firm boundaries with their children. For Ferber, independence rather than interdependence is a primary goal of healthy child development.

Tied to his masculinist understanding of development, Ferber completely ignores the question of touch. Neither touch nor any synonyms for touch are listed in his index, nor is touching or the need for physical contact discussed anywhere in his text. The closest Ferber comes to discussing touch is in his several fairly brief discussions of "separation anxiety." The first time Ferber addresses separation anxiety, he acknowledges it as a reason some children have trouble sleeping alone. He recognizes separation anxiety as a problem.

Yet, for Ferber, children must go through this "stage"—separation anxiety—to individuate. "Bedtime means separation, which is difficult for children, especially very young ones. Simply sending a toddler or young child off to bed alone is not fair and may be scary for him." Ferber proposes that parents spend "ten to thirty minutes to do something special with [their] child before bed." Yet he argues that parents must let their child know that the "special time together will not extend beyond the time [they] have agreed upon." He warns parents, "don't go beyond those limits. . . . Don't give in for an extra story. Your child will learn the rules only if you enforce them."[22] He believes that rather than "giving in" to your child's anxiety and spending more time, or even sleeping with the child, parents should encourage their child's attachment to a "transitional object." Ferber thinks the child needs to get over separation anxiety. He proposes alleviating the bedtime anxiety minimally by spending time with the child, without "giving in" to the child's anxiety by holding the actual bedtime separation in place. This thinking is inextricably connected to Ferber's belief in the need to "individuate."

Ferber believes that separation anxiety should be gotten over by teaching a child to be independent. His masculinist approach includes the use of "transitional objects" to help a child reach the goal of independence and to get one's child to sleep alone. Indeed, objects—things—are what children must learn to depend on rather than relationships and physical contact with other human beings. Ferber writes, "Better than lying with your toddler or young child until he falls asleep at night is for him to fall asleep with a 'transitional object'—a stuffed animal, a doll, a toy, a special blanket. The toy will often help him accept the nighttime separation from you and can be a source of reassurance and comfort when he is alone. It will give him a feeling of having a little control over his world because he may have the toy or blanket with him whenever he wants, which he cannot expect from you." Things, unlike people, can be relied upon. "His toy will not get up and leave after he falls asleep and it will still be there whenever he wakes."[23] Ferber argues against allowing "yourself to be used in the manner of such an object—to lie with him, to nurse or rock him, to be held, cuddled, or caressed by him, or let him twirl your hair whenever he tries to fall asleep." For if you do, Ferber warns that your child "will never take on a transitional object, because he won't need to."[24] Objects help children reach the goal of independence from their parents.

Ferber's focus on the process of individuation is not merely masculinist; it springs from a larger mainstream middle-class way of understanding development and touch. Ferber, mirroring the prevalent middle-class value system, believes that individual people need their own separate physical space, their own beds, their own rooms. "Healthy" individuals must learn to spend time alone, boundaried and separate from one another.

Ferber is probably the most popular child-rearing expert on this issue, but he is not alone in his mandate to sleep separately. Most mainstream medical and other behaviorist-leaning child-rearing experts argue against sharing sleep. As one might expect in our masculinist, mainstream culture, most of the other experts cite individuating as a primary reasons for sleeping separately. *The Self-Calmed Baby* (1989), a child-rearing book by pediatrician William A. H. Sammons, claims on its back cover, "It's surprisingly simple to make your infant an equal partner in creating a contented family." Of primary concern in his book, Sammons cautions parents not to be manipulated by their babies. Even for two-month-old infants, crying "becomes an important manipulator of attention," and manipulating babies can be quickly "spoiled."[25] Sammons warns parents, "Spoiling can occur at any age, even with a newborn."[26] Instead of being manipulated, "help" the baby learn to "self-calm." Sammons argues that all babies, even newborns, can self-calm. "Self-calming is a skill system, learned through practice. . . . As the infant learns to self-calm, he relies typically on sucking, vision, and body motion or position as his favored mode."[27] Although many health care providers consider infant body rocking—rocking her or his body back and forth while on all fours or while seated—to be an indication of psychological distress, Sammons claims it is sign of a healthy, individuated baby, a baby who can self-calm. One imagines Sammons's babies with small boots pulling themselves upward by their tiny bootstraps.

In another child-rearing book, *Healthy Sleep Habits, Happy Child* (1987), author Marc Weissbluth claims that babies must sleep a certain set number of hours—how many depending on their age—to be healthy and happy and to develop properly. For example, according to Weissbluth, three-year-old children need 1.9 hours of daytime sleep and 10.6 hours of nighttime sleep. Weissbluth's method of teaching a child to sleep this set period of hours is straightforward and clearly set against touch. Whether your child is four months old or four years, you must put him or her in the crib or bed, shut the door to the room—like other behaviorist child-rearing experts, Weissbluth assumes that the child has her or his own room—and not return until morning. Weissbluth writes, "Once down, down is down, no matter how long she cries. Please do not return, until your baby falls asleep."[28] Like Sammons, Weissbluth argues that babies and children will develop self-calming behaviors. These range from sucking on a hand to extensive self-rocking. Weissbluth's own son was a head-banger. He writes, "My third son banged his head against the crib every night when we moved into a new house. . . . My solution was to use clothesline rope and sofa cushions to pad both ends and both sides completely." Weissbluth followed his own expert advice, and responded by leaving the child to work things through on his own. Happily, Weissbluth claims success: "Now, when he banged away, there was no racket, no pain, and no parental attention."[29]

Touch is, at best, a nonissue; at worst, it is something hazardous for the masculinist thinkers. Whereas other child-rearing experts like William Sears advocate parents, particularly mothers, touching their children as much as is possible, Ferber does not mention touch. However, in Ferber's schema, touch is not merely unimportant: touch is dangerous.

William Sears

In sharp contrast to Ferber, for Sears, touch is of central importance, and sharing sleep is not only an acceptable practice, it is also a vital component of good parenting. Sears, popular parenting organizations such as La Leche League International, and other "naturalist" child-rearing experts such as Katie Allison Granju advocate strongly for parents sharing sleep with their babies and children.

The pro-sharing-sleep advocates tend to come from the larger parenting movement called attachment parenting that emerged in the middle part of the twentieth century. Currently, Sears is a very important figure in this movement, including becoming in the 1980s the expert of the day for La Leche League International, the largest attachment-parenting organization to date. As discussed in chapter 3, scientific experts such as Sears play a significant leadership role in La Leche League. One might expect that an organization like La Leche League, predominantly run by and for women, would make a particular effort to find female leadership. However, Sears and La Leche League essentialize women and women's roles in society. In other words, they believe there is something inherent in women that differentiates them and their sociobiological roles from men. Linked to their thinking about sex and gender roles, heterosexuality is assumed. Further, for these naturalist thinkers, women are "naturally" meant to be in the domestic realm and care for their children, man, and home. They understand women as closely connected to "nature." Given this, women should trust their "instincts." In contrast, men are the rational authorities one turns to for scientific information; Sears is the current scientific backup for La Leche League.[30] And although La Leche League International founded "attachment parenting" in the 1950s, it was Sears who gave it its name decades later.

Sears named the La Leche League style of parenting "attachment parent-ing" with an obvious reference to Bowlby's "attachment theory."[31] Attach-ment parenting, according to Sears, helps parents "to know their child," and this helps parents "to help their child feel right." Sears writes, "A child who feels right acts right and is a joy to parent. I want you as parents to enjoy your child."[32] Knowing one's child, helping the child "feel right," and parents en-joying their children are all rather ambiguous goals. People probably have vastly different ways of defining what it means to know a person or to feel right. In fact, Sears never makes clear what he means by these goals. One can imagine many ways to communicate with, and to be with, a child. One might emphasize discussion and reading out loud to or with a child. One might focus on activities done together with a child, such as art projects or sports. Yet for Sears, the crucial element of a healthy parent–child relationship is touch. Over and over in his book Sears discusses the importance of touching, or what he also calls "skin-to-skin contact."

Sears describes the attachment-parenting philosophy as involving "rules" such as "making a commitment to your marriage and your child" and, more concretely, breastfeeding with child-led weaning, responding promptly to your baby's cries, carrying or "wearing" your baby continuously, and, finally, shar-ing sleep with your baby.[33] Sears focuses on the importance of babies touching their *mothers,* not only through sharing sleep, but also through breastfeeding and being carried on their mothers' bodies—their mothers "wearing them"—throughout the day. It is not surprising, given the essentializing of women in attachment-parenting philosophy, that Sears uses gender-exclusive language throughout his book. The child is always referred to as male or "he," and the parent, the mother, is always "she." For Sears, it seems children are always boys and parents are always women.[34]

Before the baby comes, Sears offers several "attachment tips," simultaneously making various assumptions that do not fully reflect contemporary social realities. "Promise your faithful attention to two relationships: to yourselves as a married couple and to your child as his parents. One of the greatest gifts you can give your new baby is a home built on the foundation of a stable and fulfilled marriage."[35] Once again, profoundly conservative social assumptions accompany a challenge to middle-class values regarding relationships and bodies: Sears never considers the possibility that the parent he addresses has no spouse, much less that that parent has a same-sex partner. And although his advice about how to make the commitment is clear and grounded in a relationship-oriented worldview that involves human connection through *touching,* ultimately Sears exhibits his association of women with (mother) bodies, and babies and men with (male) humanness:

> To strengthen these commitments during pregnancy, I advise couples to follow a custom we have enjoyed in our own family. I suggest that each night before going to bed you as a couple lay your hands on the pregnant uterus. Talk about your commitment to each other as a married couple and your commitment to this tiny life inside. This beautiful nighttime ritual gets to be a habit that is likely to continue after your baby arrives. After the birth of our baby, I had become so accustomed to laying my hands on my unborn baby that I couldn't get to sleep at night unless I would go over and lay my hand on the head of our little newborn and reaffirm my commitment to fathering her. I was hooked! I was already attached before our infant was born.[36]

Sears refers to the "unborn baby" or the "pregnant uterus" as though they exist separate from the woman's body. One imagines putting one's hands directly on the uterus with no woman-body in the way. His language implies that the fetus floating in its home, the uterus, has a life of its own disconnected from her.

Once the baby comes, Sears offers even more "attachment tips." He emphasizes breastfeeding with child-led weaning, and he suggests that parents be open to various sleeping arrangements. Sears also argues that parents should respond promptly to their baby's crying. Further, parents "should travel as a father-mother-baby unit." Traveling as a unit entails the mother carrying the baby next to her body so that the baby has constant physical contact with her mother. Sears writes,

> While traveling on a speaking tour of Australia I began to appreciate the "marsupial mothering" style of kangaroos, whose babies are nearly always in touch with the mother because they live in a pouch on the mother's abdomen. I advise couples not to succumb to the usual outside pressure to "get away from your baby," but instead to become accustomed to "wearing" the baby in an infant sling or baby carrier. As you get used to being a unit you will feel right when you are together and not right when you're apart. Functioning together by day makes it easier to function together by night.[37]

In response to this, one informant said, "What planet is he from? Can't I feel good *both* with my baby, *and* away from her?" What's more, nowhere does Sears address the exhausting nature of "wearing" one's baby around the clock.

Nor does he address the physical wear and tear on one's back and body from carrying a heavy weight in a front pack, a sling, or other baby carrier. Clearly, Sears concerns himself with what he deems good for the baby, and not necessarily with what might be good for the mother.

Finally, Sears argues that parents should be wary of what he calls "detachment parenting," to which he contrasts his style of parenting—attachment parenting. Detachment parenting is a "restrained style . . . that warns parents against taking cues from their child. The advocates of detachment parenting preach: 'Let the baby cry it out. He has to learn to sleep through the night.' 'Don't be so quick to pick your baby up. You're spoiling her.' . . . 'Don't let your baby in your bed. You're creating a terrible habit.'" Sears argues that attachment parenting builds family harmony, while "detachment parenting leads to disharmony."[38] Sears takes an indiscreet stab at Richard Ferber. Referring to Ferber's behaviorist sleep program for children, Sears writes, "Besides being full of negatives, this style of parenting also features quick and easy recipes for difficult problems." Sears warns parents, "Let me caution you. Difficult problems in child rearing do not have easy answers. . . . In my experience, parents who practice detachment parenting are at risk of losing their intuition."[39] While Sears claims that difficult problems in raising one's children "do not have easy answers," one might question Sears's own easy answer: intuition. In a certain sense, "intuition" is the easiest answer of all.

Sears's central reason for adults sharing sleep with their children is that it allows for extensive touching, but there are other rationales as well. For example, he claims that the baby *and* the parents will all sleep better. Sears refers to the desperation of "millions of tired parents who struggle nightly with the dilemma of wanting to be a good nighttime parent yet longing for a full night's sleep."[40] He claims that he wrote his book to address this dilemma and to help everyone in the family to sleep better. "One of the goals of this book is to help parents and children achieve **sleep harmony**. . . . Difficult sleepers can exhaust the whole family, put a strain on their parents' marriage, and contribute to parent burn-out."[41] In other words, even for parents' most "selfish" reason to cure their child's sleep problems—they want more sleep—sharing sleep is the answer. Sears use of the word "harmony" evokes his ideological focus on relationships and intersubjectivity. Instead of the clash of individuals, the assumption behind Ferber's doctrine of separation, Sears focuses on balance and the equilibrium of individual needs.

After this brief diversion into parental selfishness, Sears returns to his mother-focused child-rearing philosophy. According to Sears, another reason to share sleep with one's child is that being kept physically apart from his mother at night leaves the child isolated, which is psychologically damaging to the child's development. Sears writes, "Children who sleep alone . . . often grow up regarding sleep as a fearful time, a time of separation."[42]

In a later section titled "Sharing Sleep Has Long-Term Effects," Sears makes the implicit argument that mothers who sleep with their children raise healthier, happier children *and* they are better mothers. He writes,

> There are many variables which contribute to children's growth and development. However, *psychologists agree that the quantity and quality of mothering does affect the emotional and intellectual development of the child.* . . . One of these effects [of sharing sleep] is on the quality of intimacy. Many psychologists and marriage counsellors report that one of the common problems of contemporary teenagers and adults is that they have difficulty forming genuinely close and intimate relationships with another person. . . . A childhood need for intimacy that is not filled never completely goes away but reappears in later years. Psychologists report that many adult fears and sleep problems can be traced back to uncorrected sleep disturbances during childhood.[43]

For Sears, good mothering is synonymous with "intuitive" or "natural" mothering. Sears argues that it is not only harmful psychologically for the child to sleep alone, but goes against the mother's "natural instincts" as well. Sears believes that mothers' "instincts" compel them to sleep with their children. To sleep apart from her child denies this maternal instinct or intuition and leaves the mother worried and restless, affecting not only her own sleep but also her very capacity to mother. He writes, "This may come as a surprise, but not only does baby sleep better in the family bed, most parents do also. Certainly mother usually does. Baby is not the only one who is separation sensitive at night. A new mother, too, experiences anxiety when her baby is not nearby. She lies awake and wonders, 'Is my baby all right?' The farther away she is from her baby the deeper is the anxiety."[44] Eventually, claims Sears, the mother's very capacity to mother will be diminished by her not responding to such basic needs as to sleep with her child. She will begin to shut down, or numb out, to mothering in general. He argues that a vicious cycle develops where nonnatural mothering leads to "bad mothering."

> If a mother consistently goes against what she feels, she begins to desensitize herself. . . . The less intuitively a mother responds, the less confidence she has in the appropriateness of her responses. The less confidence she

has, the less likely that her responses are appropriate, and the less she enjoys mothering. A mother who restrains from responding to her baby gradually and unknowingly becomes insensitive. This is a vicious cycle of detachment which I urge new mothers not to let themselves get into. Once you allow outside advice to overtake your own intuitive mothering you and your child are at risk of drifting apart. . . . Parenting with restrained responses hinders the development of your motherly intuition.[45]

For Sears, people will never have conflicting intuition. Intuition, mother's intuition, will always, only, say one thing: the Truth. If she is confused, then she is out of touch with her intuition. At this point, her best bet is to simply do what Sears says to do.

Yet another reason for sharing sleep is that sleeping with one's child allows for continuous unrestricted breastfeeding. Here is another tenet of Sears's attachment-parenting philosophy, an element that excludes working women of all classes. Children should breastfeed on demand, without restriction, and until they are ready to wean. Calling upon biology, Sears names this unrestricted breastfeeding "natural," and argues that both unrestricted breastfeeding and sharing sleep allow for increased touching. Sears claims both also stimulate the release of the hormone prolactin, heighten physical and emotional intimacy between mother and child, and aid in developing feelings of "well-being," security, and "rightness" on the part of the child. And finally, any breastfeeding, but particularly unrestricted breastfeeding, along with sharing sleep lowers the risk of Sudden Infant Death Syndrome (SIDS).

Sears is willing to use something as awful as the potential death of one's child by SIDS to argue for his sleep-sharing philosophy. Sears claims that shared sleep—by itself, aside from the breastfeeding benefit involved—lowers the risk of SIDS. It is, he argues, dangerous to sleep apart from one's child. He uses the risk of SIDS to push for sharing sleep even though the evidence here is very shaky. Interestingly, both pro- and anti-sleep-sharing experts use the potential for child death in making their arguments. As discussed earlier, a poignant example of the counterargument came out in a study by the Federal Consumer Product Safety Commission that concluded that parents "should never sleep in the same bed with infants or toddlers under the age of 2 . . . because sleeping together poses a significant risk of accidental smothering or strangling."[46] Chair of the commission Ann Brown emphasized the scientific merit of the study. She wrote in a *New York Post* letter to the editor that "the American Medical Association found it to be of such value that it published it in the *Archives of Pediatric and Adolescent Medicine.*" She continued by quoting the *Archives of Pediatric and Adolescent Medicine* editor, Catherine DeAngelis, who wrote, "The results of this study should be shared with all parents of all infants and toddlers younger than 2 years. I was surprised by the extent of the problem; can you just imagine the state of a parent who overlays a child, resulting in his or her death?"[47] Sears's argument that sharing sleep with one's child may prevent the child's death is as weak as the Federal Consumer Product Safety Commission's evidence that it may cause such a death. Critics of the report claim that, for a variety of reasons, the study's methods were faulty. Dr. Abraham B. Bergman, a professor of pediatrics at the University of Washington, argued that primary among these reasons is that "because no one knows exactly how many babies sleep with their parents in adult beds, the study gives no indication of relative risk."[48]

One of my interviewees, Karen, claimed that the smothering worry is a myth and that "it has never happened." Most of her "facts" seem to come from La Leche League, so as with most evidence in the sleep debate, it is hard to know if it is reliable (or for that matter, what constitutes "reliable"). Karen asserted that in feudal times women used to smother their infants as a form of birth control. They used the excuse of an "accidental" smothering as a way to cover up killing the child. She said that the Catholic Church began to advocate sleeping separately from one's children—which was unusual—to stop people from using "accidental" smothering as an excuse for child murder. Karen argued that the myth of the possibility of smothering your child if you sleep with it came from these times. She said that it is impossible to accidentally smother a baby and claimed that we have "instincts" that stop us from doing it.

About SIDS, Sears also uses science—rather than merely instincts—to further his child-rearing philosophy of sharing sleep. In sharp contrast to the equally "scientific" Federal Consumer Product Safety Commission's report, Sears argues, "In those infants at risk for SIDS, natural mothering (unrestricted breastfeeding and sharing sleep with baby) will lower the risk of SIDS."[49] He claims that SIDS has been classified as a sleep disorder where the infant "may be unable to arouse from sleep in response to a breathing problem."[50] Babies have immature automatic breathing mechanisms, so it is normal for new infants to have episodes, called apnea, where they stop breathing for as long as ten to fifteen seconds. At times, breathing fails to start again. When this happens, Sears writes, "Infants who are monitored show signs that the oxygen in the blood is at a dangerously low level: the heart rate becomes alarmingly slow, and the infant turns pale, blue, and limp. An observer must intervene and arouse the infant. Sometimes a simple *touch* will trigger the self-starting mechanism; sometimes the infant must be aroused from sleep in order to breathe."[51] Sharing sleep means more extensive touching between mother and infant—touching that may save the life of an infant experiencing apnea.

In his heavy-handed style, Sears continues, "Infants who have experienced an apnea episode that required outside intervention to restart their breathing are called near-miss SIDS. In other words, they would have died had someone not intervened. Tragically some infants stop breathing permanently, succumbing to SIDS."[52] Certain infants are at a higher risk for SIDS. These babies, writes Sears, "have two breathing abnormalities . . . they don't breathe when they need to . . . [and] high risk infants don't awaken when their breathing stops."[53]

Sears claims that if "SIDS is related to a diminished arousal response during sleep in some infants, it follows that anything which increases the infant's sensitivity or the mother's awareness of her baby may decrease the risk of SIDS." He continues, "This is exactly what sharing sleep and night nursing do. Infants show REM sleep patterns during sucking, and mothers also go into REM sleep when their babies nurse during the night. This harmony of sleep cycles gives the nursing pair a heightened awareness of each other."[54] Breastfeeding infants who "share sleep with their mothers suck more often throughout the night, which also gives mothers and babies an increased sensitivity to each other." Drawing on science, Sears continues, "An interesting study which sheds more light on the sleep harmony of the nighttime nursing pair concluded that the sleep periods of nursing babies and their mothers are synchronized so that 'they tend to dream simultaneously during the night from twelve weeks postpartum until the time of weaning.'"[55] In contrast, Sears argues that nonnursing mother and baby pairs do not coordinate their sleep and dream cycles.

"Natural mothering," implies Sears, is also correct—good—mothering, and if one is unsure as to what "natural mothering" might be, then simply read Sears's books. His mothering technique is *the* natural and good one. Adding a heavily moralizing component to the question of "good mothering," Sears goes as far as to say, "While inadequate mothering is certainly not the cause of SIDS, it may be a contributing factor in those infants already at risk. Studies have shown a much higher incidence of SIDS among infants of less committed and less skilled mothers."[56] Although at points in his book Sears claims not to cast judgment, nonetheless he argues that bad mothers—mothers who choose not to mother his way—put their babies' very lives at risk.

Sears's child-rearing method is explicitly gendered and heteronormative. He sees mothers' and fathers' roles in very traditional terms, and he never considers the possibility that families might be made up of queer parents, single parents, or other caretakers such as grandparents. Sears never actually says that women should stay home and parent while men go off to earn the family living. Yet this thinking is implicit in his writing. Most of it is addressed to women/mothers, rather than to men/fathers or to parents generally. He speaks repeatedly about how important the mother–child relationship is, thus making clear his thinking that women/mothers are the primary and most important parent—but only in the context of a heterosexual relationship with a man. One might imagine that, given the importance of mother-bodies in Sears's thinking, two mothers would be even better than one. Yet two lesbian mothers are outside the realm of possibility for Sears.

According to Sears, "normal" (heterosexual) women do and should stay home to raise their children; normal (heterosexual) men do and should work outside the home in the public sector, taking care of their wives' and children's financial needs. Not only is this thinking conventional, research has shown that it is also incorrect. United States middle-class women no longer stay home as full-time mothers and homemakers, and men are no longer the primary breadwinners. Anthropologist Maxine L. Margolis writes that women have become an additional family breadwinner. "Dual income families are now the norm in this country. Today so much of the typical middle-class family's consumption is dependent on women's earnings that one must wonder what the consequences would be for the American economy were large numbers of women ever to return to full-time domesticity, a *very* unlikely event in any case."[57] Margolis continues, "A few figures highlight this. In 1960, 38 percent of all adult women held jobs, a figure that rose to 46 percent in 1975, and 60 percent by the late 1990s. More striking is the increase in employed mothers. In 1960, 39 percent of women with school-age children had jobs, in 1975 the number was 55 percent, and by 1995 it had reached nearly 77 percent."[58]

However out of touch with reality and deeply conservative his thinking in terms of gender, at the same time, Sears's work is "anti-masculinist." In sharp contrast to Ferber, Sears emphasizes attachment and dependency as normal and healthy parts of human relationships rather than something to be overcome. Sears argues that development should happen in a context of what I call "normalized dependency." He argues that in a safe, dependent relationship, children will experience "well-being" and feeling "right." Because Sears believes that babies need to be with their parents, particularly their mothers, almost all the time, they should not be left alone at night or at other times. For Sears, "separation anxiety" is a normal and healthy response children have when they are separated from their caretakers. Separation anxiety should be avoided by not forcing premature separations on the child. The anxiety never need arise. The child should be allowed to take the initiative in separating when he or she is ready and in ways that he or she can manage.

Sears believes children *should* be attached to their parents "in the manner of such an object," as Ferber puts it. For Sears, the attachment of children to "transitional objects" such as pacifiers is a sign that the child is being forced prematurely into separation from the human "objects" of their love. Sears's philosophy advocates that children should attach with their parents, siblings, and other human beings, but especially with their mothers. One gets the sense that a child attaching to "things" such as transitional objects might be a sign of child neglect. Sears advocates that healthy children need the near-constant physical presence of their mother.

Indeed, Sears focuses on this *interconnection* of parents (really, mothers) with their children. It is only within this context of dependency that Sears believes normal and healthy development will happen. He writes that parents who use his style of parenting—attachment parenting—ensure that their child "learns to bond with persons, not things. The infant who is accustomed to being in arms, at breast, and in mommy and daddy's bed receives security and fulfillment from personal relationships. This infant is more likely to become a child who forms meaningful attachments with peers and in adulthood is more likely to develop a deep intimacy with a mate." And Sears warns, "The child who is often left by himself in swings, cribs, and playpens is at risk for developing shallow interpersonal relationships and becoming increasingly unfulfilled by a materialistic world."[59]

This is the position taken not only by Sears but also by the larger attachment-parenting movement. Sears, La Leche League International, and other attachment parents argue strongly against a "thing" becoming that to which one's child attaches. Indeed, "People not things" is an often-stated La Leche League motto. In a La Leche League book by Diane Bengson, *How Weaning Happens,* one mother tells the following story about transitional objects.

> "Of course I weaned my baby," the mother told me. "I had already nursed him for a full five months longer than my first two sons. Now that he is eating solid food, he doesn't need me any more. The last thing I want to be is a human pacifier!"
> The first thing that flashed through my mind when she said this was the odd way our society has recognized the artificial pacifier as the normal object and the mother's breast as the substitute. In advertisements, baby-shower gifts, and store displays, pacifiers are promoted as necessary items of infancy.

Thinking further about pacifiers and motherhood, I considered just what it is that pacifies, that "brings peace." I thought of calm in a storm, or the renewal of sleep, of the bridging of cultures. When a child is crying, she is asking for peace in her young life in the only way she knows, from the mother who is uniquely able to provide it. Learning to give and receive peace in this way equips the mother and child to face anxiety and conflict later, long after an artificial pacifier is discarded. Do I want to be a human pacifier? Now that I think about it, I am sure I do. When all is said and done, that's the best kind.[60]

For Sears, independence—a central goal of masculinist understandings of human development—will happen if and when the child is ready for it to happen. Sears writes, "Your child will not grow up to be less independent because he slept in your bed. . . . Children who are given open access to the family bed in infancy become more secure and independent in the long run. They reach the stage of independence when they are ready. Independence is not, in itself, one of our most important parenting goals. It is not the parents' responsibility to make a child independent but rather to create a secure en-vironment and a feeling of rightness which allows a child's independence to develop naturally."[61] Forcing independence on the child will only harm the child's development. Sears sees such imposed independence as one of our society's deepest problems. We are, he believes, a society of people unable to attach with one another in normal, healthy ways.

In these ways, Sears's work is nontraditional and does not fit within the larger mainstream middle-class way of understanding human development and adult–child touch. In contrast with contemporary American middle-class beliefs in individualism and private space, Sears advocates for family members sharing space, sharing rooms, and even sharing beds. He argues that instead of pushing children to be independent and individualistic, children need to be with, and attached to, other people, sharing spaces, beds, and rooms along with bodies.

Whereas Ferber and the behaviorists are wary of sharing sleep because it involves physical contact, Sears argues that sharing sleep is beneficial in large part *because* it involves extensive touching: "The skin is the largest organ in the human body, and tactile stimulation or the lack of it can have a profound effect on how the baby develops." Sears continues, "Tactile stimulation is beneficial to the entire baby, physically, emotionally, and intellectually. The extra touching that a baby receives by sleeping with his parents definitely has a beneficial effect on his development. I suspect that infants who sleep with their mothers grow better."[62] According to Sears, touch is central to the child's physical and emotion well-being. To deprive a child of touch is not unlike depriving a child of other basic physical needs such as food and drink. With touch, children "grow better."

Ironically, at the same time that Sears offers these challenges to middle-class beliefs, Sears's attachment-parenting philosophy excludes people without the resources to have one parent stay home and focus on child rearing full time. Attachment parenting requires mothers to stay home with their children, forgoing work and careers outside the home. For Sears, the "good mother" devotes herself, her body, and her time fully to her child. Although Sears seems to assume this lifestyle of full-time mothering is possible for all women, it is probably only women of the middle to upper class who can afford to fulfill his vision.[63] Poor and working-class women may sleep with their children; but women who have to work outside the home, away from their children, violate Sears's belief that women should be home with their children full time. Some feminists argue for a national guaranteed income so that everyone makes a living wage, whether they work outside the home or not.[64] However, unlike his forebear Bowlby, Sears assumes a middle-class standard of living and offers no solutions to poor or working women (unless one considers guilt a solution).

In spite of, or perhaps because of, this, Sears's thinking on "attachment parenting" is very popular within the white middle class. Sears deeply challenges a twentieth-century site of power, science and the medical establishment, at the same time as he uses science to make and reinforce his arguments. Sears advocates a "return" from science to the body, to intuition, to instincts, and to that which is "natural." Insofar as Sears's work challenges the authority of science, he argues that people should trust themselves and their "instincts" rather than the experts. Like more traditional scientific experts such as Ferber, Sears claims to offer a way to better health and better parenting. However, unlike most scientific experts, Sears advocates what he calls "natural" parenting, which means trusting oneself rather than looking to the experts for guidance. Sears's writing contains an anti-expert ethos while simultaneously making use of science and the scientific expert—himself—to back his claims.

Interestingly, Sears and his opponent Ferber use *identical* "scientific" information about sleep to argue that children should (Sears) or should not (Ferber) be allowed to sleep with parents in the parents' bed. Both Ferber and Sears describe rapid eye movement or REM sleep and non-REM sleep. Both discuss the four stages of non-REM sleep and the percentage of time babies versus adults spend in REM and non-REM sleep each night. Then, making starkly apparent the ideological nature of interpreting scientific data, Ferber uses this scientific information to argue that babies and children should *not* sleep with their parents, and Sears uses this same scientific information to argue that they *should.* Ultimately, neither expert has a foothold on the Truth. Both are deeply embedded in their own ideological agendas.

In the end, Sears seems to argue that if you trust your "instincts," you will parent in the manner proposed by Sears. In other words, good parenting is Sears's method of parenting. You can listen to Sears and "trust your instincts." Or, just in case your instincts let you down, you can circumvent "nature" and simply listen to Sears, parenting in the manner he proposes. Either way, the end result is Sears—Sears the advocate for parental intuition, Sears the pediatric expert.

Sears clearly perpetuates the dualistic thinking of mainstream culture. Women, who are associated with the body, have intuition to teach them how to live and rear children. Men, who are associated with the mind, have rationality. Sears, the rational male scientist, was taught by another rational male scientist to listen to intuitive females who mother—men do science, women mother. From intuitive females, Sears learned about the "natural," of-the-body process of child rearing. Indeed, Sears begins his book describing his awakening to "intuition" over science.

> Twelve years ago when I started pediatric practice, I was faced with the reality that doctors receive the *least* training in the problem areas which bother parents the *most.* "Doctor, is it all right for our baby to sleep in our bed?" "When our baby wakes up crying, should I go to him or am I going to spoil him?" These were real concerns from real people and they deserved real answers. *But I didn't know the answers.* There aren't any courses in medical school on where babies should sleep or why babies cry. . . . Then one day, a wise colleague took me aside and confided that when he wanted to know the answer to a difficult question on parenting, he asked an experienced, intuitive mother. Eureka! Over the next twelve years this is just what I did. I learned from experienced mothers.[65]

And what's more, Sears had one of his own at home. He writes happily, "During my learning phase, I have been blessed with five children and a wife who is an intuitive mother."[66]

The problem of incest illuminates a central tension in Sears's attachment parenting. On the one hand, Sears rejects Ferber's fear of bodies and touch. He engenders a countercultural closeness with children, physical and otherwise, including sharing beds with them. However, Sears essentializes women and with this negates women's needs as persons themselves. This is true not only in terms of negating many women's desires—and financial needs—to work outside the home. Sears negates women's needs in the home as well. For example, what if a woman likes sleeping alone? Or what if she has a partner with whom she wants to have sex in her bed?

In terms of the incest worry, one attachment-parenting expert and Sears fan, Katie Allison Granju, addresses a component of this concern in her book, *Attachment Parenting: Instinctive Care for Your Baby and Young Child* (1999),[67] under a section entitled "Questions about the Family Bed." If parents are sexual when children are present, that may be abusive. So, given this, when and where should parents be sexual, when they share their bed with children? Granju raises this among other "commonly asked questions." She writes in the voice of a concerned parent, "What about our sex life? Isn't the parents' bed supposed to provide private time for parents?" And she responds,

> The idea that the parental bed should be the locus of all sexual activity or even emblematic of the sexual relationship between mother and father is a cultural construct. Your baby's need for nighttime nurturing is a bio-logical necessity. Parents who enjoy a family bed don't stop having sex. Instead, they have sex in other areas of the house. Many couples claim that the act of seeking alternative locations for intimacy adds creativity and spontaneity to their lovemaking. . . . Lots of sleep sharing families have second, third, or even more children, so clearly the family bed isn't wrecking their sex lives![68]

Granju's response to this sexual worry might be somewhat glib for many unconvinced parents. The reality seems to be that parents who share sleep with their children do struggle with the issue of sexuality. One interviewee, Cara, was strongly for and practiced attachment parenting, and was an active member of La Leche League International. At the time of the interview, Cara had a twenty-two-month-old boy whom she still breastfed. Her child, Max, still slept with Cara and her husband, Tom. In fact, Cara told me that Max cannot sleep without her. It sounded like Max needed Cara's presence in the bed to both fall asleep and stay asleep. I asked Cara about having sex given the child in the bed. She said that La Leche League points out couples can go other places—to a couch in the living room maybe—to have sex, and that if the couple feels comfortable it is okay to have sex with babies in the bed. As Cara put it, "babies are too young to participate." Yet in spite of these two pos-sibilities, Cara said that their sexual life had been a problem for her and Tom because Max would not sleep without Cara. She made it sound as if this was mostly hard on Tom, and that that had made it a problem between them.

Although this interviewee believed it to be all right to have sex with the baby in the bed, many people would be uncomfortable with that, and maybe even view such a sexual practice as violating or abusive of the child. When I raised the child sexual abuse/incest question, Cara claimed, "it [incest] really never happens." Given the proliferation of research about the frequency of incest, one wonders if Cara's response to the incest issue is a neat defense. As some attachment-parenting experts agree, clearly, there is something sensual about having a baby or child in one's bed. In a cultural moment where there is widespread fear about incest and child sexual abuse and, I would argue, anxiety over the body's potential out-of-control-ness, Cara's response that incest does not happen frees her from having to grapple with the boundaries around her practice of sharing sleep. Unless one takes Watson's approach and gives up touching children altogether—or Cara's approach and refuses the possibility of sexually violating adult–child touch—the line between sensual and sexual is somewhat unclear. This uncertainty is bound to bring anxiety, especially in a culture that is in the first place so suspicious of sexuality, the body, and touch.

One attachment-parenting advocate and author, Deborah Jackson, recognizes this ambiguity. She writes that many people "worry that bedsharing may be connected in some way with sex abuse, a recurring and apparently growing crisis in the industrialized world."[69] In contrast to Cara, she argued that incest and child sexual abuse might be real problems, but she argues that sex with a baby in the bed is not abusive. "When parents want to be alone together, they do not have to banish the child from the room. When the baby is asleep nearby, there is nothing whatsoever to prevent intimacy. There is no need to whisper unless you want to, because a baby is used to sleeping through noise in the womb." She continues, "Parents in many cultures make love when their babies are awake alongside them, a practice which—contrary to Western belief—does not scar them for life, and makes a nonsense over our embarrassment over sexual education."[70]

Jackson argues that the answer is not to give up on adult–child touch—nor it seems, to deny abuse—but to make touching *more* a part of our lives; in particular, more touching between mother and child. Lots of healthy mother-child touching allows the child to grow into a healthy adult, an adult who will not abuse his or her own children. Jackson writes, "The problem is not whether or not our babies are beside us when we make love. It is that society does not know where to draw the line between 'healthy' loving, constructive, reproductive relationships—and violent, abusive, uncontrolled desire. Once again, we need to look back at our own infancy, when all we needed was our mother's loving touch. That is where a healthy sex education begins."[71]

For some attachment parents, the answer to the contemporary anxiety over child sexual abuse is to touch one's children more. Lots of wholesome touching leads children to grow up healthy so that they will not sexually abuse their children. However, the flip side of Jackson's argument is to, once again, blame mothers. If mothers do not touch their children enough, their children will grow up to be confused about touch and become sexual abusers. This, Jackson claims, "is the result of unresolved mothering."[72]

Conclusion

Ultimately, both Sears and Ferber let mothers down. Neither empowers women—economically and otherwise—to make their own choices while simultaneously supporting and valuing human relationships. Sears challenges the traditional medical model of child rearing while using science to substantiate his argument; of course, he himself is a scientific expert. Sears argues that women know best, yet he proposes a child-rearing method that he claims *is* best. He fails to empower women because he does not open a space for them to make *their own* decisions about how to rear their children.[73] Instead, he claims that if women were to listen to their intuition, they would raise their children in the manner he proposes—a method that is deeply restrictive to women, the options being stay home and mother, or be a "bad mother." Sears relegates women to the role of mother, and Mother who has or does nothing without Baby, quite literally, attached at the hip (or, really, breast). And, of course, Sears's child-rearing advice excludes many women who simply cannot afford to stay home full time, whether or not this is what they want.

Ferber's child-rearing method allows women more freedom to leave children and work away from home. However, in contrast to Sears, Ferber's thinking is masculinist and disparages the importance of human relationships. Ferber argues that babies and children should not sleep with their parents primarily so that they can learn to be alone (although he left science behind when he made his clearly unresearched claim). If one does choose to bring one's child into the parental bed, he suggests questioning one's own preference about the practice. Ferber argues, "If you find that you actually prefer to have your child in your bed, you should examine your own feelings very carefully."[74] In other words, if you prefer the practice, then the practice is suspect; one should never prefer—enjoy too much—physical contact, sharing sleep or some other contact, with one's child. That enjoyment equals getting something out of it for oneself, and good mothers always act selflessly.

It is a no-win situation for American mothers. If you follow Ferber and put your baby in a crib in her or his own room to sleep, you are not a natural mother, not a loving mother, not a good mother. If you follow Sears and sleep with your baby in your bed, you are a mother without boundaries, a mother using your baby to fulfill your own needs, potentially an incestuous mother. The sleep debate, much like certain strands of contemporary feminism, has split into binary and oppositional positions. As a first step toward being truly useful to mothers, to open up choices for women while simultaneously supporting human relationships, the sleep debate must reposition itself in non-dualistic—both/and rather than either/or—terms, and frame the sleep options as *options* to choose from in a way that fits each mother's and each child's particular needs while taking into account their economic and relationship-bound context.

FIVE

Violent Touch: Feminists, Conservatives, and Child Sexual Abuse

These days, children are thought to be in grave danger of being touched violently, abusively, or sexually in public places like day-care facilities and schools. The result of this collective fear of touching is that children who spend significant time in (for example) day care may not be receiving the physical contact they need to thrive. At the same time, real dangers to children, such as malnutrition and hunger, poor schooling, and violence at home, are often overlooked. And although most child sexual abuse happens within homes, public concern over violent or sexually abusive touching of children in families has decreased even as media attention and fear about public touching remains extremely high.[1]

So far I have discussed the perceived "danger" versus understood "necessity" of parents, particularly mothers, touching children (primarily) in the home. In this chapter, I explore how we in the United States got to a place where touching children is understood to be so dangerous in the public sphere. I locate and explore the roots of this mind-set in an unlikely assemblage of American conservative mainstream thinkers and second-wave radical feminists—undeniably strange bedfellows. By examining conservative and feminist literature on touch, I show the progression of thinking from the early-twentieth-century behaviorist school, through the mid-century naturalist movement, to the emergence in the 1960s and 1970s of a second-wave feminist analysis that treated touch as an instrument for enacting social power between unequally situated individuals—men and boys over women and girls.[2] I then explore the ensuing conservative backlash, which focused attention on abusive touch in the public sphere while exempting the traditional family—the locus of the majority of touch problems—from scrutiny. I expose the dualistic nature of the debate, which boils down to a "to touch or not to touch" dichotomy.

In my view, the radical feminists were correct in their social analysis of gender relations, and in their uncovering—or, rather, as Linda Gordon notes, "rediscovery"—of the phenomenon of incest.[3] However, I argue that this rediscovery had unintended consequences because the radical feminists focused on touch *only* as problematic rather than as a social phenomenon that embodies multiple elements: good and bad, healthy, necessary, and potentially dangerous all at once. They brought intense public attention to how adults (men) use violence in touching, but neglected how people express love through touch. They grabbed hold of one side of the dualism in ways of thinking about touch. Unfortunately, the conservative movement has now fundamentally distorted the earlier achievements of the feminist movement in its struggle to expose and combat child sexual abuse. Conservatives fundamentally misused the feminist analysis to defend the traditional family, claiming that abusive touch is rampant against children outside the family. This fueled the contemporary fires of anxiety about touching children in public places, like day cares and schools, that we still experience today. As an alternative to conservatives, and dualistic ways of thinking about touch more generally, I propose a transformative view of adult–child touch that would allow the feminist movement to identify and promote the positive—possibly necessary—forms of touch that are not merely instruments of power reinforcing oppression, but also mediums of pleasure that promote health, growth, and well-being.

Radical Feminism and Ideologies of Adult–Child Touch: Child Sexual Abuse and Incest

As discussed earlier, the naturalist and Kinsey schools of thought came into the public realm in the 1940s and 1950s, before the second-wave feminist movement gained prominence in the late 1960s, and moved the public discourse on touch to an entirely different plane. The behaviorists, naturalists, and Kinsey all presented problematic issues for the feminist movement: the behaviorists for their revulsion of feminine traits, the naturalists for their focus on traditional at-home mothering roles, and Kinsey for his uncritical promotion of touching—which, as we shall see, for the feminists exemplified the manifestation of a patriarchal social order.

The second-wave feminist movement that emerged in the late 1960s and thrived through the 1970s differed from all the prevailing discourses by framing touch not in terms of child rearing—which smacked of compulsory parenting that relegated women to the home—but in terms of power. The two most prominent second-wave feminist factions, liberal feminism and radical feminism, along with other important second-wave feminist groups such as the eco-feminists, simply did not address child rearing. The eco-feminists came the closest to dealing with child-rearing matters as they focused on essentialist and naturalist ideas of the maternal and matrilineal. However, even in their literature, there was little explicit discussion of child rearing per se, or of adult–child *touch* in child rearing (such as the touch involved in breastfeeding versus bottle-feeding, or sharing a bed with children versus the crib), the focus of my study, and indeed the focus of many mainstream child-rearing debates in the United States.[4]

In sharp contrast to the behaviorists' and naturalists' focus on child-rearing issues related to women's lives, second-wave feminists had little to say about breastfeeding and children's sleep. In particular, radical feminists, a prominent second-wave feminist faction, focused on the relationship between touch and *power*—social and familial power, and especially its abuse. It should be noted that the radical feminists may not have thought about their work in terms of issues of touch so much as issues of *violence*. However, most of the violence they addressed happens through the medium of touch, and in the case of child sexual abuse, adult–child touch. The issues they raised became prominent and mainstream concerns, and these concerns that were addressed in popular literature regarding adult–child touch, including child-rearing literature, in ensuing decades.

For the radical feminists, touch—that is, *violent* touch—was a medium through which a dominant male culture exerted power. Radical feminism argued that intimate relationships, and the ways those relationships were lived in the everyday through institutions like the family, were inextricably connected to larger gendered systems of power. Men and boys had power over women and girls.

Expressing grief and anger at women's oppression in society, radical feminists strongly affirmed women and women's special worth within a society that devalued them. They argued that contemporary social institutions such as the nuclear family were an intricate part of the web of oppression that they called the patriarchy. Radical feminists wanted to dismantle these institutions, and the way to do so, they believed, was through a fundamental reworking of women's consciousness. These activists were mainly concerned with touch as a violent instrument of patriarchy: "Violence exists whenever one group controls in its own interests the life chances, environments, actions, and perceptions of another group, as men do women. . . . But the theme of violence as overt physical cruelty lies at the heart of radical feminism's linking of the patriarchy to violence: rape, sexual abuse, sexual slavery in enforced prostitution, spouse abuse, incest, sexual molestation of children . . . and the explicit sadism in pornography."[5]

In the radical feminists' view, although the patriarchy used economic, political, psychological, and ideological power to sustain male dominance, physical force was the bottom-line defense. To bring this backdrop into view, radical feminists exposed rape, enforced prostitution, domestic violence, and sexual harassment in the workplace, on the streets, and in the schools.[6] They fought against what they considered the "violence" of pornography.[7] And they uncovered the most silenced secret of all, incest and child sexual abuse.[8] Incest was a prime example of male oppression, often enacted through male control over, and abuse of, female bodies.

"Female children are regularly subjected to sexual assaults by adult males who are part of their intimate social world," Judith Lewis Herman argued. "The aggressors are not outcasts and strangers; they are neighbors, family friends, uncles, cousins, stepfathers, and fathers. To be sexually exploited by a known and trusted adult is a central and formative experience in the lives of countless women."[9] And Herman wrote, "Father–daughter incest is not only the type of incest most frequently reported but also represents a paradigm of female sexual victimization. The relationship between father and daughter, adult male and female child, is one of the most unequal relationships imaginable. It is no accident that incest occurs most often precisely in the relationship where the female is most powerless."[10] Ultimately, radical feminists argued that incest was more than simply a result of the patriarchy; it was a means to re-create the patriarchy. Girls learned to be girls—they became girls—through a socialization process that included male violation of their bodies and selves.

> Thus did the victims of incest grow up to become archetypally feminine women: sexy without enjoying sex, repeatedly victimized yet repeatedly seeking to lose themselves in the love of an overpowering man, contemptuous of themselves and of other women, hard-working, giving, and self-sacrificing. Consumed with inner rage, they nevertheless rarely caused trouble to anyone but themselves. In their own flesh, they bore repeated punishment for the crimes committed against them in childhood.[11]

Certainly, the radical feminists did not deny that the more commonly acknowledged phenomenon of child sexual abuse by a pedophile—the crazy deranged stranger—occurred; in their view, it too was a manifestation, as was rape of an adult woman by a stranger, of patriarchal power. Yet for radical feminists, family incest and child sexual abuse were particularly insidious instruments of the patriarchal order—in large part, because society didn't recognize how common they were. "The unholy silence that shrouds the interfamily sexual abuse of children and prevents a realistic appraisal of its true incidence and meaning is rooted in the same patriarchal philosophy of sexual private property that shaped and determined historic male attitudes towards rape," radical feminist Susan Brownmiller wrote. "For if woman was man's corporal property, then children were, and are, a wholly owned subsidiary."[12]

To counter this void, radical feminists explored the limited research already done on child sexual abuse, and they initiated their own research to document the prevalence of sexual abuse inflicted on women and girls. Brownmiller cites particularly damning evidence in three studies: a Washington, D.C., study in which 12 percent of rape victims—a group ranging from eighteen months to eighty-two years in age—were children age twelve and younger. Of rapes reported to the Memphis police department, 6 percent of all victims were age twelve and under. Of reported rapes in Philadelphia, 8 percent of all victims were age ten and under, and 28 percent were age fourteen and below.[13]

Brownmiller also unearthed an analysis of adult sex crimes against children in Brooklyn and the Bronx done by the Children's Division of the American Humane Association in 1969. Among other things, the Brooklyn-Bronx study found that the "sexually abused child is statistically more prevalent than the physically abused, or battered child; the median age of the sexually abused child is 11, but infants have not escaped molestation; ten girls are molested for every one boy."[14] Further, noted Brownmiller, 97 percent of the offenders were male and "in three-quarters of the Brooklyn-Bronx cases the offender was known to the child or her family. Twenty-seven percent lived in the child's home (father, stepfather, mother's lover, brother). Another 11 percent did not live in the home but were related by blood or marriage. . . . Only 25 percent of the offenders were reported to be total strangers."[15] Additionally, over 40 percent of the cases entailed abuse that occurred over an extended period of time including, in one case, seven years.

Of all the issues raised by the second-wave feminists, child sexual abuse and incest had the greatest resonance with the general public, or at least with the mass media. Suddenly incest was "everywhere." Movies began to regularly address the issue. Novels and memoirs were written about incest and child sexual abuse. Maya Angelou's well-known memoir, *I Know Why the Caged Bird Sings,* exemplifies an early version of such work. Angelou describes the ongoing sexual abuse she experienced at the hands of her mother's boyfriend with whom they lived, Mr. Freeman.

> He grabbed my arm and pulled me between his legs. His face was still and looked kind, but he didn't smile or blink his eyes. Nothing. He did nothing, except reach his left hand around to turn on the radio without even looking at it. Over the noise of the music and static he said, "Now, this ain't gonna hurt you much. You like it before, didn't you?"
>
> And then there was the pain. A breaking and entering when even the senses are torn apart. The act of rape upon an eight-year-old body is a matter of the needle giving because the camel can't. The child gives, because the body can, and the mind of the violator cannot.
>
> I thought I had died—I woke up in a white-walled world, and it had to be heaven. But Mr. Freeman was there and he was washing me. His hands shook, but he held me upright in the tub and washed my legs. "I didn't mean to hurt you, Ritie. I didn't mean it. But don't you tell. . . . Remember, don't you tell a soul."[16]

Mr. Freeman told Angelou that if she ever told anyone what he had done, then he would kill her beloved brother, Bailey. But, after being hospitalized, Angelou did tell. Then, she quit talking altogether except to her brother. "I had to stop talking. . . . I had discovered that to achieve perfect personal silence all I had to do was to attach myself leechlike to sound. I began to listen to everything. I probably hoped that after I had heard all the sounds, really heard them and packed them down, deep in my ears, the world would be quiet around me."[17]

The radical feminists echoed Angelou's story. They spoke about male violence, often the violence by familiar males sexually violating the little girls in their lives. They spoke about silence, about not telling. And in this, a space opened for more and more voices. This chance to speak and be heard was profoundly liberating for many, many women.

For the first time, women everywhere began speaking out about their hidden childhood experiences, horrible secrets often long remembered but forcibly silenced. Other women began to remember that which they had been forced to forget. With the help of a growing body of feminist psychotherapists, these women claimed to have repressed their memories of child sexual abuse. Feminist psychologists argued that "recovered memory syndrome" was the result of children experiencing something too horrible for them to handle psychically.[18] The abused children repressed the abuse memories as a means of survival. With the second wave of feminist thought, a safe place was suddenly opened up in society for the women to re-remember what they had forgotten.

In the early 1980s, the "incest survivor movement" grew and, with it, popular journals, self-help groups, and the publication of a plethora of pop psychology books on incest and child sexual abuse.[19] Talk shows exploited the incest theme for its juicy, heavily emotional elements. Over time, the incest theme only grew more popular in the mass media. Indeed, in the late nineties, Karen De Witt wrote in a *New York Times* article, "If a dozen movies, television dramas and memoirs are any indication, incest, one of humanity's last taboos, is taboo no longer." Incest "is now openly explored in a spate of new books and movies."[20] James B. Twitchell, author of *Forbidden Partners: The Incest Taboo in Modern Culture,* noted "the obvious reason behind the current trend . . . [was] the women's movement." But he also argued about the incest theme: "In a highly competitive entertainment world, this is one that will quickly grab you."[21] This rush of mass media attention, starting in the early 1980s, became a flashpoint for the conservative movement, which would co-opt the achievements of the feminist movement for its own ends. Through these widespread public examples of abusive physical contact, touch—already problematic in mainstream culture—acquired even more overwhelmingly negative associations.

Given radical feminists' intense focus on undoing efforts to downplay the evidence of violence against women and girls, there was little incentive—indeed, there existed a preponderance of counterincentives—to examine manifestations of healthy touch. Thus, in the canon of important second-wave radical feminist texts, only two texts, both by the Boston Women's Health Book Collective, even briefly discussed positive forms of adult–child touch—and they did so with great caution. One of those books, *Ourselves and Our Children: A Book by and for Parents*, devoted only one page to breastfeeding versus bottle-feeding. Taking no stand on which was better, the authors were careful to point out the benefits of each alternative:

> Breast-feeding involves a special and very important physical closeness at feeding times, it is convenient and always available, and some babies may have less trouble digesting human milk than formula. . . . Bottle feeding is much less demanding on the mother's schedule, makes it easier for her to return to work, and has the particular advantage of allowing the father or another adult to participate fully in the care and feeding of a young baby.

And holding and cuddling can provide similar physical closeness to that experienced during breast feeding. Babies can thrive either way.[22]

The texts mentioned beneficial physical contact through infant feeding and immediately following birth, but there was no further reference to any form of positive touch such as during sleep or when the child is carried.[23] The feminists' near-omission of positive discussion of adult–child touch is striking, in contrast to the vast amounts of popular and scholarly writing available on breastfeeding, sleeping with children, holding children, and other positive forms of adult–child physical contact. And, in contrast to feminist work, most of this popular and scholarly writing relegated women to the role of mother; not following popular child-rearing advice meant one was a "bad mother," and ultimately a "bad woman."

Given the feminists' focus on violent touch, their reaction to Kinsey's already-controversial work should not be surprising. Brownmiller pointed out that Kinsey found, "One in four women interviewed . . . had reported an unwanted preadolescent sex experience of some sort with an adult male." And she noted that, of these women, "80 percent reported that they had been frightened."[24] Given this, Brownmiller, Herman, and other radical feminists such as Florence Rush were stunned by Kinsey's beliefs that adult–child sexual contact was not inherently harmful. They argued that Kinsey exhibited yet one more example of patriarchal thinking. "With the usual male arrogance, Kinsey could not imagine that a sexual assault on a child constitutes a gross and devastating shock and insult, and so he blamed everyone but the offender," Rush wrote.[25]

The response to Kinsey's work highlights the tension in radical feminism around issues of adult–child touch. Clearly, Kinsey's thinking about adult–child sexual contact was deeply problematic. The radical feminists rightly used Kinsey to confirm their argument about abusive power, gender, and touch. Nonetheless, the radical feminists did not acknowledge what might be useful in Kinsey's work in terms of touching as important and healthy for children (or, for that matter, in his challenge to heteronormativity via his celebration of all touch, including that involved in diverse sexualities). They did not consider the ways in which Kinsey's thinking about touch might also be liberating. In a world where bodies and female bodies in particular were often understood to be "dirty" and dangerous, they rejected a viewpoint that could have challenged a negative ideology about women-bodies.

I believe the radical feminists were fundamentally right in their social analysis and in exposing the reality of incest. Their far-reaching argument about adult–child touch had the potential to rupture the mainstream dualistic ways of thinking about adult–child touch that had existed through the century. Yet by limiting their focus to violent touch, the radical feminists reinforced the view that the body is bad and touching is dangerous; ironically, this is the side that conservatives and the feminist backlash would embrace within the rigid dualism through which the United States mainstream culture viewed touch.

Feminists and Dualisms

The dualistic thinking about adult–child touch that I uncover in radical feminism can be identified with a broader problem in feminism explored by other scholars. Yet my interest in feminism goes beyond the scholarly. I am, of course, a feminist. I call myself a socialist feminist. And for me, feminism has been both an intellectual, and literal, lifeline. I come from three generations of Irish American Catholic women—my own, my mother's, and my grandmother's generation. My mother became a feminist, a radical feminist, in the early 1970s, and this was the beginning of the end of my family. And this was a very good thing. So for me, the story of my family is a story of the profound value of second-wave radical feminist thought. Feminism allowed my mother both to see, and to open, a door that led out of our family history, our multigenerational family story of violence. And I, like many women, owe to radical feminism the possibility of revisiting my childhood and re-remembering the violence, including the sexual abuse that happened there.[26] So, given this deep personal debt, I criticize a lack, a gap, I see in feminist thought with some trepidation. Feminism is so under siege by the larger mainstream and conservative culture, I have an impulse to simply defend it and ignore any legitimate critiques I, or others, may have. Yet this defensive and rigid response merely replicates the larger culture's dualistic thinking that I am invested in debunking.

Radical feminists, in particular, focused on the question of male violence, and they developed complicated analyses of the oppressive system, the patriarchy, which included a deeply critical study of contemporary capitalism. Yet there were also problems with second-wave radical feminist thought; in particular, there was an element of simplicity in it. It was, to some extent, dualistic.

Some second-wave radical feminists laid the world out in either/or terms. They reproduced a "deeply embedded cultural habit of thinking."[27] This dualistic thought had, at its core, an anti-touch element. For some second-wave radical feminists, the oppressive order of things was at once complex and simple. Men violate through touching. Men violate women's bodies and women's bodies are violated: touching is problematic. If nothing else, the movement had an inclination to understand touching as dangerous because it never examined other possibilities.

Indeed, second-wave radical feminist thought had a dichotomous ethos that has been carefully examined and critiqued by today's third-wave and other feminists like Lynn Chancer, Susan Bordo, bell hooks, and Audre Lorde. Third-wave feminists have complicated our understanding of oppression. Like Foucault, they argue that oppression is multifaceted; power is not a physical thing to hold on to, but like a dynamic force that flows through society configuring to assume particular historical forms. In one moment, in one place, physical contact may be harmful. Yet in another context, it may be healthy, healing, even necessary. Bodies touching bodies *are* sites for prospective violence, and yet also, sites with the potential for deep pleasure.

Not only did radical feminists tend to reproduce a broad cultural dualistic ideology, but feminist thought dichotomized within feminism as well. One side of the split, the "sexism feminists," focused on structural sexism and the patriarchy. The other school of thought, the "sex feminists," which developed during the anti-feminist backlash of the 1980s and 1990s, focused on sexual freedom rather than on sexism and violent oppression. If these diverse focal points were to work together in "both/and" instead of splitting into "either/or" theoretical positions, they had the potential to fundamentally challenge dualistic thinking about touch and women's bodies.[28]

As early as 1984, Carole S. Vance, in her essay "Pleasure and Danger: Toward a Politics of Sexuality," described this same split—between the feminist concern over pleasure versus that of danger—as running through the nineteenth and twentieth centuries. Her essay came out of a historically important conference for feminism, the Scholar and the Feminist IX conference, "Towards a Politics of Sexuality," held at Barnard College on April 24, 1982. At the conference, feminists attempted to explore "the ambiguous and complex relationship between sexual pleasure and danger in women's lives and in feminist theory."[29] The conference represented an explosive moment of articulating the pleasure/danger split in feminist thought. About the split, Vance wrote:

Since the nineteenth century, feminist theorists have disagreed on how to improve women's sexual situation and, even more basically, on what women want sexually. Some have been broadly protectionist, attempting to secure some measure of safety from male lust and aggression, assuming either that women's sexuality is intrinsically muted or at least that it cannot flower until greater safety is established. Others, more often in the twentieth century than the nineteenth, have been expansionist and exploratory, believing that women could venture to be sexual in more visible and daring ways, especially as material changes which favored women's autonomy in general (wage labor, urbanization, contraception, and abortion) also supported sexual autonomy.[30]

The "pleasure"—or in Chancer's terms, "sex"—feminists realized that, in part, males had exercised their power to repress women's sexuality and women's desires. "Because of this history of sexual repression, many feminists feel strongly, and understandably so, that procuring sexual freedom for all women must be a central concern of the feminist movement," she writes. "This goal of sexual freedom is often pursued through individual defiance: here, sexual practices that challenge traditional constraints become a mode of rebellion and a quite personal politics. To seek and find physical pleasure is believed to be a good, even in a sexist present."[31]

Hence, on one side of the divide within radical feminism, the sex feminists challenged the ways in which "male-dominated societies" restricted and controlled women's desires.[32] On the other side, the sexism feminists contested the male-dominated and oppressive social structures of the capitalist patriarchy.

The split within feminism continues to haunt the feminist movement today, playing out along a number of political fault lines, which include the areas discussed by Chancer—pornography, beauty, sadomasochism, and rape—and ultimately have created unexpected alliances, not unlike the radical feminist/ conservative alignment over touch. In the 1980s and 1990s, for example, some sexism-focused radical feminists, such as Catherine MacKinnon and Andrea Dworkin, argued that pornography oppresses women by objectifying them, and that this reinforces/reproduces violence against them.[33] With this argument, the anti-pornography—sexism—feminists found themselves in some ways aligned with the religious right and, simultaneously, criticized by many third-wave "pro-sex" feminists.

In sharp contrast to both anti-pornography feminists and the religious right, "pro-sex" feminists argued that pornography has a *liberating* potential.

They pointed out that we live in a deeply repressed Protestant society, where the body and things of the body, such as sexuality, are seen as fundamentally bad. Women in particular have been limited in this anti-body binary thinking. They are either pure, madonna mother-bodies or impure, sexual whore-bodies. For the "pro-sex" feminists, pornography could be a celebration of the body and of sexuality. It could be understood as a place where women challenge the "whore" image of sexual women by explicitly celebrating their own sexual bodies. Yet, like the sexism feminists, the sex feminists also never looked at affirming, healthy, adult–child touch.

Early and later radical feminists—both sexism and sex-focused—never examined the healthy, perhaps necessary, side of touching children. Ultimately, the radical feminist dualistic approach to touch was rooted in the limits and broader agenda of second-wave feminism; namely, their concentration on freeing women from compulsory parenting. Second-wave feminists did not want to examine ways to better touch—or generally better parent—children. They wanted to loosen the social ties binding women to parenting.

Families and Values: The Conservative Backlash

In the 1970s, after more than a decade of radical change, things shifted once again. The conservative right began an intense backlash that continues today. In the aftermath of the turbulent sixties and seventies, Watergate, Vietnam, energy crises, inflation, and economic stagnation, people became nostalgic for an imagined perfect past—"the stability, order, and tradition of a lost golden age," as Skolnick put it.[34]

In assigning blame for the supposed fall from paradise, conservatives focused on the feminist challenge to the "traditional" nuclear family. Clearly, the feminists' exposure of widespread incest and child sexual abuse struck to the heart of American faith in the family—the bedrock of conservatives' world. Conservatives, much like Sears, La Leche League International, and other naturalists, argued that the so-called traditional family is a *natural* entity through which men and women achieve their differing biological destiny and even their biblical meaning. For conservatives, the radical feminist critique of the family was an attack on the basis of social harmony and civilization. Conservatives deflected this criticism by blaming feminists and the sexual revolution for the decline of marriage and stay-at-home mothering. They also refocused the widespread concern over sexual abuse away from the family—despite the overwhelming evidence that this was the locus of the problem—into a popular hysteria about pedophiles, strange men outside the family who molested children.

Well-known conservative George Gilder, in his important and early work responding to the feminist second-wave movement, *Sexual Suicide* (1973), and again in his 1986 update of that work, retitled *Men and Marriage,* argued that women socialize men within the heterosexual institution of the nuclear family, and thereby tame men's natural promiscuous sexuality.[35] Gilder wrote, "Modern society relies on predictable, regular, long-term human activities corresponding to the sexual faculties of women. The male pattern is the enemy of social stability. This is the ultimate source of female sexual control and the crucial reason for it. Women domesticate and civilize male nature. They can jeopardize male discipline and identity, and civilization as well, merely by giving up this role."[36]

According to conservatives such as Gilder, when women leave the home to go to work, two disastrous events occur. First, men's status in the family as provider is undermined and men drift from their families at loose ends in the amoral public world. "A man without a woman has a deep inner sense of dispensability, perhaps evolved during the millennia of service in the front lines of tribal defense. He is sexually optional. Several dominant males could impregnate all the women and perpetuate the tribe."[37] Not only does the male provider role end, but these dispensable men also cease to protect the women and children (who had composed the "natural" nuclear families). Second, and perhaps most important, men's moral socialization by women ends. This means male sexuality runs amok. Men return to their primal barbarian state, raping, pillaging, and fundamentally threatening the social order. According to Gilder and other conservatives, all human societies throughout time face this struggle. Women must socialize men or confront the terrible consequences. "Biology, anthropology, and history all tell the same essential story. Every society, each generation, faces an invasion by barbarians. They storm into the streets and schools, businesses and households of the land, and, unless they are brought to heel, they rape and pillage, debauch and despoil the settlements of society. . . . These barbarians are young men and boys, in their teens and early twenties."[38] In the modern world, marriage and the "traditional" nuclear family represent the only place where this "taming" of men may occur. "A young man enters the decisive phase of his life when he resolves on marriage and career. . . . At this point, economic incentives and bureaucratic rules alone are impotent to make him a useful citizen. He becomes law-abiding and productive, in essence, because he discovers it is the only way he can get sex from the women he wants, or marriage from the one he loves. It is the sexual constitution, not the legal one, that is decisive in subduing the aggressions of young men."[39]

For Gilder and other conservatives, the feminist advocacy of universal day care (leaving women free to work outside the home) equals a step toward social collapse. Day care—not surprisingly, the center of 1980s scandals involving alleged sexual abuse and pedophiles—became emblematic of a social Armageddon. Focusing on the damage supposedly done to children when subjected to day care, another important 1980s conservative, Gary Bauer, Ronald Reagan's director of the Office of Policy Development for the administration's family policy, argued that "mothers should stay home for the sake of the children." Bauer—whose own children attended day care for nine years—described day care as Marxist, and claimed that children who attend suffer "long-term damaging effects."[40]

In a recent article in the conservative *National Review Online,* editor Rich Lowry elaborated on mothers' natural obligation to stay home with their children: "Why is it so hard to admit that mothers are central to child-rearing, so important, in fact, that they should stay home when their kids are little? It probably has a lot to do with the problem liberals have admitting that biology sometimes is inescapable, that nature imposes certain obligations that can't be got around with clever alternate arrangements."[41] Linking day care to abortion, Lowry continues sarcastically, "Why should anyone be burdened with an inconvenient child? . . . If liberals think awkwardly timed children can be sucked away into eternity, why would they think that mothers should have to go too far out of their way to nurture them once they are actually here?"[42]

Other conservatives place the problem of day care in the context of threats to children. Some took Gilder's work and focused on how men, unsocialized by women and freed from the domesticating effects of wife and home, would potentially become dangerous sexual predators. These men represented an immense threat to children. Not only were children unprotected by their mothers—who were purportedly busy fulfilling themselves in the work world—but also fathers had drifted from the private realm where they no longer felt needed as providers. Children had neither mothers nor fathers to protect them. David Blankenhorn, a well-known social conservative, argued in the 1990s that "the spreading risk of childhood sexual abuse is directly linked to the decline of married fatherhood."[43] And in the public world of day care, where children were forced to go unshielded, they were at risk of coming into contact with unsocialized, sexually predatory males. Quoting and then condemning Judith Lewis Herman, Blankenhorn attacked what he considered a feminist and mass media fantasy that sexual abuse is fundamentally a problem of fathers. He wrote, "The weight of the evidence is clear. What magnifies the risk of sexual abuse for children is not the presence of a married father but his absence."[44] Blankenhorn concedes that some fathers may sexually abuse their children but contends that most fathers protect their young. Without a father to protect them, children are left unshielded from mothers' boyfriends and "poorly protected from sexually opportunistic males in the surrounding community."[45]

In an article, "Home-Alone America," that she wrote for the *Policy Review,* conservative Mary Eberstadt also identified sexual abuse as a problem stemming from the decline of the traditional family. Eberstadt argued that most of the troubles faced by United States youth (including adolescent suicide, psychological trouble, bad conduct, and child sexual abuse) find their source in "mother abandonment"—in other words, mothers working outside the home. She used various examples—a young San Diego man who opened fire in a high school in March 2001, the Columbine high school killers, Jeffrey Dahmer, and Timothy McVeigh—to point out that what all of these young white males had in common was that, as teenagers, they were left at home alone, while their mothers went to work.[46] Working mothers caused these children to kill.

Eberstadt argued that since 1980—since the end of the second-wave feminist movement—child sexual abuse has increased enormously because of the rise in mothers working outside the home, leaving the children alone and accessible to predatory males. "A connection to home-alone America seems undeniable. . . . In order for predatory males (and they are almost always males) to abuse, they must first have access; and that the increasing absence from home of biological mothers . . . effectively increases the access of would-be predators." She cited a 1997 Heritage Foundation study that calculates that child sexual abuse had increased by 350 percent since 1980.[47] This date would seem important for the conservative argument because the second-wave feminist movement and its—in conservative opinion—bad influence had been around for a decade. In other words, with feminism, rates of child sexual abuse go up.

In fact, the "increase" in child sexual abuse was merely an increase in social awareness and a changed definition of abuse—thanks, one might add, to the second-wave feminist movement. Kinsey's research in 1953 reinforced this: he had found a similar rate of "child sexual abuse" in the 1930s and 1940s, but simply did not call it "abuse." (In her essay, Eberstadt briefly acknowledged the possibility of changing social awareness but insisted that the numbers would have risen dramatically even without those changes.)

For conservatives, children face immense danger when unprotected by the "traditional" nuclear family—father working and providing, mother at home caring for the children. In this thinking, alone—without mothers—and faced with a world full of predatory men, children are at grave risk. Conservatives have invented a threatening public world of rapacious, unsocialized men. Indeed, I argue that the emergence of numerous false claims of day-care abuse in the 1980s and 1990s fits in the growing conservative conviction of danger faced by children away from home, outside motherly care, and subject to supposedly abusive strangers.

In the late 1980s and 1990s, the popular culture reflected conservative fears about working mothers, neglected children, and pedophiles. A cable channel for women, Lifetime, continues to air a rich collection of made-for-television movies about pedophiles and the children they abuse. These programs tend to be shown during the day to women who work at home. Some tell stories about other mothers (bad mothers) who go off to work and leave their children to become helpless victims of a depraved world. One 1991 made-for-television movie, *Don't Touch My Daughter,* tells a standard right-wing story of child sexual abuse: an eleven-year-old white middle-class girl, Dana, is kidnapped and molested by a working-class man, Eddy Ryter, from the same city. Of course, her mother, a divorcée, works outside the home, leaving her young daughter alone all too often.

George Gilder's fantasy—barbarian, unmarried, uncivilized, always grubby and unshaven Eddy Ryter—exists in sharp opposition to Linda and Dana. He has kidnapped, molested, and murdered untold numbers of little girls. He threatens to do it again with Dana. And the (liberal) legal system permits it. Finally, the mother is forced to take justice into her own hands. She breaks into Eddy's home and shoots and kills him. Of course, it never would have come to this if Linda had not been away at work in the first place, leaving her daughter alone.

Don't Touch My Daughter speaks to widespread conservative fears about evil pedophiles, out there somewhere, lurking, waiting for the opportunity to snatch up our daughters and defile them with their dirty touch. There is little that everyday people can do to protect themselves—except, at the very least, mothers must be where they are supposed to be, with their children.

The dangerous world of *Don't Touch My Daughter* was alive in many people's imaginations and in popular anxiety about child molestation by strangers. It surfaced in cases of extensive abuse thought to have occurred in numerous day-care centers across the nation. One of the most notorious of these involved a southern California preschool run by the McMartin family. This case started in the summer of 1983 with allegations of child molestation and ritual satanic abuse. The trial ran from April 1987 until July 1990. The charges included 354 counts of molestation and/or abuse, 41 witnesses, and 369 alleged victims, but eventually deteriorated into a series of acquittals, deadlocks, and declarations of mistrials.[48] When the McMartin trial was finally abandoned, it "and copycat cases that came in its wake, left a permanent mark on day-care operations . . . and on those who need their services."[49] Cultural critic James R. Kincaid wondered, "How much more guilt do working mothers need shoveled on them. . . . [Yet] often it is worse than guilt, a judge in Michigan actually remov[ed] a three-year-old girl from her mother because the mother was using day care thirty-five hours a week while taking classes in Ann Arbor."[50]

In another high-profile day-care abuse case in 1984, Frank Fuster and his young wife Ileana were charged with sexually abusing more than twenty children in their home day-care center. Eventually, more than twenty children reported being raped and molested. Fuster's five-year-old son from a previous relationship, Noel, provided the "most damning" evidence against Fuster in an interview that was biased at best. The taped interview includes scenes in which "the interviewers—apparently stymied by Noel's insistence that no one abused him—ask the child if it's possible that he was abused but simply doesn't remember it because he was hypnotized or asleep at the time." Noel Fuster today insists that he was never abused by his father.[51] Nonetheless, Frank Fuster is still serving his 165-year sentence.

Lately, some conservative commentators lay the blame for these scandals—which have been more recently called hysterical witch hunts—on feminism because of the second-wave feminist focus on child sexual abuse.[52] In reality, the day-care scandals and popular cultural phenomena like *Don't Touch My Daughter* were born from the conservative vision: a world constituted by predatory men, the only response to which could be the reestablishment of the "traditional" family and the rolling back of the advances of feminism.

The conservative insistence that danger lurks outside the home and the "traditional" family meshes with contemporary legal perspectives and anxieties about sexual dangers to children. As we have seen through the past century, fears about child sexual abuse and the sexual body out of control have been embedded within ways of thinking about touching children. Conservative anxiety about children being sexually abused outside the home reflected one of two historical currents running through the twentieth century. One involved the concern with cruelty to children within families, of which the more hidden and less recognized type of child sexual abuse—the abuse brought to public attention in the 1970s by second-wave feminists—is incest. The second was the sexual abuse of children by strangers; this type of child sexual abuse, pedophilia, has been more socially recognized throughout the century. Accordingly, legal attention given to child sexual abuse of children by unfamiliar persons has a longer history.

Society and the legal system alike treat "child molesters"—that is, those who abuse children to whom they are *not* related—very differently from "incest offenders," those who abuse child relatives. Child molesters are viewed as more wicked, ill, and abnormal than incest offenders, who are subject to less public contempt and media attention. Within the legal system, child molesters are charged in criminal court, whereas incest offenders are likely to be charged in family or juvenile court. In the United States, both the federal government and each of the state governments have their own court systems. Federal courts deal with what are understood as federal matters, such as cases that involve the violation of federal law, constitutionality of laws, or disputes between states. Most criminal cases are handled in state courts. Further, most states have courts that handle specific legal matters. For example, what are seen to be "family matters"—such as incest—are handled in family courts. In contrast, child molestation is simply viewed as a criminal matter and thus handled in the regular state criminal court system. This is significant because family courts tend to lean toward therapeutic solutions to problems, whereas criminal courts lean toward punishment. Thus, because they are likely to be charged in family court, incest offenders have a chance at rehabilitation through treatment. In contrast, because they are charged in criminal court, child molesters are likely to face imprisonment as well as civil commitment laws, invasive medical treatment, and community notification and registration laws. Sociologist Juliana M. Blome claims, "Child molesters are almost seven times more likely to be imprisoned than their intrafamilial counterparts."[53] Blome argues that many convictions of child molesters seem way out of proportion to the harm committed. For example, one California man received a 129-year prison sentence for molesting an eleven-year-old girl. Another child molester was sentenced to 527 years. This man's defense attorneys remarked that had the defendant killed the child, he would have served less time.[54]

Popular movies mirrored life. In *Don't Touch My Daughter,* Eddy is clearly a criminal, and for this he dies. In contrast, in another child sexual abuse movie aired regularly on television, *Something about Amelia,* a white middle-class father is disclosed as an incest perpetrator who had sex with his young daughter repeatedly. This kind of child sexual abuser—a man abusing his own daughter instead of someone else's child—is understood as needing help. He is treated therapeutically.

The second-wave radical feminist movement in the 1970s represented a cultural moment where child sexual abuse in the family, incest—the type of sexual abuse shown by research to happen most—was more widely recognized. Since then, conservatives have used the second-wave feminist exposure of child sexual abuse to argue against feminist goals; in particular, in the 1980s, it used the radical feminists' exposure of child sexual abuse in its backlash against feminism. Coinciding neatly with the conservative backlash, our social focus has recentered on the fear of the—less common—child molester outside of the family. Ultimately, the various movements to end child sexual abuse have had the result of ending the touching of children in public places while doing very little to stop child sexual abuse in the home where, according to research, it actually seems to happen.

Nationally, the response to the child sexual abuse terror has been fearful vigilance against the possible presence of pedophiles, increased pressure on women to stay home with their children, and an intense focus on the touching of children by adults outside the home. One of numerous dangers here lies in the possibility that we persecute the innocent—underpaid day-care workers, working mothers, women who practice extended breastfeeding or sharing sleep—rather than acknowledge where the real danger lies, even as we risk stopping the touching of children in the nurturing ways that children probably do need to be touched. Indeed, there is an ethos of danger around adults touching children at all. In the late 1980s and 1990s, many child-care workers were told not to touch or have physical contact with the children in their care. Teachers became increasingly careful not to touch their students for fear of being misunderstood. Even those who work with very young children—children who may need to be touched for healthy development to occur—became cautious and began to avoid physical contact.[55] In 1993, I worked for several months in an urban institution with young girls who had reached the end of the institutional rope. They had been tossed out, or had run away from, one too many foster families and could no longer be placed. This institution was a holding place until the girls turned eighteen and the state was relieved of its troublesome responsibility. The institution's staff was not allowed to touch the girls; even a tap on the shoulder or a brush of the arm was frowned upon. Furthermore, the girls were not allowed to touch each other. Sitting next to each other on the couch or resting an arm around another girl's shoulders received the quick reprimand, "Hey! No pc!" (physical contact). These girls all came from extremely abusive backgrounds, the majority had histories of sexual abuse and some had been both abused and the abuser of other smaller children. Thus, the institution was very concerned that the girls not misinterpret any touch. Its simple institution-style solution was to allow *no* touching to occur. This solution merely reinforced the existing dualistic ways of thinking about touch.

SIX

Touching Problems

One human being sucking on another's breast, or one snuggled up to another in bed, are acts containing multiple and significant meanings. Like other forms of adult–child touch, beliefs about breastfeeding and sharing sleep (or not) have been and continue to be deeply contested in the mainstream United States.

In this book I have sought to reveal the ideological and dualistic structure of ideas about adult–child physical contact. Unlike Bernice Hausman, I do not advocate any position on touch; rather, I examine the power-laden context of the various positions. I depend on thinkers like Susan Bordo, who captures the structure of dualistic thinking in the Western tradition. Because touching involves bodies, the mind–body split plays a central role in ideologies of touch. Like Bordo, I don't consider the body a fundamentally stable, acultural constant against which one might contrast other culturally relative forms. The body, like everything in culture, is always in the grip of cultural practices, as Michel Foucault argues. Indeed, the problem is not cultural repression of the natural instinctual body; there is no "natural" body. Our bodies, and all that is human, are largely made by our culture.

Bordo reminds us of the importance of this split, and, implicitly, how ideologies of touch can reinforce more general dualistic patterns. Women are associated with the body, understood to be "instinctual," spontaneous, wild, and in danger of flying out of control. By contrast, the male as mind or spirit is identified with control and rationality: "Dualism here appears as the offspring, the by-product, of the identification of the self with control, an identification . . . lying at the center of Christianity's ethic of anti-sexuality. The attempt to subdue the spontaneities of the body in the interests of control only succeeds in constituting them as more alien and more powerful, and thus more in need of control."[1]

There are multiple meanings to these gendered mind–body associations. Bordo proposes that one is abhorrence for traditional female roles and cultural limitations, and that another springs from a deep fear of "'the Female,' with all its more nightmarish archetypal associations of voracious hungers and sexual insatiability."[2] Adolescent anorectics often express a fear of growing up to be mature, sexually developed women. "'I have a deep fear,' says one, 'of having a womanly body, round and fully developed. I want to be tight and muscular and thin.'" Another anorectic believes that if she could only stay thin, she would "'never have to deal with having a woman's body.'" She claims, "'[L]ike Peter Pan I could stay a child forever.'" Bordo writes, "The choice of Peter Pan is telling here—what she means is, stay a *boy* forever."[3]

In mind–body dualistic thinking, the body is not merely evil. As our culture has romanticized the so-called primitive person-as-body in stories of the "noble savage," we have also romanticized the female-as-body. In the mind–body dualism, on the one hand, the "bad" female body is understood to be out-of-control animalistic sexuality, while the "good" (but still animalistic) female body is the instinctual mother. Feminist scholars have dubbed this opposition within the mind–body dualism "madonna–whore." Women may be good, mothering, nurturing bodies or bad, excessively sexual, out-of-control bodies. In this projection, there is no room to be fully complex human beings. Indeed, women are understood to be all that men are *not:* Good women are virtuous, nurturing mother figures. Bad women are out-of-control, sexual "sluts."[4]

There are many ironies in binary thought. One surrounds women's labor. Women are belittled for putting their children in day care, yet there is almost no social assistance to help women (or men) stay home with their children. If nonaffluent women stay home with their children and use the very limited—at this point, almost nonexistent—resources of welfare, they are called lazy welfare mothers. If they go to work, chances are very good that one job will not cover their living expenses and, further, they are considered selfish for leaving their children in someone else's care. In fact, the very work women often do as home workers—service work, including sex work, cleaning, child care, and cooking and serving food—is considered good and a "labor of love" *unless* they get paid for it. When women get paid for such labor, they are often looked down upon for doing something "dirty" or "lowly."

The Boundaries of Touch

Social understandings of what it means to be female and what women's work is have changed over time. As discussed in chapter 2, with industrialization, women and men began to have separate spheres. More and more, men went out to the public realm of the workplace, while women stayed in the newly private world of the home. The factory and public world was rational, calculating, and competitive. The private home, surrounded by firm ideological boundaries, was the place of connection, caring, and love. "Love" was understood to be women's work.

With industrialization, women's work increasingly involved child rearing and home work such as cleaning rather than producing the goods of life. Production was now done in the public world of industry. Yet one "product" was left to women, especially the growing middle class—the child. And child-rearing advice was meant to help women to "produce" the very best child possible. This ideal (boy) child was to function successfully in the regimented, competitive world of industrial capital.

Child-rearing advice as dualistic ideologies of adult–child touch occur within the two primary mainstream American child-rearing schools, the "naturalist" and the "behaviorist," which exist at either end of the touch continuum, and run throughout the twentieth and into the twenty-first century. For the fundamentally pro-touch naturalists, the body is to be celebrated. For the more or less anti-touch behaviorists, the body is to be controlled and contained. I argue that neither of the two schools has its finger on the pulse, so to speak, of the "right," actual, or "true" body. Indeed, both play a role in body practices and in shaping our bodies and making our body-selves part of culture.

For the behaviorists, science represented the opposite of the female's out-of-control female-body. Like the male mind, science was understood to be rational, ordered, and in control. Children raised by science (as symbolic of men) would grow up to reflect scientific, male-identified traits. They would be controlled, strong, rational, firm, and heterosexual; in a word, masculine. Watson believed that children raised—as almost all children were—by women were weak, emotional, and out of control. Watson was, in fact, deeply misogynistic. And in his heteronormative framework, although Watson never said it explicitly, the underlying worry was that these children (who were somehow always boys), having been touched too much by women, would be feminine, "sissies," and gay.[5]

Throughout the twentieth century, the behaviorists, such as Watson and Ferber, championed a masculine and heteronormative ideal in human development. They believed a healthy child grows up to be a rational, nonemotional, controlled and controlling, strong, independent, and heterosexual adult. Behaviorists argue that children are born as relatively blank slates and must be trained to be become the people we want them to be; that is, masculine and heterosexual grown-ups.

The behaviorists appropriate and claim for science an area of expertise that once belonged to women. Ironically, in trampling upon women's "traditional" knowledge, and in so doing, disempowering women, the behaviorists helped open up the possibility for second-wave feminism to ideologically free women from obligatory child rearing as they entered the workforce in the second half of the twentieth century. Indeed, with the second wave, increasingly, women not only worked outside the home, but also felt (somewhat) entitled to focus on their own careers, to understand themselves in terms of work away from home.

Recently, an academic friend and mother told me I was the only mother she knew who practiced attachment parenting. I asked her what the other mothers she knows do for a living. They were all either academics or other professionals, or else were the women who worked *for* the professionals doing child care. Of course, these two groups are not likely to practice attachment parenting. Attachment parenting makes it fairly difficult for a woman to have a career. Indeed, much attachment-parenting literature is explicitly against women working outside the home. Women who *must* work away from their own children out of financial necessity (the situation of many childcare workers and other working women) and women strongly committed to their careers (as are many child-care workers, professionals, and others) are less likely to be interested in or able to do attachment parenting. Ironically, behaviorist theories make working away from home and children a little easier for women through their encouragement of weaning or not breastfeeding at all and through sleep training with the goal of getting children to sleep by themselves through the night.

The naturalists, like La Leche League International discussed at length in chapter 3 and William Sears discussed in chapter 4, essentialize women and their roles. This may stem from their Christian religious background (La Leche League was founded by seven Catholic white middle-class women who met through a Christian association). Yet insofar as they essentialize women's roles, naturalists also challenge the hegemony of science over child-rearing expertise and reclaim this expertise for women. They offer women power, albeit limited, in that they celebrate women's supposedly traditional and "instinctual" knowledge. The naturalists also challenge two key aspects of twentieth-century mainstream American thinking: the masculine ideal and the materialism of middle-class consumer culture.

Although they challenge mainstream science, naturalists still use science to make their arguments. Indeed, all of the various ideologies of touch make use of scientific research and findings in their claims. In other words, science can and is used for a variety of ideological positions.

In their child-rearing philosophy, naturalists follow the lead of the child. For naturalists, the child *naturally* knows what she or he needs from birth. Parents are charged with simply learning to listen to their children's language or "cues." Crying is one such cue, and because of this, a parent's response must be quick.[6] Naturalists believe children will become healthy, happy adults if their needs ("needs" as defined by the naturalists) are met. A primary need is to be touched. Among many benefits, touching induces intimacy and connection. And, for naturalists, being connected to and having relationships with others is a fundamental need of human infants. Through healthy connections in infancy and childhood, human beings learn to be healthily related, interdependent and independent adults. Whereas behaviorists value masculine ideals, like learning to be alone in childhood, naturalists are anti-masculinist. They value dependency in children and, through inter/dependency, children learning to be related to and in relationships with others.

Naturalists challenge materialism by arguing for connection to "people not things." Naturalists object to the behaviorist's independence-inducing tool, the "transitional object," a blanket or toy meant to help babies and children separate from their parents and be content on their own. It is fascinating that in a consumer society such as ours, the behaviorists and naturalists split over the questions of *things*. Behaviorists argue that things should be used as a psychological aid in raising healthy children. For behaviorists, like in mainstream society, property is, quite literally, a good thing. Naturalists argue that babies and children should be aided in attaching to their parents, particularly their mothers, and never to material objects. They believe that when children attach to transitional objects, it is a sign that the child's (natural) needs are not being met.

The second-wave radical feminist movement in the 1970s ruptured both the naturalists' and the behaviorists' perfect image of the middle-class family. They introduced a cultural moment in which child sexual abuse in the family—incest, the most frequent type of sexual abuse—was more widely acknowledged. Radical feminists argued that, to some extent, the sexist oppression of women and girls is enacted in the adult male touching of girls. Radical feminist thought linked power with touch, and in this they ruptured previous ways of thinking about touching children.

Yet, due in part to the either/or elements of their own thinking, radical feminists never developed a positive view of touch. And their argument unintentionally fed into a deep-rooted Anglo-American anti-sexuality, anti-touch ethos. However unintended, the social response to this argument has been sur-veillance over, and a wariness toward, adult–child touch. And insofar as some radical feminist thought had a one-sided focus on touch as problematic, these radical feminists ended up, in a funny way, (mis)used by the right wing.

Conservatives co-opted feminists' deeply critical social analysis of adult–child touch, the nuclear family, and power and used second-wave feminist exposure of child sexual abuse to argue against feminist goals. In the 1980s and 1990s, in the New Right's backlash, conservatives focused their attention on the family. They claimed that the so-called traditional family was being destroyed, and blamed that for many of the other social problems we faced. According to conservatives, there were good families and bad families, and the bad families were destroying our society. Social historian Hester Eisenstein writes, "The New Right ideology creates a stark polarization between Good versus Evil. On the side of the angels is the traditional nuclear family with the nurturing mother at home raising her 2.1 children to believe in the traditional values, and the hardworking breadwinner father out there in the difficult but rewarding world of the paid workforce, bringing home the bacon. On the side of Satan and the forces of evil are the lesbians, the homosexuals and the women in the paid workforce."[7] Anti-feminist conservative Phyllis Schlafly exemplified this thinking in her belief that "America is a two-class society, divided not between rich and poor but between those who hold decent family values and those who do not."[8] Akin to Schlafly, a similar "two-class society" exists for the child-rearing experts as well. There are the good mothers and the bad mothers. The good mothers parent in the manner prescribed by the experts; the bad mothers do not.

Nationally, the conservative backlash and terror of child sexual abuse has led to fearful vigilance for pedophiles, increased pressure on women to stay home with their children, and avoidance of the touching of children by adults outside the home. Indeed, there is an aura of danger associated with adults touching children in any way. In the late 1980s and 1990s, many child-care workers were told not to touch the children in their care. Teachers became increasingly careful not to touch their students for fear of being misunder-stood. For example, a high school teacher near Tacoma, Washington, reported to Oxenhandler, "Basically we've been taught that there's a little piece of a student's forearm that it's okay to touch, briefly, but nowhere else."[9] Oxen-handler writes, "My own thirteen-year-old daughter . . . happened to mention to me the other day, 'Did you know that P.D.A.'s aren't allowed at my school?' 'P.D.A.'s?' I asked. For a moment, I actually thought I might be reassured by her answer, as if she were being protected from something noxious—something like an S.T.D. (sexually transmitted disease), or P.I.D. (pelvic inflammatory disease). But then she explained: "Public Display of Affection."[10] Even those who work with very young children, children who may need touch in order to develop in a healthy way, have begun to avoid physical contact. Oxenhandler writes, "What of the small children who are spending the greater part of their most formative years in day-care centers where touch is so highly restricted that adults are not permitted to hold children on their laps or to hug them tightly in their arms? What effect does this have, day in and day out, on children who spend most of their waking hours apart from their families?"[11]

The movements to end child sexual abuse have resulted in efforts to end the touching of children in public places while doing very little to stop child sexual abuse from occurring in the home where, according to research, it seems to happen most. Day-care centers, schools, camps, and other places in the public sphere have become extremely restrictive about how their staffs may touch children. This, as the naturalists argue, might be a problem. Children probably need to be touched—and more than they will be if they spend most of their time in public places where touching is not allowed.

By way of conclusion, I wish to expand on two fundamental problems with dualistic ways of thinking about adult–child touch. One involves the political economy and other more concrete realities of women's and children's lives. Amid all the ruckus, in all the child-rearing and other advice, there is very little focus on the real issues women and children face—issues such as poverty, inequalities of gendered labor, and violence (for example, as discussed in chapter 5, violence where it actually seems to happen most: not at day care, but at home). I explore how dualistic thinking about touch distracts us from these issues. Two, binary ideologies of touch normalize. They shape women and children as mother- and child-subjects. And in this, they create intense anxiety in mothers. Women believe they must "produce" a particular kind of child. Yet no matter what they do, mothers can't win. They are blamed for too much touching; they are condemned for too little.

Dualisms and the Political Economy

We would benefit from comparing child-rearing advice to advertising. Advertising played a role in "civilizing the self." In part, advertising in the 1920s and 1930s was the response of big business to labor agitation for a more fair and equitable world. Advertising argued that the way to the "good life" was through consumption. Advertising encouraged workers to look to their own consumptive practices—buying this toothpaste versus that, this brand of clothing versus that—to solve their problems rather than fighting for an altered socioeconomic situation. Yet beyond simply consuming, advertising also pushed workers to define—and "civilize"—themselves and their "desires in terms of the good of capitalist production."[12] This way, workers would not only support big business through buying its mass-produced goods but would also "implicitly accept the foundations of modern industrial life."[13] Child-rearing advice functions like advertising. It urges us to focus on ourselves as the locus of solutions to most child-rearing problems. Thinking in terms of individual solutions is born from a larger tradition in American political thought that advocates individual answers to most problems, including social problems. If only the individual mother parents well, the children will grow up right, even though she may not have access to the resources necessary to feed and house her children or to protect them from violence. Instead of demanding a different social order, with subsidized child care, pay for women's domestic labor, and so on, the advice calls upon us to try a different child-rearing method, much like using a new toothpaste was offered as the individual solution to social dissatisfaction.

The *real* problems women and children face—poverty, overwork, lack of social or financial support, lack of child care, and violence—are outside the experts' focus. Nor are these the issues that the white middle class concentrates on. In the United States, we focus on beliefs about adult–child touch, beliefs that are bound up with larger sociocultural concerns with gender and sexuality, the body, and what it means to be human. We make touching—or not—the issue rather than tackling the real issues. And we hold women responsible for children's well-being without giving them the assistance they need for children to grow up healthy and well.

One central area where women need assistance is in child care. Women do the lion's share of child care in the United States and in most of the rest of the world. The child-rearing books that I examine reflect this reality. They almost all, explicitly, address *mothers*. Crittenden writes, "Despite the media's fondness for Mr. Mom, he remains an aberration. Of the 20.5 million American children under the age of five, only about 320,000 have fathers as their primary guardian—a minuscule 1.5 percent."[14] Women are the primary caretakers of children and they do most other domestic work as well.[15]

Maybe the gendered nature of child care shouldn't be a problem. But for all kinds of reasons, it *is*. As a culture, we consider *mothers* individually responsible for the well-being of their children. Rather than understanding children as the responsibility of society, we hold the individual women accountable. This is not a new phenomenon. In 1831, popular writer Lydia Maria Child argued that each mother must "take the entire care of her own child."[16] "Children whose mothers did not 'take the entire care of them,'" opined the author of an 1841 *Parents* magazine article, faced real danger; a mother "cannot be long relieved without hazard or exchanged without loss."[17] This is problematic, in part because women are working themselves to the bone. Child rearing and homemaking are hard work.[18] Even so, many women with children do not want, or cannot afford, to put paid work aside. "Almost 18 million, roughly half of all women with children under eighteen, do work full-time; that is, at least thirty-five hours a week."[19] Mothers who work outside the home toil longer than nearly anyone else in our economy. "On average, they are estimated to work more than eighty hours a week. Time-use surveys confirm that as women enter the workplace, they take on the equivalent of two full-time jobs, forcing them to cut back on everything in their lives but paid work and children."[20]

Besides being overworked and squeezed for time, contemporary American mothers have money problems. Single mothers, in particular, work extensive hours for little money, yet their whole family has to live on what little they bring in. There are many reasons why women in the United States today make less money than men. One is that women do "at least twice as much of the world's unpaid labor as men. This is the principal distinction between 'women's work' and 'men's work': men are paid for most of the work they do, and women aren't," Crittenden says. United Nations statistics show that in industrialized countries, "women spend roughly one-third of their total working time on paid work and two-thirds on work that is unpaid and unrecognized. For men, the proportions are reversed."[21]

The United States is one of the wealthiest nations in the world, yet we have almost no social assistance for mothers and children. And not only do we *not* offer assistance; women's work caring for children is uncounted and unpaid, even though female caring labor is at both the center of families and the heart of the national economy. Recent studies have shown "that the amount of work involved in unpaid child care is far greater than economists ever imagined. Indeed, it rivals in size the largest industries of the visible economy. By some estimates, even in the most industrialized countries, the total hours spent on unpaid household work—much of it associated with child-rearing—amount to at least half of the hours of paid work in the market. Up to 80 percent of this unpaid labor is contributed by women."[22] Because women work so many hours for free, they are significantly poorer than men. Indeed, women suffer from poverty much more than men, "even though they work longer hours than men in almost every country in the world."[23]

Because women with children spend so many hours doing unpaid work, they have less time to do paid work, and the paid work is more likely to be part time. Women with children often do not take—or aren't offered—positions that demand a child-free schedule, such as those with excessively long hours. These are the positions that tend to entail more responsibility, more power, and higher pay. Further, many women take time off from their careers to mother, which means a longer-term loss in pay, pensions, and other benefits.

Women with children suffer most from the wage gap. Childless women, whose work patterns are more likely to be similar to men, have a significantly smaller wage gap than mothers. Jane Waldfogel found that women who were thirty and had no children were making 90 percent of men's wages. In contrast, thirty-year-old women with children were making only 70 percent. Waldfogel found that all factors being equal, the more children a woman had, the lower her earnings.[24]

Women do most of our child care and pay for it in money, time, and endless anxiety. But instead of agitating, resisting, and demanding pay and recognition for their labor, many women spend a lot of time and energy worrying over child-rearing advice and methods. Child-rearing advice is a kind of mirage that disappears when we get close to it. It keeps us busy looking in the wrong direction. It keeps us focused on ourselves and our individual child-rearing situation and choices rather than on the social world within which we rear our children.[25]

Coontz offers an example of how, in the frantic middle-class focus on child-rearing advice, we lose track of the real issues. In the United States, a very large percentage of the population cannot afford health care. Even so, in the 1980s and 1990s, there was a movement to punish pregnant women who did not seek prenatal care. "A number of states . . . jailed women because authorities estimated that they would not otherwise seek prenatal care."[26] Herein lay a "catch-22 for many modern mothers, just as there was for those accused of child neglect one hundred years earlier. By the end of the 1980s, growing numbers of pregnant women could not *find* prenatal care. To punish women for not getting prenatal care when we do not recognize public responsibility for providing it is uncomfortably close to the turn-of-the-century practice of penalizing poor mothers for not giving their children the benefits of affluence."[27]

Dualisms and the Shaping of Heteronormative Parent-Subjects

Twentieth-century ideologies of adult–child touch have worked, in part, to socially construct heteronormative gender roles. Women learn to be women—

and we all learn to be heterosexual—through these ways of thinking. Ultimately, dualistic beliefs about gender and sexuality lie at the bottom of most of them. These are deeply problematic, partly because they leave no room for ambiguities, and life and parenting are full of ambiguities. Instead, they serve as moralizing, normative discourses about how people "ought" to live. Dualisms train women to be women in a certain way; as a consequence, women feel responsible for the child-rearing method and ideology they choose and often believe themselves to be completely responsible for the outcome, as if how their child "turns out" depends almost entirely upon them. One might call this a "productivist" view of children; the child does not develop; rather, the mother uses touch as a way to "produce" the child to fit a preset notion (for example, independent or community-oriented, and always heterosexual). Further, dualisms engender anxiety in women about their child-rearing choices because the questions become: "Am I doing the right thing in the right way to produce the right child?" "Am I as good a mother as I could be (and so also as good a women)?"

Because I myself have a small child, I have experienced the intense pressure women often feel. At the beginning of my son's life, I was less concerned with what I *should* do and more concerned with what I *could* do to get him to calm down, be quiet, and sleep. That moment passed quickly. Soon, I was as caught up with the "best" way to do things as were all the other new mothers I knew. In the mother–infant group I attended that was led by Arlene Eisenberg (whose work I discuss in chapter 3), I sought advice about the "best" way to do things. I also started a new mothers' group that met weekly in our homes. In the beginning, the women came from my birthing class. Over time, the group grew to include many women with babies the same age from around the neighborhood. More and more women who had babies born within a month of February 2000, when my son arrived, appeared seemingly out of nowhere. In what was supposed to be one of the biggest, coldest, loneliest cities in the world, women exchanged telephone numbers with me before they even knew my name.

Connections with other mothers was one of the best things about the social world I entered when I became a mother. Women offered each other friendship and support, a chance to talk, and time together to ease the sometimes crushing loneliness of caring for a baby. On the other hand, all of the adult parents I met in my two, and later three, new parents' groups *were* women. There was no rule banning men. I simply did not know any male parents who were the primary caretakers of their small children. Apparently, the other women in my groups didn't either.

Even now, I can name only one single male primary caretaker. My own male partner has done a large amount of our child care, but it is certainly not equal. Of course, this is anecdotal; unfortunately, it is also reflective of the larger society. And for this responsibility, women pay a price. Of course, the price entails money and time, but it also involves a kind of personal angst. Many mothers—and certainly those I focus on in my study, white middle-class mothers—*worry* endlessly about their children. A large part of that worry involves wondering if they are making the right child-rearing choices.

Most of these choices are set out in either/or terms. Women are told there are clear "right" and "wrong" ways to mother because the ideologies about "correct" parenting tend to frame themselves in dichotomies of right versus wrong. The two primary ideological child-rearing schools, the behaviorist and the naturalist, insist on opposing advice. One school argues that mothers should breastfeed but stop at one year; the other that mothers should breastfeed indefinitely, letting the child wean at her or his own pace, whenever she or he is ready. One says mothers should have their children in bed with them (or risk SIDS); the other that mothers should never bring the children into their bed (or risk SIDS). Within these oppositions, often women do not feel that they have a real choice or that there are a variety of "good" ways to mother. They feel obligated to buy into one or the other of the ideologies. Indeed, they feel judged no matter what they do.

The kind of adults a culture's children become is influenced by a variety of factors. A culture's belief about the "good life" and what it means to be human; whether the child is male or female, white or of color, rich or poor; and the child's individual experiences play an enormous role in determining who a child will one day be. This has little to do with any particular touching or child-rearing practice but rather with how the child experiences the world and what normative structures the world imposes on him or her, and what the child can or cannot do, based on his or her surroundings and resources.

This may seem boringly self-evident. Nonetheless, women in our society are told, and many believe, that the kind of adult their child becomes results from the child-rearing choices they make. A "good mother"—whatever that means—will have a "good child." Women become extremely anxious over whether or not to breastfeed, to use a crib, and so on, and their incredible anxiety is fed by the proliferation of child-rearing books with their conflicting advice.

I argue that child-rearing advice functions, in part, to nourish this "mother-worry." Both the worry and the advice act as distractions from the realities of women and children's lives. We don't have to keep raising our children the way we do today. It is certainly not "natural" to leave the total care of children to individual mothers. This contemporary reality is the outcome of a particular social order. Some people benefit from this order. Others, many of them women and children, do not. Meanwhile, we act as though if only we pick the right child-rearing method, our children will grow up right.

Dualistic ideologies of touch work to produce mothers: "good" mothers who do things "right" and, conversely, "bad" mothers who rear their children incorrectly, dangerously, incestuously, selfishly. Moreover, as they produce mother-subjects, in Foucault's terms, they engender anxiety or "mother-worry." One primary anxiety is that women believe that *they* need to produce particular kinds of children: individualistic and masculine children or relationship-oriented children; children without needs or "centered" and attached children—and either way, "normal" heterosexual children. In these ideologies, touching is an important means to create the "right" kind of child. On the one side, more touching leads to an attached and "healthy" child, one who is able to be in relationships. On the other side of the touch debates, less touching leads to an independent and "healthy" child who is able to meet his own needs on his own.

Oxenhandler offers us an alternative to both behaviorist and naturalist ideologies of touch. She argues against binary thinking and challenges us to think in terms of both/and rather than either/or.[28] Clearly, touching children holds the potential for being both life-giving *and* dangerous. We probably cannot afford to give up touching children, as we have in so many public locations where children live and grow and spend significant amounts of time, such as day cares, summer camps, and schools. Nor should we deny the violent potential inherent in touch; as radical feminists made us realize, it is still experienced too often in our most intimate institution, the family.

As an alternative to binary thinking, Oxenhandler proposes that we work at an ongoing process of "trial and error" to be attuned to our children, and to ourselves. "Trial and error: the attitude of attunement is the very opposite of dogmatic attitude. For the latter begins in certainty, with beliefs that it imposes like a grid on what it encounters," she says. Oxenhandler argues that between parent and child (or, we might add, between all adults and children; indeed, between all persons), "there is no such single, preordained point of departure, but rather, an ever-changing series of states—hunger, repose, restlessness, excitement, delight—through which the two continually adjust to one another."[29] Thus we neither give up touching nor deny the need to be alert to its harmful potential.

Oxenhandler moves away from dualistic "right" versus "wrong" frameworks for touching. For her, there is no "preordained point of departure" for touching, be it touching as much as possible (through, for example, child-led weaning and sharing sleep), avoiding touch (through never having the child in the parental bed and weaning early), or any other such touch dictate. In one sense, naturalist thinkers might claim that they practice attunement; they are attuned to the "natural" child and their own "instincts." Yet ultimately, for naturalists, the rules are not about attuning, but touching. Naturalists believe they know already (before any particular moment where one might attempt to be attuned) that the natural thing to do is touch, and touch a lot. Oxenhandler's attunement framework seems to reduce both this type of dogmatism and anxiety about touching children. Her attunement framework also challenges the idea of the "production" of children because attunement is not goal oriented, at least not in the sense of what one's child will become in the future. Attunement is about a shared experience between parent and child in the present moment.

Nonetheless, albeit a move away from the dogmatism of dualisms, Oxenhandler does not fully replace the dualistic "right" versus "wrong" framework for touching. With Oxenhandler's attunement, parents now might replace a previous dictate for "right" touching with anxiety about "attuned" touching. One might constantly worry about being "attuned enough" in all one's touching interactions. It is still a kind of dictate; in other words, "attunement," the idea of striving to be "attuned," is also normative. Parents are "right" when attuned, and otherwise "wrong." One might wonder: Am I attuned with my child in this moment, or am I merely projecting attunement because this is physical contact that I want or do not want (contact—or lack thereof—that might actually be damaging to my child)? How do I *know* if I am attuned? What if I am never sure, or simply do not experience attunement?[30]

In his later thought, Foucault presents a way to move beyond both dualistic thinking and Oxenhandler's attunement. In his essay, "On Enlightenment," Foucault challenges us to treat

the instances of discourse that articulate what we think, say, and do as so many historical events. And . . . not deduce from the form of what we are what it is impossible for us to do and to know; but . . . separate out, from the contingency that has made us what we are, the possibility of no longer being, doing, or thinking what we are, do, or think. It is not seeking to make possible a metaphysics that has finally become a science; it is seeking to give new impetus, as far and wide as possible, to the undefined work of freedom.[31]

In this Foucauldian definition of "enlightenment," Foucault challenges its traditional formulation understood as bringing light, "truth," or seeing things "as they are." Indeed, Foucault rejects enlightenment as providing any final truth, any perfect and clear vision. In this, Foucault rejects dualistic ideologies of touch as they posit their own enlightenment. For example, Sears argues that he offers the "truth" of naturalist parenting. Via this Truth, Sears believes that optimal parenting is achieved, and the child is produced completely whole and with the correct social orientation. Simultaneously, Ferber and the behaviorists view science as the ultimate tool of enlightenment. Like Sears, albeit a different method of touching, they claim that their version of enlightenment informs a finished parenting and an individualized and happy child.

Does Foucault's above definition of enlightenment imply an alternative way of thinking about the boundaries of adult–child touch? What he suggests, I believe, is that our thinking about touching is never finished. It is never not a problem; it is always dangerous. For Foucault, "the undefined work of freedom" would mean, in this case, being aware of how both our desire for touch and our fear of it are historically generated, ridden with politics, ridden with power, and must to be subject, always, to our own criticism.

We want to be free of ambiguities and to touch our children "correctly," without danger. And this is not possible. Touch is indeed dangerous, as much as it is deeply necessary and potentially life-giving. The freedom Foucault suggests is a freedom from the illusion of certainty, and therefore, freedom from the anxiety that the frantic search for certainty produces. If a mother fears the impact of extended breastfeeding on her child, but thinks she "should" breastfeed later than most of her contemporary culture, I challenge both the belief in a clear "should," a perfect solution, *and* the anxiety surrounding that belief. Thus, we experience the danger and joy of touch simultaneously. There is no way around ambiguity. We have the feelings we have; I suggest that we struggle, not to stop feeling both danger and joy, but to limit the impact of anxiety or of any self-satisfied belief in a final truth by understanding our ideas as born from a historical, power-laden context.

Epilogue

As I said earlier, I am a mother, a white middle-class mother. Having the cool, detached eye of a researcher has helped me only marginally, if at all, to stay calm and clear-headed when it comes to child-rearing advice. I worry, and I worry over each alternative. Every decision about feeding or sleep seems to carry the weight of my son's future happiness and well-being. And no matter which way I go, I always wonder, anxiously, if it was the "right" choice.

As a graduate student whose partner worked full-time hours for part-time pay adjuncting, we were very squeezed financially when my son was born. Nonetheless, I wanted to stay home for the first year or so with my son. We together were living on $20,000 per year in New York City, which is not much, I assure you, but is still a lot by many, many people's standards. For help, I decided to look into social services. We were three people—one adult was teaching four classes a semester at a local university and the other adult was staying home to take care of the third (tiny) person. At our income level, there was only one service available to us and for which we qualified: Women, Infants, Children (WIC). After going through numerous forms and bringing them duplicates of everything down to my great-grandmother's cat's birth certificate, they finally gave me my official WIC card.

The only step left was the training. Training? Yes, I had to sign up for a breastfeeding training to begin to get my checks. As I said in chapter 3, there is a cultural imperative to breastfeed right now; furthermore, for WIC it makes financial sense. When women breastfeed, WIC does not supply them with formula and thus saves a great deal of money. A very young woman, who had probably never held a baby much less breastfed one, led the training. To begin, she passed out a plethora of pamphlets and informational sheets covered with images of white women sporting wedding rings and breastfeeding babies. The pamphlets were about how to breastfeed, why to breastfeed, the benefits of breastfeeding, and, after all that encouragement, how we should be sure to stop breastfeeding at one year. Next, the trainer made our group of six pregnant women spilling out of our metal folding chairs—four African American women, one Latina with her mother, and myself—watch a short video on happy smiling white women with their happy white babies, breast-feeding. Then she went around the circle and made us say whether we were going to breastfeed. Everyone said no except for me. I felt like I was letting the other women down, buckling to the WIC program's pressure. But the truth was that I *was* going to breastfeed, or at any rate, try. Next, each of us had to practice holding and "breastfeeding" a life-size white baby doll. It was a bit humiliating, but at least we did not have to take our shirts off. At the end of all this, we received our WIC stamp of approval—checks.

The checks meant I would be given food assistance in the form of very particular food options. As the saying goes, beggars can't be choosers. Well, at WIC, they take that saying quite literally. The food "options" were not necessarily nutritious, just particular. I could get so many of a certain brand of eggs (white only), so many ounces of two different kinds of bright orange American cheese, lots and lots of cow's milk (it had to be full-fat, and there was too much for anyone except maybe bovine babies), and cereal (only a certain brand, and within that brand, only the ones that were 99.9 percent sugar).

As you know, I did breastfeed my son. And I breastfed, and I breastfed. And here I am, still breastfeeding. My son is four years old, and even now, very attached to breastfeeding. Having read most available child-rearing literature for my study, I was angered at the bigotry of all of it, and even so, I was swayed by the attachment-parenting movement. I decided to do child-led weaning. I must admit, it sometimes seems as if my son is never going to stop breastfeeding. But then, I look back and see that he is nursing much less than six months ago, and even less than six months before that. Anyhow, this is probably not what the WIC trainer had in mind.

As you might imagine, my partner and I "share sleep" with our son as well. Indeed, one day, at eighteen months, my son came across his hardly used crib, which was serving time as a dresser drawer/bookshelf, and asked, "What's dat!?" Maybe he would have been this way anyway, but in the case of my son, what the attachment parents claim has come to fruition. He is very smart and very calm. And he is probably the most cheerful, friendly person I have ever met. If I were still on WIC, I wonder if the WIC people would approve.

Notes

Preface

1. "Teacher's Pet," *Buffy the Vampire Slayer,* 1996.
2. Erving Goffman, *Frame Analysis,* 1–2.

Chapter 1: To Touch or Not to Touch

1. Foucault, *Discipline and Punish,* 304.
2. Foucault, *Power/Knowledge,* 98.
3. Foucault, *Discipline and Punish,* 27.
4. Foucault, *Power/Knowledge,* 93.
5. For a rich and detailed discussion of the second shift, please see Hochschild, *Second Shift.*
6. Foucault, "On the Genealogy of Ethics," in Rabinow, *Michel Foucault,* 256.
7. This was reflected in a personal e-mail conversation I had with health communications researcher Andrew Maxfield, who then worked with Peter Hart Research (June 5, 2005). Maxfield, who took part in conducting forty focus groups in California with diverse cohorts of people that included questions about touch, said that the very term "touching" held negative connotations for many White and African American participants. In contrast, Maxfield said that both Koreans and Latinos in the study were more "open toward touching" their children, and many had "established behaviors [such as] stretching and massaging the child [that they associated] . . . with healthy parenting." Maxfield claimed that the difference between the groups who were more comfortable and those who were less comfortable with touching seemed to reflect acculturation into the contemporary mainstream culture. The Koreans and Latinos in the study who were more comfortable with at least discussing touching their children were more recent immigrants and had more insular cultures.
8. Oxenhandler, *Eros of Parenthood,* 266.
9. Freund, McGuire, and Podhurst, *Health, Illness, and the Social Body,* 6.
10. Ibid., 218.
11. Ibid.
12. "Study Links I.Q. and Breast-Feeding," *New York Times,* A27.
13. Coburn, "Formula for Profit," 61.
14. Lorber, "Believing Is Seeing," 569.
15. Rich, "Compulsory Heterosexuality," in Snitow et al., *Powers of Desire,* 191.
16. The use of personal or autobiographical data is increasingly common in

sociological writing. As feminist and other scholars have argued, such writing offers alternative methods of knowing to traditional scholarly writing practices where the researcher attempts, and inevitably fails, to stay outside the frame of the study. My book concerns dualistic ideology; my own experiences offer a lived story of that ideology. For further examples of autoethnographic scholarship, see Cho, "Regression Analysis"; Halley, "Cleaning Lady"; and Vidal-Ortiz, "On Being a White Person of Color." For a fascinating critique of traditional ethnography, see Clough, *End(s) of Ethnography*.

17. Stearns, "Breastfeeding and the Good Maternal Body."

18. National Center on Child Abuse and Neglect, *Child Maltreatment 1994*; Haugaard and Reppucci, *Sexual Abuse of Children*.

19. Bordo, *Unbearable Weight*, 149.

20. Ibid., 140.

21. Ibid., 140–41.

22. Ibid., 5.

23. Lorber, "Believing Is Seeing," 569.

24. Warner, *Fear of a Queer Planet*, xxi.

25. Ibid., xiii.

26. For additional research on heteronormativity, see Sedgwick, "How to Bring Your Kids Up Gay," in Warner, *Fear of a Queer Planet;* and Rich, "Compulsory Heterosexuality," in Snitow et al., *Powers of Desire*.

27. Bordo, *Unbearable Weight*, 6.

28. See Becky W. Thompson's research involving in-depth interviews with women who have eating problems; Thompson, *Hunger So Wide*.

29. Ehrenreich and English, *For Her Own Good*.

30. Watson, *Psychological Care of Infant and Child*, 12–13.

31. Ibid., 12 (emphasis original).

32. Ibid., 87.

33. Ibid., 6.

34. Mosse, *Image of Man*.

35. Stearns, "Breastfeeding and the Good Maternal Body," 318.

36. Blum, *At the Breast*, 96.

37. Finkelhor, *Child Sexual Abuse*.

38. Oxenhandler, *Eros of Parenthood*, 266.

39. Hulbert, *Raising America*, ix.

40. Ibid., x.

41. Bobel, *Paradox of Natural Mothering*, 1.

42. Ibid., 164.

43. Ibid., 1.

44. Blum, *At the Breast*, 2.

45. Hausman, *Mother's Milk*, 16.

46. Blum, *At the Breast*, 11.

47. For an interesting exploration of some of these issues, see Blum, *At the Breast*. For example, Blum notes that "most public health efforts to promote breastfeeding, even the most well-meaning, have ignored the meanings of not breastfeeding for African-American working-class mothers" (193). She writes, "African-Ameri-

can mothers . . . face a particular legacy of embodied exploitation, in which their sexuality and reproduction were appropriated by white men or demonized as dangerous and out of control. Although some Black women were caregivers for white children, and were then seen as 'naturally' maternal, their own children were neglected, even sent or sold away. Breastfeeding, in which the Black baby was denied its mother's milk as she nursed the white infant, is a particularly charged symbol, at once metaphoric and literal, of these historic relations" (147–48).

48. Alford, *Craft of Inquiry*.

49. I do not examine the practice of spanking children, as none of the popular child-rearing experts I study advocate spanking. This makes sense given the ideologies of science, rationality, and control within which the experts write. Spanking may still be popular, but it is no longer a given in mainstream child-rearing ideology. Like other physical, pain-producing, "cruel and unusual" punishments, the legitimacy of spanking diminished with the advent of the Enlightenment. People may still spank their children; however, in the U.S. white middle class, spanking is not considered a "civilized" child-rearing technique. Indeed, because of this anti-spanking ethos, a turn-of-the-century Italian immigrant to the United States claimed, "I came to learn that I have almost no power over my own children. . . . Oh, how often I know too well, that a good spanking can cure the bad habits of my children. Yet I must think twice before I do this. Here in America I may be taken to court for having administered punishment on my own son" (quoted in Grant, *Raising Baby by the Book*, 73).

50. Between 1900 and 1940, only a handful of social scientists, such as Holt and Watson, wrote about adult-child touch. But after Spock wrote his famous child-rearing book in the 1940s, more and more people became child-rearing "specialists." During the 1960s and 1970s, child-rearing literature joined the glut of self-help books.

51. In *Harmful to Minors: The Perils of Protecting Children from Sex,* Levine shows the degree to which the threat of child sexual abuse by strangers has been overstated and that the danger of child sexual abuse by family members has been dramatically understated. She includes a very useful discussion of the day-care sexual abuse panic. Levine places her argument in the context of a more general defense of the sexuality of children and criticism of a contemporary and widespread anti-sexuality, or de-sexed, view of childhood. Although the specifics of her argument go beyond the scope of this study, her work is an extremely valuable contribution to a critique of dualisms in contemporary life.

52. Margolis, *True to Her Nature*.

53. Ibid., 6.

54. Grant, *Raising Baby by the Book*, 72.

55. See Margolis, *True to Her Nature*; Grant, *Raising Baby by the Book*; and Degler, *At Odds*.

56. Coontz, *Way We Never Were*, 6.

57. Sernau, *Worlds Apart*, 92.

58. Skolnick, *Embattled Paradise*, xix–xx.

59. Ibid., xx.

60. Ibid.

Chapter 2: The Rise of the Expert, the Fall of the Mother

1. Margolis, *True to Her Nature*; Blum, *At the Breast*; Grant, *Raising Baby by the Book*; and Ehrenreich and English, *For Her Own Good*.
2. Bordo, *Unbearable Weight*, 5.
3. Margolis, *True to Her Nature*; Blum, *At the Breast*; Grant, *Raising Baby by the Book*; and Ehrenreich and English, *For Her Own Good*.
4. Lynd and Lynd, *Middletown*, 131.
5. Crittenden, *Price of Motherhood*, 47.
6. Ibid., 48.
7. As quoted in ibid., 49.
8. Ibid.
9. Ibid., 51.
10. Ibid.
11. Ewen, *Captains of Consciousness*.
12. Crittenden, *Price of Motherhood*, 51.
13. Freund, McGuire, and Podhurst, *Health, Illness, and the Social Body*, 214.
14. Ibid.
15. Ibid., 218.
16. For historical arguments related to this claim, see Ewen, *Captains of Consciousness*; Blum, *At the Breast*; and Grant, *Raising Baby by the Book*.
17. Skolnick, *Embattled Paradise*.
18. Ibid.
19. As quoted in ibid., 11.
20. See Coontz, *Way We Never Were*, and Skolnick, *Embattled Paradise*.
21. Skolnick, *Embattled Paradise*, 12.
22. Quoted in Ehrenreich and English, *For Her Own Good*, 200.
23. Holt, *Care and Feeding of Children*.
24. Lynd and Lynd, *Middletown*, 149.
25. Ibid., 151.
26. Ibid.
27. Ehrenreich and English, *For Her Own Good*, 112.
28. Ibid.
29. Ibid., 76.
30. Mosse, *Image of Man*.
31. Ehrenreich and English, *For Her Own Good*, 77.
32. Ibid.
33. Mosse, *Image of Man*.
34. Ehrenreich and English, *For Her Own Good*, 157.
35. As quoted in Ibid., 157–58.
36. Ibid., 170.
37. Ibid.
38. Holt, *Care and Feeding of Children*, 91.
39. Ibid.
40. Ibid., 84.
41. Ibid.

42. Ibid., 88.
43. Ibid., 89.
44. Ibid.
45. Ibid., 82.
46. Ibid., 83.
47. Ibid.
48. Ibid., 103.
49. Watson, *Psychological Care of Infant and Child,* 3.
50. Ibid., 1.
51. Ibid., 11.
52. Ibid., 81–82.
53. Ibid., 71.
54. Ibid., 75.
55. Ibid., 38.
56. Ibid., 87.
57. Ibid., 43–44.
58. Mosse, *Image of Man,* 9.
59. Ibid.
60. Ibid.
61. Ibid., 3.
62. Ibid., 4.
63. Watson, *Psychological Care of Infant and Child,* 5–6.
64. Ibid., 6–7.
65. Ibid., 121.
66. Ibid.
67. Ibid., 121–22 (emphasis original).
68. McCarthy, *The Group,* 238.
69. Ibid., 241–42 (emphasis original).
70. Ibid., 248–49.
71. Ibid., 248.
72. Watson, *Psychological Care of Infant and Child,* 7–8.
73. Horwitz, "Always with Us," 317.
74. Kealey, "Black Student's Primer," 114.
75. Grant, *Raising Baby by the Book,* 56.
76. As quoted in ibid.
77. Ibid., 117.
78. Watson, *Psychological Care of Infant and Child.*
79. Ehrenreich and English, *For Her Own Good,* 214.
80. As quoted in Maier, *Dr. Spock,* 91.
81. Ibid., 153.
82. Spock and Parker, *Dr. Spock's Baby and Child Care.*
83. Maier, *Dr. Spock.*
84. Ibid., 153.
85. Ibid., 171.
86. Spock, *Common Sense Book of Baby and Child Care,* 19–20 (my emphasis).
87. Ibid., 103–4.

88. Maier, *Dr. Spock*.
89. Ibid., 141.
90. Spock, *Common Sense Book of Baby and Child Care*, 33.
91. Ibid.
92. Margolis, *True to Her Nature*; Blum, *At the Breast*.
93. Spock, *Common Sense Book of Baby and Child Care*, 34.
94. Ehrenreich and English, *For Her Own Good*, 261–62.
95. As quoted in Gibbs, "Who's in Charge Here?" 45.
96. Margolis, *True to Her Nature*, 44.
97. Spock, *Common Sense Book of Baby and Child Care*, 61.
98. Ibid., 41.
99. Ibid., 3 (my emphasis).
100. Ibid., 90–91.
101. Ibid., 17.
102. Ibid., 484.
103. Weiss, "Mother, the Invention of Necessity, 56."
104. Maier, *Dr. Spock*, 359.
105. Skolnick, *Embattled Paradise*, 41.
106. Ibid.
107. Ibid.
108. Kinsey et al., *Sexual Behavior in the Human Female*, 121.
109. As quoted in Jones, *Alfred C. Kinsey*, 326.
110. Ibid., 261.
111. Kinsey et al., *Sexual Behavior in the Human Male*, 167.
112. Herman, *Father–Daughter Incest*.
113. Kinsey et al., *Sexual Behavior in the Human Female*, 117, 119, 120, respectively.
114. Ibid., 116.
115. Ibid., 117.
116. Ibid., 121.
117. Herman, *Father–Daughter Incest*, 16.
118. Jones, *Alfred C. Kinsey*.
119. Ibid., 507.
120. Ibid.
121. Ibid.
122. Ibid.
123. Kinsey et al., *Sexual Behavior in the Human Male*, 160.
124. Ibid., 167.
125. Jones, *Alfred C. Kinsey*.
126. Kinsey et al., *Sexual Behavior in the Human Male*, 185.
127. Jones, *Alfred C. Kinsey*.
128. Kinsey et al., *Sexual Behavior in the Human Male*, 161.
129. Ibid.
130. Harlow, "Nature of Love," 673.
131. Blum, *Love at Goon Park*, 216.
132. Ibid., 217.

133. Luria et al., *Human Sexuality,* 351.
134. Harlow, "Nature of Love," 678.
135. Ibid., 679.
136. Ibid., 679–80.
137. Ibid., 677.
138. Blum, *Love at Goon Park,* 140.
139. Ibid.
140. Harlow, "Nature of Love," 678.
141. Ibid., 677.
142. Ibid., 685.
143. Ibid.
144. Ibid.
145. For a clarifying overview of the various elements of the twentieth-century U.S. feminist movements, see Lengermann and Neibrugge-Brantley, "Contemporary Feminist Theory," in Ritzer, *Sociological Theory.*
146. Ibid.

Chapter 3: Breasts versus Bottles and the Sexual Mother

1. Holt, *Care and Feeding of Children,* 27–66.
2. Watson, *Psychological Care of Infant and Child,* 108.
3. Blum, *At the Breast.*
4. Grant, *Raising Baby by the Book.*
5. Blum, *At the Breast,* 21.
6. Ibid., 20.
7. Ibid., 21–22.
8. Ibid., 22–23.
9. Grant, *Raising Baby by the Book,* 72.
10. Ibid., 46 (emphasis original).
11. Blum, *At the Breast,* 23.
12. Ibid.
13. Ibid., 24.
14. Ibid.
15. Ibid., 24–26.
16. Ibid., 26.
17. Ibid.
18. Ibid.
19. As quoted in ibid., 27.
20. Freund, McGuire, and Podhurst, *Health, Illness, and the Social Body,* 218.
21. Blum, *At the Breast,* 27.
22. Ibid.
23. Ibid., 28.
24. For further information and analysis of differences in rates of breastfeeding, see the American Academy of Pediatrics, "Breastfeeding and the Use of Human Milk"; Hausman, *Mother's Milk*; Bobel, *Paradox of Natural Mothering*; and Blum, *At the Breast.*

25. Blum, *At the Breast,* 31.

26. Ewen, *Immigrant Women in the Land of Dollars,* 138.

27. Ibid.

28. Blum, *At the Breast,* 30.

29. Ibid.

30. Ibid.

31. As quoted in ibid., 29.

32. As quoted in ibid., 32.

33. Granju, *Attachment Parenting,* 109.

34. Ibid., 108.

35. Ibid.

36. Ibid (emphasis original).

37. Ibid.

38. Blum, *At the Breast,* 31.

39. Pantell, Fries, and Vickery, *Taking Care of Your Child,* 14.

40. Ibid.

41. In my interviews and in the interviews done by Stearns in her article "Breast-feeding and the Good Maternal Body," women repeatedly discussed their struggles with breastfeeding in public (or not) and the extensive social pressure they experienced not to breastfeed outside their home or even at home in the presence of others.

42. Blum, *At the Breast,* 19.

43. Blum, *At the Breast*; Carter, *Feminism, Breasts and Breast-Feeding*; Department of Health and Human Services, "Breastfeeding."

44. American Academy of Pediatrics, "Breastfeeding and the Use of Human Milk."

45. Blum, *At the Breast,* 28.

46. Ibid., 13.

47. Ibid., 14.

48. Ibid.

49. Ibid.

50. American Academy of Pediatrics, "Breastfeeding and the Use of Human Milk."

51. Blum, *At the Breast.*

52. American Academy of Pediatrics, "Breastfeeding and the Use of Human Milk," 496.

53. Ibid., 499.

54. Ibid., 496–97.

55. Ibid.

56. American Academy of Pediatrics, "Breastfeeding and the Use of Human Milk (RE9729)," 1035.

57. Ibid.

58. Ibid.

59. American Academy of Pediatrics, "Breastfeeding and the Use of Human Milk," 497.

60. Pantell, Fries, and Vickery, *Taking Care of Your Child,* 14 (emphasis original).

61. Granju, *Attachment Parenting*, 142.

62. La Leche League International, *Womanly Art of Breastfeeding*, 7th ed., 393.

63. Ibid., 201.

64. Giles, *Fresh Milk*, 185–86.

65. Ibid., 190.

66. Ibid., 190–91.

67. Shanley, "Milkmen."

68. Ibid.

69. Bowlby, *Maternal Care and Mental Health*, 71.

70. Ibid., 72–73.

71. Ibid., 25.

72. Blum, *At the Breast*, 33.

73. Bowlby, *Maternal Care and Mental Health*, 86.

74. Ibid., 87.

75. La Leche League International, *Womanly Art of Breastfeeding*, 35th anniversary ed.; La Leche League International, *Womanly Art of Breastfeeding*, 7th ed.

76. La Leche League International, *Womanly Art of Breastfeeding*, 7th ed., 391–92.

77. Ibid., v.

78. Blum, *At the Breast*, 65.

79. Ibid.

80. Bengson, *How Weaning Happens*, 3.

81. Ibid., 9–11.

82. Ibid., 12.

83. Ibid., 47.

84. Lewin, "Breast-Feeding: How Old Is Too Old?" 5.

85. Blum, *At the Breast*, 128.

86. Stearns, "Breastfeeding and the Good Maternal Body."

87. Associated Press, "Woman Kicked Off Plane."

88. Ibid.

89. Ibid.

90. Hart, "And Now, Breast-Feeding Rights?"

91. Bengson, *How Weaning Happens*, 61.

92. American Academy of Pediatrics, "Breastfeeding and the Use of Human Milk."

93. IRIN HIV/AIDS News Report, "Breastfeeding Ups Death Risk in HIV Mothers."

94. Ibid.

95. Bengson, *How Weaning Happens*, 38.

96. Ibid., 40.

97. Stearns, "Breastfeeding and the Good Maternal Body."

98. Lewin, "Breast-Feeding: How Old Is Too Old?" 5.

99. American Academy of Pediatrics, "Breastfeeding and the Use of Human Milk."

100. As quoted in Epstein, "Questioning the 'Deadline' for Weaning," F8.

101. La Leche League International, *Womanly Art of Breastfeeding*, 3rd ed., 55.

102. La Leche League International, *Womanly Art of Breastfeeding,* 7th ed., 167–68.

103. La Leche League International, *Womanly Art of Breastfeeding,* 3rd ed., 55.

104. La Leche League International, *Womanly Art of Breastfeeding,* 7th ed., 170.

105. As quoted in ibid.

106. La Leche League International, *Womanly Art of Breastfeeding,* 3rd ed., 271.

107. Eisenberg, Murkoff, and Hathaway, *What to Expect,* 31.

108. Ibid.

109. Ibid.

110. Ibid.

111. Ibid., 32.

112. Ibid.

113. As quoted in Lewin, "Breast-Feeding: How Old Is Too Old?" 5.

114. Stearns, "Breastfeeding and the Good Maternal Body," 321.

115. Eisenberg, Murkoff, and Hathaway, *What to Expect,* 32.

116. Traina, "Maternal Experience," 1–2.

117. Mader, *Human Reproductive Biology,* 74.

118. Ibid., 77.

119. Lewin, "Breast-Feeding: How Old Is Too Old?" 5.

120. Corbett, "Breast Offense," 84.

121. Ibid., 85.

122. McKinney, "Mom Targeted by DCFS."

123. Ibid.

124. Ibid.

125. Ibid.

Chapter 4: Babies in Bed

1. Indeed, the debate has not slowed since 1999. In 2005, the American Academy of Pediatrics explicitly advocated "a ban on babies sleeping with their parents. . . . [A]n expert committee convened by the academy concluded that the new recommendations [for babies to sleep in their own beds] are necessary to save more infants from crib death, known formally as sudden infant death syndrome (SIDS)"; Stein, "To Cut Crib Deaths," A01. The American Academy of Pediatrics also recommended for the first time that babies be put to sleep using a pacifier. Of course, the naturalists protested. They argued, "The evidence that pacifiers are helpful and bed sharing is dangerous is far from conclusive." The naturalists claimed, "The recommendations will hinder breast-feeding and mother–child bonding, which are clearly beneficial"; Stein, "To Cut Crib Deaths," A01.

2. Goode, "Baby in Parents' Bed," A22.

3. Leach, "Beware the Parenting Police," A25.

4. Seabrook, "Annals of Parenthood," 57.

5. For example, in New York City, an informational service called the New Mommies' Network sponsored a talk on "The Sleep Debate: Ferber vs. Sears (and Is There an In-Between?)—Tough Love vs. Attachment Parenting" (presentation done by Lois Nachamie, author of *Big Lessons for Little People,* in 2000). Ferber is a practic-

ing pediatrician and he teaches at Harvard Medical School. When one searches Google for the name "Richard Ferber," 49,600 hits or sites (December 13, 2006) are retrieved that explore various aspects of Ferber's thinking on children and sleep.

Sears is a no less important popular thinker. He is probably the central contemporary expert spokesperson for La Leche League International as well as for the larger grassroots attachment-parenting movement. On December 13, 2006, a Google search of the name "William Sears" gets 395,000 hits. Sears probably has many more sites than Ferber because his advice spans most aspects of child rearing—including feeding, discipline, and general care—not just sleep. Amazon .com currently has 395 different child-rearing books for sale that were authored or coauthored by Sears (Amazon.com, December 13, 2006), although this includes reissues of some books.

6. For examples of liberal feminist arguments, see Bernard, *Future of Marriage;* and Epstein, *Deceptive Distinctions.*

7. For examples of this left feminist critique of liberal feminism, see Bologh, *Love or Greatness;* and Bordo, *Unbearable Weight.*

8. Sleep-sharing advocates like Sears often use this point—that historically in many parts of the world, infants and children seem to have always slept with their parents, and that they still do so today—to make their case that sharing sleep is "normal" for human beings. For example, in her book, well-known within the attachment-parenting movement, *The Continuum Concept: Allowing Human Nature to Work Successfully,* Jean Liedloff argues, "At this moment in history, with our customs as they are, sleeping with one's baby seems a wildly radical thing to advocate. . . . But in light of the continuum and its millions of years, it is only our tiny history which appears radical in its departures from the long-established norms of human and prehuman experience"; Liedloff, *Continuum Concept,* 157.

9. National Institute of Health, "Study Finds Bed Sharing."

10. Ibid.

11. Ibid.

12. Ibid.

13. Ibid.

14. Ferber, *Solve Your Child's Sleep Problems,* 253.

15. Ibid., 38.

16. Ibid., 39.

17. Ibid., 38–39.

18. For research and arguments related to this point, see Bobel, *Paradox of Natural Mothering;* Bordo, *Unbearable Weight;* and Oxenhandler, *Eros of Parenthood.*

19. Blum, *At the Breast.*

20. Bologh, *Love or Greatness,* 5.

21. For a fascinating history of modern Western masculinity, see Mosse, *Image of Man.*

22. Ferber, *Solve Your Child's Sleep Problems,* 37.

23. Ibid., 40.

24. Ibid., 41.

25. Sammons, *Self-Calmed Baby,* 167.

26. Ibid., 233.

27. Ibid., 185.

28. Weissbluth, *Healthy Sleep Habits,* 123.

29. Ibid., 202.

30. Originally, the La Leche League published most of Sears's numerous child-rearing books. As Sears developed in popularity, he began to use bigger, for-profit publishers.

31. Bowlby, "Maternal Care and Mental Health."

32. Sears, *Nighttime Parenting,* 1.

33. Ibid., 2.

34. Nonetheless, heterosexuality is assumed in Sears's work. Parents may be women, but they are always married to men.

35. Sears, *Nighttime Parenting,* 2.

36. Ibid.

37. Ibid., 6.

38. Ibid., 6–7.

39. Ibid., 7–8.

40. Ibid., xvii.

41. Ibid., xix.

42. Ibid., 31.

43. Ibid., 33–35 (my emphasis).

44. Ibid., 27.

45. Ibid., 79.

46. Goode, "Baby in Parents' Bed," A1.

47. Brown, "Safe Slumber," 36.

48. Goode, "Baby in Parents' Bed," A22.

49. Sears, *Nighttime Parenting,* 161.

50. Ibid., 156.

51. Ibid., 157 (my emphasis).

52. Ibid.

53. Ibid., 159.

54. Ibid., 162.

55. Ibid., 163.

56. Ibid., 161.

57. Margolis, *True to Her Nature,* 148.

58. Ibid., 149.

59. Sears, *Nighttime Parenting,* 10.

60. Bengson, *How Weaning Happens,* 75.

61. Sears, *Nighttime Parenting,* 38.

62. Ibid., 29–30.

63. For further discussion and research on socioeconomic class and mothering, particularly in terms of breastfeeding, see Blum, *At the Breast.*

64. Chancer, "Benefiting from Pragmatic Vision."

65. Sears, *Nighttime Parenting,* xvii–xix (emphasis original).

66. Ibid., xix.

67. About the title of Katie Allison Granju's *Attachment Parenting: Instinctive Care for Your Baby and Young Child* (1999), Jacob Segal commented that it was very funny

that "instincts" require a guidebook. He imagined a similar fictitious book entitled *Keep Breathing: A Self-Help Guide to the Preservation Instinct.*

68. Granju, *Attachment Parenting,* 196.

69. Jackson, *Three in a Bed,* 182.

70. Ibid., 186–87.

71. Ibid., 196.

72. Ibid., 193.

73. See chapter 6 for a more detailed discussion as to what it might mean for mothers to make "their own" decisions.

74. Ferber, *Solve Your Child's Sleep Problems,* 39.

Chapter 5: Violent Touch

1. For examples of research addressing sexual abuse and its more common occurrence in the home, see the U.S. Department of Health and Human Services Administration for Children and Families, "Victims"; Blome, "The Socially Constructed Perpetrator"; Herzberger, *Violence within the Family,* 18; National Center on Child Abuse and Neglect, *Child Maltreatment*; Haugaard and Reppucci, *Sexual Abuse of Children,* 47–49; Herman, *Father–Daughter Incest*; and Brownmiller, *Against Our Will.*

2. Please see Angelides, "Feminism, Child Sexual Abuse," for his examination of the feminist response to child sexual abuse. Angelides argues, "Feminists worked hard to reverse the tendency to blame the victims of child sexual molestation, and they did it by reinterpreting child sexual abuse 'in terms of male power' and child powerlessness. This move was an extension of radical feminist analyses of rape, which had been redefined not as a sexual act but as an act of violence and an assertion of power" (147).

3. Gordon argues, "The 'discovery' of child sexual abuse in the last decade has been only a rediscovery of a problem well known to social workers in the nineteenth century and the Progressive era"; *Heroes of Their Own Lives,* 7. For further exploration of the histories of child sexual abuse in the United States, also see Robertson, *Crimes against Children.* For a very interesting examination of understandings of child sexual abuse in England and Wales between 1910 and 1960, see Smart, "History of Ambivalence."

4. For more information on United States second-wave feminist thought, including eco-feminist, see Clough, *Feminist Thought;* and Lengermann and Neibrugge-Brantley, "Contemporary Feminist Theory," in Ritzer, *Sociological Theory.*

5. Lengermann and Neibrugge-Brantley, "Contemporary Feminist Theory," in Ritzer, *Sociological Theory,* 474.

6. Barry, *Female Sexual Slavery*; Brownmiller, *Against Our Will*; Dworkin, *Pornography*; Dworkin, *Intercourse*; Russell, *Politics of Rape.*

7. Dworkin, *Pornography*; Morgan, *Going Too Far.*

8. Brownmiller, *Against Our Will*; Butler, *Conspiracy of Silence*; Herman, *Father–Daughter Incest*; Herman, *Trauma and Recovery*; Herman and Hirschman, "Father–Daughter Incest"; Rush, *Best-Kept Secret*; Russell, *Secret Trauma.*

9. Herman, *Father–Daughter Incest,* 7.

10. Ibid., 4.

11. Ibid., 108.

12. Brownmiller, *Against Our Will,* 281.

13. Ibid., 272–73.

14. Ibid., 277–78.

15. Ibid., 278.

16. Angelou, *I Know Why,* 65–66.

17. Ibid., 73.

18. For more information on recovered memory syndrome and the debate about it, see psychologist Jennifer J. Freyd's *Betrayal Trauma: The Logic of Forgetting Childhood Abuse.* Freyd argues from the perspective of the recovered memory syndrome. There is a countermovement, the false memory movement—interestingly, it is grounded in behaviorist psychology—that argues against the possibility of recovered abuse memories. For a perspective from the false memory movement, see Crews, "Revenge of the Repressed." Freyd's own mother and father founded the popular branch of this movement, the False Memory Syndrome Foundation. They then proceeded to "out" her as someone claiming—falsely, according to them—to have been sexually abused (by her father). Freyd writes that, whereas she had chosen not to discuss her private life in public, she "lost the ability to choose privacy" (198). "Approximately eight months after I first presented betrayal trauma theory, my parents, in conjunction with Ralph Underwager and others, formed the False Memory Syndrome Foundation (FMSF). Before the organization was formed, my mother, Pamela Freyd, had published an article presenting her version of family history" (198). This was a history Jennifer Freyd had wished to keep private. Nonetheless, Freyd writes, her mother circulated the article to her professional colleagues and the media, thus making "public allegations about [Jennifer Freyd's] professional and personal life" (198) and simultaneously helping start the false memory movement. Following in the footsteps of Watson, who of course was never one to take women's claims seriously, behaviorist psychology has taken on the academic end of the false memory movement. The popular component of the movement is, as one might imagine, particularly popular among those accused of child sexual abuse (such as Jennifer Freyd's father).

19. Probably the most popular of the incest survivor movement books was *The Courage to Heal: A Guide for Women Survivors of Child Sexual Abuse* by Bass and Davis. Other such books include those by Fraser, *My Father's House*; Bass and Thornton with Brister, Hammond, Huntley, and Lamb, *I Never Told Anyone*; Rush, *Best-Kept Secret*; Butler, *Conspiracy of Silence*; and Forward and Buck, *Betrayal of Innocence.*

20. De Witt, "Incest as a Selling Point," 6E.

21. As quoted in ibid.

22. Boston Women's Health Book Collective, *Ourselves and Our Children,* 238.

23. Ibid.

24. Brownmiller, *Against Our Will,* 276.

25. Rush, "Sexual Abuse of Children," in Wilson and Connell, *Rape.*

26. For this personal history in autoethnographic form, see Halley, "This I Know"; "To Speak of My Mother"; "The Cleaning Lady"; and "Ranch Style."

27. Chancer, *Reconcilable Differences,* 24.

28. Ibid.
29. Vance, *Pleasure and Danger,* 3.
30. Ibid., 2.
31. Ibid.
32. Ibid.
33. Ibid.
34. Skolnick, *Embattled Paradise,* 4–5.
35. Gilder, *Men and Marriage,* 12.
36. Ibid.
37. Ibid., 16.
38. Ibid., 39.
39. Ibid.
40. Faludi, *Backlash,* 265.
41. Lowry, "Day Care PC."
42. Ibid.
43. Blankenhorn, *Fatherless America,* 39.
44. Ibid., 39–41.
45. Ibid., 41. Meanwhile, children are being sexually abused. However, contra the conservative focus, studies indicate that child sexual abuse is more likely to happen at home by family members and friends instead of by stranger abuse or abuse at a day care; Herzberger, *Violence within the Family,* 18; National Center of Child Abuse and Neglect, *Child Maltreatment.* Indeed, national "incidence studies indicate that child sexual abuse is primarily intrafamilial"; Blome, "Socially Constructed Perpetrator," 1. Despite this, conservatives are not as much interested in child sexual abuse as in criticizing women for working outside the home. This is true in spite of the fact that most women have no choice, and many are working dead-end jobs with few benefits and low pay.
46. Eberstadt, "Home-Alone America."
47. Ibid., 6–7.
48. Kincaid, *Erotic Innocence,* 195.
49. Ibid., 200.
50. Ibid.
51. Kirk, "Did Daddy Do It?" *Frontline.*
52. See, for example, Rabinowitz, *No Crueler Tyrannies.* Rabinowitz, a member of the conservative editorial board of the *Wall Street Journal,* has written a journalistic account of the most unjust of the day-care scandals. Conservative commentators have linked these scandals and Rabinowitz's account of them to the feminist focus on incest. See also Isaac, "Our Witch Trials."
53. Blome, "Socially Constructed Perpetrator," 14.
54. Ibid.
55. Bennett, *Touching Children*; Oxenhandler, *Eros of Parenthood.*

Chapter 6: Touching Problems

1. Bordo, *Unbearable Weight,* 146.
2. Ibid., 155.

3. Ibid.

4. For interesting research on binary gender ideology, "sluts," and "slut-bashing," see Tanenbaum, *Slut!*

5. Tragically, this insistence that boys must be masculine and reject any "feminine" qualities and that touching boys (nonviolently) will lead them to be feminine continues today. The organization GenderPAC recently issued an e-mail statement about Ronald Paris Jr., who is currently awaiting sentencing for the murder of his three-year-old son, Ronnie. GenderPAC writes that "Paris didn't want Ronnie to grow up to be a 'sissy'" and that he "instructed his wife not to hug their son." The child died after receiving fatal injuries while his father was "teaching the boy how to fight"; GenderPAC, "A Father's Lesson in 'Manhood.'"

6. It is very interesting that, in the past century, beliefs about crying, much like beliefs about touching, have varied extensively in the mainstream United States. Crying has been and continues to be understood to be a sign of a "spoiled" child, a necessary means to exercise for human infants, a cue or way of indicating some need, and even a "late indicator" of hunger (in other words, infants should not need to go as far as crying to indicate their need for food) according to a 2005 statement by the American Academy of Pediatrics.

7. Eisenstein, *Gender Shock,* 86–87.

8. As quoted in Coontz, *Way We Never Were,* 107.

9. Oxenhandler, *Eros of Parenthood,* 261.

10. Ibid., 262.

11. Ibid., 264.

12. Ewen, *Immigrant Women in the Land of Dollars,* 42.

13. Ibid.

14. Crittenden, *Price of Motherhood,* 26.

15. Crittenden writes, "Even when a wife earns more than half of the family income, the husband will typically contribute no more than 30 percent of the domestic services and child care. And that estimate comes from surveys based on men's own statements about their family contributions, surveys that experts agree are biased on the upside. . . . In families with preschool children, mothers appear to be putting in roughly three to four *times* as many hours as fathers. One study of thirty-seven families of young children, representing various classes, races, and work patterns, found that the man rarely had primary responsibility for any *single* child-rearing duty. In no household did a father take responsibility for *all* child-rearing tasks"; Crittenden, *Price of Motherhood,* 24–25 (emphasis original).

16. As quoted in Margolis, *True to Her Nature,* 24.

17. Ibid.

18. Many women give up or do not have their own careers outside of the home in order to focus fully on these jobs. Indeed, "homemaking, the fundamental task associated with raising the young, is still the largest single occupation in the United States. . . . Even among women in their thirties, by far the most common occupation is full-time housekeeping and caregiving. . . . The persistence of traditional family patterns cuts across economic, class, and racial lines"; Crittenden, *Price of Motherhood,* 17.

19. Crittenden, *Price of Motherhood,* 18.

20. Ibid., 22. In spite of conservative hype, mothers who work outside the home do not seem to spend less time with their children. Regardless of the huge movement of women into the workforce, studies show that mothers spend as much if not more time with their children today than they did in the 1960s. Research that goes as far back as the 1920s shows that mothers in the 1980s spend as much if not more time with their children than did mothers in the 1920s; Bryant and Zick, "Are We Investing Less," 365–91. Their time is crunched but the time they spend with their children is not. Instead, working mothers cut back on sleep and housework; Crittenden, *Price of Motherhood*; Garey, *Weaving Work and Motherhood*.

21. Crittenden, *Price of Motherhood,* 77.

22. Ibid., 8.

23. Ibid.

24. Waldfogel, "Understanding the 'Family Gap,'" 137–56.

25. Of course, this is not *all* that child-rearing advice does. It also offers women and, ideally, men some good ideas. These various and diverse ideas are best when offered as possibilities—options—for parents to choose, reject, or use only partially.

26. Coontz, *Way We Never Were,* 112.

27. Ibid., 112–13.

28. Oxenhandler, *Eros of Parenthood.*

29. Ibid., 19–20.

30. For a poststructuralist critique of attunement as normalizing, see Connolly, *Identity/Difference.*

31. Foucault, "On the Genealogy of Ethics," 316.

References

Alford, Robert R. *The Craft of Inquiry: Theories, Methods, Evidence.* Oxford: Oxford University Press, 1998.

American Academy of Pediatrics. "Breastfeeding and the Use of Human Milk (RE9729)." *Pediatrics* 100, no. 6 (December 1997): 1035–39.

———. "Breastfeeding and the Use of Human Milk." *Pediatrics* 115, no. 2 (February 2005): 496–506.

Angelides, Steven. "Feminism, Child Sexual Abuse, and the Erasure of Child Sexuality." *GLQ: A Journal of Gay and Lesbian Studies* 10, no. 2 (2004): 141–77.

Angelou, Maya. *I Know Why the Caged Bird Sings.* New York: Bantam, 1971.

Associated Press. "Woman Kicked Off Plane for Breastfeeding: Files Complaint Saying She Was Being Discreet, Airline Disagrees." November 16, 2006, http://www.msnbc.msn.com/id/15720339.

Barry, Kathleen. *Female Sexual Slavery.* Englewood Cliffs, N.J.: Prentice-Hall, 1979.

Bass, Ellen, and Laura Davis. *The Courage to Heal: A Guide for Women Survivors of Child Sexual Abuse.* New York: Harper and Row, 1988.

———, and Louise Thornton with Jude Brister, Grace Hammond, Jean Huntley, and Vicki Lamb, eds. *I Never Told Anyone: Writings by Women Survivors of Child Sexual Abuse.* New York: Harper and Row, 1983.

Bengson, Diane. *How Weaning Happens.* Schaumburg, Ill.: La Leche League International, 1999.

Bennett, Alyssa R. *Touching Children.* (Documentary video, VHS). New York: Aylett Pictures, 1994.

Bernard, Jessie. *The Future of Marriage,* 2nd ed. New Haven, Conn.: Yale University Press, 1982.

Blankenhorn, David. *Fatherless America: Confronting Our Most Urgent Social Problem.* New York: Basic Books, 1995.

Blome, Juliana M. "The Socially Constructed Perpetrator of Child Sexual Abuse: Incest Offenders and Child Molesters." Unpublished paper, 1997.

Blum, Deborah. *Love at Goon Park: Harry Harlow and the Science of Affection.* Cambridge, Mass.: Perseus, 2002.

Blum, Linda M. *At the Breast: Ideologies of Breastfeeding and Motherhood in the Contemporary United States.* Boston: Beacon Press, 1999.

Bobel, Chris. *The Paradox of Natural Mothering.* Philadelphia: Temple University Press, 2002.

Bologh, Roslyn Wallach. *Love or Greatness: Max Weber and Masculine Thinking—A Feminist Inquiry.* London: Unwin Hyman, 1990.

Bordo, Susan. *Unbearable Weight: Feminism, Western Culture, and the Body.* Berkeley: University of California Press, 1993.

Boston Women's Health Book Collective. *Our Bodies, Ourselves: A Book by and for Women,* 2nd ed. New York: Simon and Schuster, 1976.

———. *Ourselves and Our Children: A Book by and for Parents.* New York: Random House, 1978.

Bowlby, John. "Maternal Care and Mental Health." *Bulletin of the World Health Organization* 3 (1951): 355–34.

———. *Maternal Care and Mental Health.* New York City: Schocken Books, 1966.

Brown, Ann. "Safe Slumber for Infants." *New York Post,* October 7, 1999, 36.

Brownmiller, Susan. *Against Our Will.* New York: Simon and Schuster, 1975.

Bryant, W. K., and C. D. Zick. "Are We Investing Less in the Next Generation? Historical Trends in Time Spent Caring for Children." *Journal of Family and Economic Issues* 17, no. 3/4, (Winter 1996): 365–91.

Butler, Sandra. *The Conspiracy of Silence: The Trauma of Incest.* New York: Bantam, 1978.

Carter, Pam. *Feminism, Breasts and Breast-Feeding.* New York: St. Martin's Press, 1995.

Chancer, Lynn. "Benefiting from Pragmatic Vision, Part I: The Case for Guaranteed Income in Principle. In *Post-Work,* edited by Stanley Aronowitz and Jonathon Cutler, 81–127. New York: Routledge, 1998.

———. *Reconcilable Differences: Confronting Beauty, Pornography, and the Future of Feminism.* Berkeley: University of California Press, 1998.

Cho, Grace M. "Regression Analysis: Mother, Memory, Data." *Cultural Studies—Critical Methodologies* 5, no. 1 (February 2005): 45–51.

Clough, Patricia Ticineto. *The End(s) of Ethnography: From Realism to Social Criticism.* Newbury Park, Calif.: Sage, 1992.

———. *Feminist Thought: Desire, Power, and Academic Discourse.* Oxford: Blackwell, 1994.

Coburn, Jennifer. "Formula for Profit: How Marketing Breastmilk Substitutes Undermines the Health of Babies. *Mothering* (July/August 2000): 61.

Connolly, William E. *Identity/Difference: Democratic Negotiations of Political Paradox.* Ithaca: Cornell University Press, 1991.

Coontz, Stephanie. *The Way We Never Were: American Families and the Nostalgia Trap.* New York: Basic Books, 1992.

Corbett, Sara. "The Breast Offense." *The New York Times Magazine,* May 6, 2001, 82–85.

Crews, Frederick. "The Revenge of the Repressed: Part II." *New York Review of Books* 41, no. 20 (December 1994): 49–58.

Crittenden, Ann. *The Price of Motherhood: Why the Most Important Job in the World Is Still the Least Valued.* New York: Henry Holt and Company, 2001.

De Witt, Karen. "Incest as a Selling Point." *New York Times,* March 30, 1997, 6E.

Degler, Carl. *At Odds.* New York: Oxford University Press, 1980.

Dworkin, Andrea. *Pornography: Men Possessing Women.* New York: Perigee Books, 1979.

———. *Intercourse.* New York: Free Press, 1987.

————. *Letters from the War Zone: Writings 1976–1987.* New York: Dutton, 1989.

Eberstadt, Mary. "Home-Alone America." *Policy Review* 107 (June 2001), http://www.policyreview.org/jun01/eberstadt_print.html.

Ehrenreich, Barbara, and Deirdre English. *For Her Own Good: 150 Years of the Experts' Advice to Women.* Garden City, N.Y.: Anchor Books, 1978.

Eisenberg, Arlene, Heidi E. Murkoff, and Sandee E. Hathaway. *What to Expect: The Toddler Years.* New York: Workman, 1994.

Eisenstein, Hester. *Gender Shock: Practising Feminism on Two Continents.* North Sydney: Allen and Unwin, 1991.

Epstein, Cynthia Fuchs. *Deceptive Distinctions: Sex, Gender, and the Social Order.* New Haven, Conn.: Yale University Press, 1988.

Epstein, Randi Hutter. "Questioning the 'Deadline' for Weaning." *New York Times,* September 21, 1999, F8.

Ewen, Elizabeth. *Immigrant Women in the Land of Dollars: Life and Culture on the Lower East Side, 1890–1925.* New York: Monthly Review Press, 1985.

Ewen, Stuart. *All Consuming Images: The Politics of Style in Contemporary Culture.* New York: Basic Books, 1988.

————. *Captains of Consciousness: Advertising and the Social Roots of Consumer Culture.* New York: McGraw-Hill, 1977. Reprint, New York: Basic Books, 2001. Page references are to the 2001 edition.

Faludi, Susan. *Backlash: The Undeclared War against American Women.* New York: Doubleday, 1991.

Ferber, Richard. *Solve Your Child's Sleep Problems.* New York: Simon and Schuster, 1985.

Finkelhor, David. *Child Sexual Abuse: New Theory and Research.* New York: Free Press, 1984.

Forward, Susan, and Craig Buck. *Betrayal of Innocence: Incest and Its Devastation.* New York: Penguin Books, 1979.

Foucault, Michel. *Discipline and Punish: The Birth of the Prison.* New York: Vintage Books, 1979.

————. *Power/Knowledge: Selected Interviews and Other Writings 1972–1977.* New York: Pantheon Books, 1980.

————. "On the Genealogy of Ethics: An Overview of Work in Progress." In *Michel Foucault: Ethics, Subjectivity and Truth,* edited by Paul Rabinow, 253–80. New York: New Press, 1994.

————. "What Is Enlightenment?" In *Michel Foucault: Ethics, Subjectivity and Truth,* edited by Paul Rabinow, 303–20. New York: New Press, 1994.

Fraser, Sylvia. *My Father's House: A Memoir of Incest and Healing.* New York: Ticknor and Fields, 1987.

Freund, Peter E. S., Meredith B. McGuire, and Linda S. Podhurst. *Health, Illness, and the Social Body: A Critical Sociology,* 4th ed. Upper Saddle River, N.J.: Prentice Hall, 2003.

Freyd, Jennifer J. *Betrayal Trauma: The Logic of Forgetting Childhood Abuse.* Cambridge, Mass.: Harvard University Press, 1996.

Frye, Marilyn. *The Politics of Reality: Essays in Feminist Thought.* Trumansburg, N.Y.: Crossings Press, 1983.

Garey, Anita. *Weaving Work and Motherhood.* Philadelphia: Temple University Press, 1999.

Gender Public Advocacy Coalition. "A Father's Lesson in 'Manhood' Deals a Deadly Blow to Toddler." July 22, 2005, http://www.gpac.org/archive/news/notitle.html?cmd=view&archive=news&msgnum=0602.

Gibbs, Nancy. "Who's in Charge Here?" *Time,* August 6, 2001, 40–49.

Gilder, George. *Men and Marriage.* Gretna, La.: Pelican, 1986.

Giles, Fiona. *Fresh Milk: The Secret Life of Breasts.* New York: Simon and Schuster, 2003.

Goffman, Erving. *Frame Analysis: An Essay on the Organization of Experience.* New York: Harper and Row, 1974.

Goode, Erica. "Baby in Parents' Bed in Danger? U.S. Says Yes, but Others Demur." *New York Times,* September 30, 1999, A1, A22.

Gordon, Linda. *Heroes of Their Own Lives: The Politics and History of Family Violence.* New York: Viking, 1988. Reprint, Urbana: University of Illinois Press, 2002. Page references are to the 2002 edition.

Granju, Katie Allison. *Attachment Parenting: Instinctive Care for Your Baby and Young Child.* New York: Pocket Books, 1999.

Grant, Julia. *Raising Baby by the Book: The Education of American Mothers.* New Haven, Conn.: Yale University Press, 1998.

Halley, Jean. "This I Know: An Exploration of Remembering Childhood and Knowing Now." *Qualitative Inquiry* 6, no. 3 (September 2000): 349–58.

———. "To Speak of My Mother." *Qualitative Inquiry* 9, no. 1 (February 2003): 49–56.

———. "The Cleaning Lady: An Exploration of Class and Gender in a Rural Wyoming Family." *Qualitative Inquiry* 11, no. 2 (April 2005): 191–97.

———. "Ranch Style: A History Told in Carpets. *Qualitative Inquiry* 11, no. 4 (August 2005): 514–17.

Harlow, Harry F. "The Nature of Love." *American Psychologist* 13 (1958): 673–85.

Hart, Betsy. "And Now, Breast-Feeding Rights?" *Jewish World Review,* April 9, 2002, http://www.jewishworldreview.com/cols/hart040902.asp.

Haugaard, Jeffrey J., and N. Dickon Reppucci. *The Sexual Abuse of Children: A Comprehensive Guide to Current Knowledge and Intervention Strategies.* San Francisco: Jossey-Bass, 1988.

Hausman, Bernice L. *Mother's Milk: Breastfeeding Controversies in American Culture.* New York: Routledge, 2003.

Herman, Judith Lewis. *Father–Daughter Incest.* Cambridge, Mass.: Harvard University Press, 1981.

———. *Trauma and Recovery.* New York: Basic Books, 1992.

———, and Lisa Hirschman. "Father–Daughter Incest." *Signs* 2 (1977): 1–22.

Herzberger, Sharon D. *Violence within the Family: Social Psychological Perspectives.* Boulder, Colo.: Westview Press, 1996.

Hochschild, Arlie Russell, with Anne Machung. *The Second Shift,* 2nd ed. New York: Penguin Books, 2003.

Holt, Luther Emmett. *The Care and Feeding of Children: A Catechism for the Use of Mothers and Children's Nurses,* 2nd ed. New York: D. Appleton, 1901.

hooks, bell. *Ain't I a Woman: Black Women and Feminism*. Boston: South End Press, 1981.

Horwitz, Howard. "Always with Us." *American Literary History* 10, no. 2 (Winter 1998): 317–34.

Hulbert, Ann. *Raising America: Experts, Parents, and a Century of Advice about Children*. New York: Alfred A. Knopf, 2003.

IRIN HIV/AIDS News Report. "Breastfeeding Ups Death Risk in HIV Mothers in Developing Countries," May 25, 2001, http://iys.cidi.org/humanitarian/hivaids/01a/ixl28.html.

Isaac, Rael Jean. "Our Witch Trials." *American Spectator* 36, no. 2 (March/April 2003): 74–75.

Jackson, Deborah. *Three in a Bed: The Benefits of Sharing Your Bed with Your Baby*, 2nd ed. New York: Bloomsbury, 1999.

Jones, James H. *Alfred C. Kinsey: A Public/Private life*. New York: Norton, 1997.

Kealey, Terence. "A Black Student's Primer on the History of Eugenics." *Journal of Blacks in Higher Education* 34 (Winter 2001–2): 114–15.

Kincaid, James R. *Erotic Innocence: The Culture of Child Molesting*. Durham, N.C.: Duke University Press, 1998.

Kinsey, Alfred C., Wardell B. Pomeroy, and Clyde E. Martin. *Sexual Behavior in the Human Male*. Philadelphia: W. B. Saunders, 1948.

———, Wardell B. Pomeroy, Clyde E. Martin, and Paul H. Gebhard. *Sexual Behavior in the Human Female*. Philadelphia: W. B. Saunders, 1953.

Kirk, Michael. "Did Daddy Do It?" *Frontline*. Boston: PBS/WGBH, April 25, 2002.

La Leche League International. *The Womanly Art of Breastfeeding*, 3rd ed. New York: Plume Books, 1981.

———. *The Womanly Art of Breastfeeding*, 35th anniversary ed. Franklin Park, Ill.: La Leche League International, 1991.

———. *The Womanly Art of Breastfeeding*, 7th ed. New York: Plume Books, 2004.

Leach, Penelope. "Beware the Parenting Police." *New York Times*. October 1, 1999, A25.

Lengermann, Patricia Madoo, and Jill Neibrugge-Brantley. "Contemporary Feminist Theory." In *Sociological Theory*, 3rd ed., edited by George Ritzer, 447–96. New York: McGraw-Hill, 1992.

Levine, Judith. *Harmful to Minors: The Perils of Protecting Children from Sex*. Minneapolis: University of Minnesota Press, 2002.

Lewin, Tamar. "Breast-Feeding: How Old Is Too Old?" *New York Times*, February 18, 2001, 5.

Liedloff, Jean. *The Continuum Concept: Allowing Human Nature to Work Successfully*, 2nd ed. Reading, Mass.: Addison-Wesley, 1985.

Lorber, Judith. "Believing Is Seeing: Biology as Ideology." *Gender and Society* 4, no. 4 (December 1993): 568–81.

Lorde, Audre. *Sister Outside*. Freedom, Calif.: Crossing Press, 1984.

Lowry, Rich. "Day Care PC: Moms Should Stay Home." *National Review Online*. April 26, 2001.

Luria, Zella, Susan Friedman, and Michael D. Rose. *Human Sexuality*. New York: John Wiley and Sons, 1987.

Lynd, Robert S., and Helen Merrell Lynd. *Middletown: A Study in Modern American Culture.* San Diego: Harcourt Brace Jovanovich, 1957.

Mader, Sylvia S. *Human Reproductive Biology,* 2nd ed. Dubuque, Iowa: William C. Brown, 1992.

Maier, Thomas. *Dr. Spock: An American Life.* New York: Harcourt Brace, 1998.

Margolis, Maxine L. *True to Her Nature: Changing Advice to American Women.* Prospect Heights, Ill.: Waveland Press, 2000.

Maxfield, Andrew. Personal e-mail conversation with author, June 5, 2001, New York City.

McCarthy, Mary. *The Group.* Toronto: Signet Books, 1954.

McKinney, Dave. "Mom Targeted by DCFS Still Breast-Feeds Boy, 8". *Chicago Sun-Times,* July 10, 2002, http://www.suntimes.com/output/news/cst-nws-nurse10 .html.

Morgan, Robin. *Going Too Far: The Personal Chronicle of a Feminist.* New York: Random House, 1978.

Mosse, George L. *The Image of Man: The Creation of Modern Masculinity.* Oxford: Oxford University Press, 1996.

National Center on Child Abuse and Neglect. *Child Maltreatment 1994: Reports from the States to the National Center on Child Abuse and Neglect.* Washington, D.C.: Government Printing Office, 1996.

National Institute of Health. "Study Finds Bed Sharing among Parents and Infants on the Rise." January 13, 2003, http://www.nichd.nih.gov/news/releases/bed _sharing.cfm.

Oxenhandler, Noelle. *The Eros of Parenthood: Explorations in Light and Dark.* New York: St. Martin's Press, 2001.

Pantell, Robert H., James F. Fries, and Donald M. Vickery. *Taking Care of Your Child: A Parent's Guide to Medical Care,* 3rd ed. Reading, Mass.: Addison-Wesley, 1990.

Pasquin, John. *Don't Touch My Daughter* (made-for-television movie). Lifetime, April 7, 1991.

Rabinowitz, Dorothy. *No Crueler Tyrannies: Accusations, False Witness, and Other Terrors of Our Times.* New York: Free Press, 2003.

Rich, Adrienne. "Compulsory Heterosexuality and Lesbian Existence." In *Powers of Desire: The Politics of Sexuality,* edited by Ann Snitow, Christine Stansell, and Sharon Thompson, 177–205. New York: Monthly Review Press, 1983.

Richardson, Laurel. "Writing: A Method of Inquiry." In *Handbook of Qualitative Research,* edited by Norman K. Denzin and Yvonna S. Lincoln, 516–29. Thousand Oaks, Calif.: Sage, 1994.

Robertson, Stephen. *Crimes against Children: Sexual Violence and Legal Culture in New York City, 1880–1960.* Chapel Hill: University of North Carolina Press, 2005.

Robinson, Paul. *The Modernization of Sex: Havelock Ellis, Alfred Kinsey, William Masters and Virginia Johnson,* 2nd ed. Ithaca, N.Y.: Cornell University Press, 1989.

Rossi, Alice. "Gender and Parenthood." *American Sociological Review* 49 (1983): 1–19.

Rush, Florence. "The Sexual Abuse of Children: A Feminist Point of View." In *Rape: The First Sourcebook for Women,* edited by Cassandra Wilson and Noreen Connell. New York: NAL Plume, 1974.

———. *The Best-Kept Secret: Sexual Abuse of Children.* Englewood Cliffs, N.J.: Prentice-Hall, 1980.

Russell, Diana E. H. *The Politics of Rape: The Victim's Perspective.* New York: Stein and Day, 1974.

———. *The Secret Trauma: Incest in the Lives of Girls and Women.* New York: Basic Books, 1986.

Sammons, William A. H. *The Self-Calmed Baby.* Boston: St. Martin's Paperbacks, 1989.

Seabrook, John. "Annals of Parenthood: Sleeping with the Baby." *The New Yorker,* November 8, 1999, 56–65.

Sears, William. *Nighttime Parenting: How to Get Your Baby and Child to Sleep.* New York: Plume, 1985.

———, and Martha Sears, R. N. *The Baby Book: Everything You Need to Know about Your Baby from Birth to Age Two.* Boston: Little, Brown, 1993.

Sedgwick, Eve Kosofsky. "How to Bring Your Kids Up Gay." In *Fear of a Queer Planet: Queer Politics and Social Theory,* edited by Michael Warner, 69–81. Minneapolis: University of Minnesota Press, 1993.

Sernau, Scott. *Worlds Apart: Social Inequalities in a New Century.* Thousand Oaks, Calif.: Pine Forge Press, 2001.

Shanley, Laura. "Milkmen: Fathers Who Breastfeed." http://ucbirth.com/milkmen.htm. Accessed July 15, 2004.

Skolnick, Arlene. *Embattled Paradise: The American Family in an Age of Uncertainty.* New York: Basic Books, 1991.

Smart, Carol. "A History of Ambivalence and Conflict in the Discursive Construction of the 'Child Victim' of Sexual Abuse." *Social and Legal Studies* 8, no. 3 (1999): 391–409.

Spock, Benjamin. *The Common Sense Book of Baby and Child Care.* New York: Duell, Sloan and Pearce, 1945.

———, and Steven J. Parker. *Dr. Spock's Baby and Child Care,* 7th ed. New York: Pocket Books, 1998.

Stearns, Cindy A. "Breastfeeding and the Good Maternal Body." *Gender and Society* 13, no. 3 (June 1999): 308–25.

Stein, Rob. "To Cut Crib Deaths, Separate Beds Are Urged for Babies." *Washington Post,* October 10, 2005, A1.

"A Study Links I.Q. and Breast-Feeding." *New York Times.* May 12, 2002, A27.

Tanenbaum, Leora. *Slut!: Growing Up Female with a Bad Reputation.* New York: Perennial, HarperCollins, 2000.

Thompson, Becky W. *A Hunger So Wide and So Deep: A Multiracial View of Women's Eating Problems.* Minneapolis: University of Minnesota Press, 1994.

Traina, Cristina L. H. "Maternal Experience and the Boundaries of Christian Sexual Ethics." *Signs* 25, no. 2 (Winter 2000): 369.

Tuchman, Gaye. "Historical Social Science: Methodologies, Methods, and Meanings." In *Handbook of Qualitative Research,* edited by Norman K. Denzin and Yvonna S. Lincoln, 306–23. Thousand Oaks: Sage, 1994.

U.S. Department of Health and Human Services, Office on Women's Health. "Breastfeeding: HHS Blueprint for Action on Breastfeeding." Washington, D.C.: Government Printing Office, 2000.

U.S. Department of Health and Human Services, Administration for Children and Families. "Victims: Child Maltreatment 2004." http://www.acf.hhs.gov/programs/cb/pubs/cm04/chapterthree.htm (accessed December 14, 2006).

Vance, Carole S., ed. *Pleasure and Danger: Exploring Female Sexuality.* Boston: Routledge and Kegan Paul, 1984.

Vidal-Ortiz, Salvador. "On Being a White Person of Color: Using Autoethnography to Understand Puerto Ricans' Racialization." *Qualitative Sociology* 27, no. 2 (Summer 2004): 179–203.

Waldfogel, Jane. "Understanding the 'Family Gap' in Pay for Women with Children. *Journal of Economic Perspectives* 12, no. 1 (Winter 1998): 137–56.

Warner, Michael. Introduction. In *Fear of a Queer Planet: Queer Politics and Social Theory,* edited by Michael Warner, vii–xxi. Minneapolis: University of Minnesota Press, 1993.

Watson, John B. *Psychological Care of Infant and Child.* New York: W. W. Norton, 1928.

Weiss, Nancy Pottishman. "Mother, the Invention of Necessity: Dr. Benjamin Spock's Baby and Child Care." *American Quarterly* 29 (Winter 1977): 519–46.

Weissbluth, Marc. *Healthy Sleep Habits, Happy Child.* New York: Fawcett Columbine, 1987.

Whedon, Joss, director. "Teacher's Pet." *Buffy the Vampire Slayer,* episode no. 4, 1996.

Index

JEAN O'MALLEY HALLEY is an assistant professor of sociology in the Sociology and Anthropology Department at Wagner College. Among other publications, she has published four articles in the journal *Qualitative Inquiry*. She also assisted Patricia Ticineto Clough in editing, and has an essay in, *The Affective Turn: Toward Theorizing the Social* (2007). She is currently working on her second book, a social history of cattle ranching and the United States beef industry. Halley holds a Ph.D. in sociology from the Graduate Center of the City University of New York, and a master's degree in theology from Harvard University.

The University of Illinois Press
is a founding member of the
Association of American University Presses.

———————————————————————

Composed in 9/13 ITC Stone Serif
with ITC Stone Sans display
by Jim Proefrock
at the University of Illinois Press
Designed by Paula Newcomb
Manufactured by Thomson-Shore, Inc.

University of Illinois Press
1325 South Oak Street
Champaign, IL 61820-6903
www.press.uillinois.edu